3poolelib/0912

The Shaping of Us

How Everyday Spaces Structure
Our Lives, Behaviour, and Well-Being

Lily Bernheimer

ROBINSON

ROBINSON

First published in Great Britain in 2017 by Robinson

1 3 5 7 9 10 8 6 4 2

Illustrations on pages 29, 44, 53, 61, 93, 129, 182, 188, 209 and 239
courtesy of Grace Exley

Important Note
Some of the characters who appear in this book are fictional amalgams of people the
author has come across in real life, and a small number have had names and other
identifying features altered to protect their identity.

A CIP catalogue record for this book is available from the British Library.

ISBN: 978-1-47213-785-2

Typeset in Adobe Jenson Pro by SX Composing DTP, Rayleigh, Essex
Printed and bound in Great Britain by Clays Ltd, St Ives plc

Papers used by Robinson are from well-managed forests
and other responsible sources.

MIX
Paper from
responsible sources
FSC
www.fsc.org   FSC® C104740

Robinson
An imprint of
Little, Brown Book Group
Carmelite House
50 Victoria Embankment
London EC4Y 0DZ

An Hachette UK Company
www.hachette.co.uk

www.littlebrown.co.uk

To two people whose collaboration this book is greatly indebted to: my parents.

'We treat space somewhat as we treat sex. It is there but we don't talk about it.'[1]

– *Edward T. Hall*

Contents

Preface

The spaces we live in shape our lives. They impact our feelings, behaviour, identities, and even how quickly we can solve puzzles. The environments we spend time in can make us healthier, decrease our perception of pain, and make us less likely to litter. Space is like a secret script directing our actions. It's a script we play a part in writing by choosing where to work, who to socialise with, and how to decorate our homes. But like the actors in a play, we maintain the illusion that our actions are unscripted.

Remember the first time you went to a foreign country. Money is strange, and people stand close, and the street is a jungle of forms. You've gone off script. We know intuitively that space is essential to who we are – as individuals and societies. But oddly, we don't acknowledge how much it moulds us. This may be because it's so difficult to pin down how an environment affects us. Consider why so many people prefer older houses, and why our modern attempts to mimic them tend to fail so spectacularly. Is it the outside appearance, the craftsmanship, the building materials, the towns around them, or the way we interact with people in them?

Our behaviour is often counter-intuitive. We believe that traffic lights and curbs keep us safe, but have fewer accidents when we are forced to pay attention to our surroundings. We build promising parks that no one uses, and install energy smart meters that we then ignore. How does a desolate walkway become a bustling social centre and why do communities rally to save certain derelict buildings?

We like spaces that flirt with us – complex and mysterious settings – without threatening the achievement of our goals. The built environment supports our well-being best when it echoes the natural world in some way – through pattern, dimension, light, layout, noise – the scale and tone of the world that we were built for.

The Shaping of Us exposes how our surroundings shape us, and what the shape of our environments says about us. Through public space, housing, workspaces, healthcare facilities, and cities, I uncover how space mediates community, creativity, and identity. I examine the experiences of different cultures and personality types, and the benefits of grassroots and mainstream approaches to building. What makes spaces work and what may become of us if we don't listen to what we know is good for us. I trace how the environments we inhabit make us who we are – from the earliest moments of our evolution to the worlds we build around us.

Introduction

'We shape our buildings, and afterwards our buildings shape us.'[1]
— *Winston Churchill*

This is not a book about nature versus nurture.

It's about both.

The environments we inhabit shape us so profoundly that their influence defies this distinction.

Winston Churchill was right – to an extent. Because humans have been around far longer than buildings. And before buildings, the elements and environments of our natural habitats shaped us as well.

The Shaping of Us traces how our perceptual systems and preferences developed in relation to the environments we evolved in. How we developed shelters, aesthetics, and settlements in reaction to these inclinations. How we have slowly lost this basic ability to build and maintain environments we flourish in. And how we can get it back.

I will reveal how we are formed by our homes, streets, and neighbourhoods, and what the shape of these spaces says about us. How landscapes and cityscapes define us individually, collectively, and culturally – and how we use them to define ourselves. Even how we change from moment to moment, from one place to another.

1

We like to believe that we are consistent and logical, that our identities hold firm across our lives. But do they? We say 'What happens in Vegas stays in Vegas.' As if our actions there aren't our own – as if we aren't ourselves in foreign settings.

In 1971, two US congressmen visited Vietnam and made a disturbing discovery: large numbers of the American armed forces were addicted to heroin. Thirty-five per cent of servicemen had tried heroin, and nineteen per cent became actively addicted. The American public was horrified, and the government reacted swiftly. President Richard Nixon created a new office, the Special Action Office of Drug Abuse Prevention, to combat these new narcotic enemies.

The office first set up a system to test urine samples and treat addicts in Vietnam before they returned home. Next, they appointed a leading psychiatric researcher named Lee Robins to study the full extent and implications of the epidemic. And this is where the story takes a strange turn. Robins found that Vietnam veterans had an astonishingly low rate of relapsing to heroin addiction once they returned home. Standard relapse rates are generally around eighty-seven per cent, but only twelve per cent of veterans addicted in Vietnam had experienced *any* episode of re-addiction in the US.[2] At this time, heroin was widely believed to be so powerfully addictive that a single dose could doom its victims to lifelong dependency.

What could explain this shocking disconnect? It wasn't simply a lack of access. Half of those addicted in Vietnam had used narcotics at least once upon returning to the US, but only a small portion continued. And, surprisingly, few of the young men they interviewed attributed their drug use to the stress of warfare. Most began using before they actually entered combat, and those who were more actively involved in combat were no more likely to use heroin than those working as cooks and typists behind lines.[3]

What is startling about this story was not just how few men relapsed, but how many of them tried heroin to begin with. And these two blips have something in common. It wasn't just that heroin was cheap, readily available, and socially normalised among their peers in Vietnam. It was also that they didn't see their time there as part of their normal lives and careers. Their old friends and family were far away. And they were in sharp new steaming green scenes. The sky was made of sweat and explosives. It was a different world. And they were different people there.

Our identities are more fragile than we imagine. And they grow frailer when we remove the framework they rely upon. This is why we invest so much in building places – building ourselves – the way we think we want to be.

When Winston Churchill uttered the famous words at the head of this chapter, he was talking about the House of Commons. It was 1943 and the Commons chamber, where the lower house of Parliament meets, had been destroyed two years before. On the night of 10 May 1941, more than five hundred bombers of the second and third fleets of the Luftwaffe swarmed through London's skies – some of the very last bombs in the raid fell on the Palace of Westminster. By morning, the Commons chamber had been reduced to ruins, a shell of the structure it had been.

Churchill had spent over forty years in the old chamber, and he liked it very much the way it had been. Meeting with a special select committee on the House of Commons Rebuilding, he found some members had some big ideas about how the chamber could be improved. It could be larger, for one – the old chamber

The British House of Commons, rebuilt
© Pictorial Parade/Getty Images

The US House of Representatives
© Saul Loeb/Getty Images

had only 427 seats for 646 members of Parliament. But Churchill was deeply opposed to this idea. 'Giving each member a desk to sit at and a lid to bang' would leave the space empty and dead most of the time, he said. The undersized original filled beyond capacity at critical moments. Members spilled out into the aisles, creating a fitting 'sense of crowd and urgency'. A sense of intimacy.

The old chamber was also rectangular in shape, forcing the Conservative and Labour parties to sit on opposing sides – a confrontational stance. Some thought this should be modernised to a more egalitarian semi-circle, like the US House of Representatives. But Churchill was dead set against it. The confrontational form had helped shape the two-party system, he believed, which was essential to the function of British parliamentary democracy.

Churchill's desire to replicate the old House of Commons was partly symbolic. He wanted to prove to the Nazi regime and to his own people that British democracy had not been damaged – that the great history and culture housed in the structure would live on seamlessly. No expense was spared in recreating the quality and texture of the old building. An ancient quarry was reopened to match the original stone. Oak trees three centuries old were felled. Aged craftsmen were brought out of retirement to work their age-old wonders.[4] But it was also more than a symbolic gesture. A space can shape how we interact, how we communicate. Churchill not only wanted to recreate the building, but also the movements, the feelings, the style of communication it facilitated – the characteristically rambunctious nature of British parliamentary debate that Americans find so baffling.

It is often said that history is written by the victors. And, as scholars like evolutionary biologist Jared Diamond have pointed out, our understanding of history is often defined by architecture

– that of cultures such as Egypt, China, Rome, and the Maya, which have engraved their histories on our landscapes through large and persisting structures. We learn less in history books about ancient Mongolians and Papua New Guineans partly because they have not left a legacy of giant pyramids and Hadrian's Walls to remember them by. But cultures with a great fondness for building big structures also tend to fall apart in a big way. And we may be headed the same way, if we don't get our act together pretty quickly.

Sometimes, we use buildings to reinforce ourselves. But at other times we try to redesign ourselves through them – to change who we are. The Commons chamber was only one building out of millions that were destroyed in countries including the UK, Germany, and Japan during the war. And while it was under reconstruction in 1952, a very different idea was guiding the rebuilding of great chunks of Europe. It was called modernism.

Standing in the ruins of the old world with the enormous task of housing war-torn populations, modernist architects had a great vision. New structures would use glass, steel, and concrete. Government and institutional buildings would be open, light, and flexible – an end to the hierarchical, authoritarian structures of closed offices and ornate power centres that had led us into war. Cities would be laid out functionally and efficiently. Large tower blocks for living would be connected by superhighways to separate zones for work and commerce.

British social reformers even applied these utopian goals in miniature to the layout of public housing. New housing featured a single, open-plan living space, breaking down the antiquated distinction between the 'middle class' parlour and the more utilitarian living room. These new designs would foster openness and flexibility for the modern age of class and gender mobility.

This was also the guiding rationale across the sea in North America and in growing cities around the globe.

These were lovely visions. But in our haste to build a new efficient, egalitarian civilisation, we left something behind. When buildings surpass a certain height – around six storeys – we lose the ability to communicate with people on the ground. The cars that promised freedom became personal prisons, insulated from the gridlock and pollution they propagate. Rates of asthma, obesity, depression, and attention-deficit disorder have skyrocketed. The environments we inhabit have become further and further removed from the scale and tone of the world we were built for. They have become less biophilic.

'Biophilia' literally means 'love of the living world', but it refers to the innate attraction humans have for the natural world. It explains why we love ocean views, spring flowers, and canopies of trees. We are especially drawn to elements that signalled sources of nourishment or shelter to our predecessors. But it's not just that we *like* these natural forms and settings. They intimately impact our ability to think, heal, and create. Gazing at a tree can swiftly reduce blood pressure and the circulation of stress hormones. And over time, the effects are compounded. Patients recovering from surgery in a room with a view of a tree can recover more quickly and experience less pain than those without one.

But the benefits of biophilia also come from sources less obvious than forests and potted plants. The form of older structures and settlements was often more innately biophilic. Buildings used natural materials such as wood and stone. Roads followed the contour of the land. Places grew slowly. There was more mystery, variety, and malleability. And much of this was lost in the fast pace of twentieth-century life.

Today, we're redesigning our world anew around the goal of sustainability – at least, we seemed to be until a certain climate-change-denying property tycoon became the 'leader of the free world'. But once again, we're not paying enough attention to how we interact with our buildings. How they impact our well-being and behaviour. How we feel about them.

I moved to New York City after college thinking that I wanted to become an urban planner. I thought, as many people do, that this was like being an architect for cities and public spaces. So I got a job at an innovative non-profit organisation that was working to make New York and other cities more 'liveable' by making streets safer for cyclists, pedestrians, and children. Bringing in more trees, benches, and bike lanes – making the public realm a place for people rather than cars.

New York City has a world-class public transport network, and only forty-six per cent of its households even own a car. But the sprawling nature of US development and generally poor public transport means there are few other places one can so easily get around without a vehicle. Nationwide, American car ownership is at ninety-two per cent, so shifting to more sustainable, less car-dependent lifestyles would require different types of housing as well.[5] It would require people to live more densely so they could walk places and support more frequent-running buses.

In 2009, I attended a sustainable transportation conference in San Francisco, and had the opportunity to visit one of these dense developments across the bay in my hometown of Berkeley. My colleagues seemed to think the soulless slick tower was a great success. It was walking distance from the local BART metro train station, close to shops and restaurants, and offered a limited number of bookable car-club vehicles in the basement. From a transportation perspective, it did appear to be a success.

The developments were based on the simple assumption that if we built more compact housing people would drive less. But there seemed to be little consideration of who would actually live there and what their lives would be like. Would they have children? Would they like to garden? And would this new incarnation of high-rise towers really work any better than the modernist version if it still didn't account for well-being, feelings, and sense of identity? Redesigning our homes, workplaces, and cities to make them more resource-efficient presents an invaluable opportunity to make them work for the people in and around them. But unfortunately, this isn't happening on the scale needed.

These are the questions that led me to study environmental psychology – to examine the relationship between people and their environments. But environmental psychology is sadly something of a well-kept secret. Even architects, builders, urban planners, and interior designers rarely benefit from this great evidence base. Not to mention office managers, hospital administrators, teachers, and anyone with a place to call home – or looking for one.

This is partly because environmental psychology, a distinct subfield within psychology, is a young discipline. The University of Surrey, where I studied for my MSc., was the first in the world to establish a post-graduate programme in 1973. It is still the only Masters programme of its kind in the UK or US, and one of few around the world.

It's also a secret because psychologists have historically shied away from focusing their research instruments on the environment – the context, as they called it. Psychologists like to study people, especially individuals. We can isolate individuals, put them in laboratories, run brain scans, diagnose them. We can even put a few people or a large group together in a laboratory and watch what happens. But you can't bring a person and their house into a laboratory so easily. Or set up a one-way mirror inside their living room to observe them.

Can we disentangle the social environment from the physical environment? We can't, completely. This is one of the things that make the study of environmental psychology difficult, and interesting. Sometimes, research confirms what we already knew. But other times, we discover our assumptions are the reverse of reality.

Traditionally, psychologists drew mathematical-looking diagrams attempting to explain the relationship among individuals, groups, values, identity, and behaviour. And in these diagrams you would find a little floating box labelled 'context' or 'facilitating conditions'. Context was what stood in for the kaleidoscope of streetlights and savannahs, sounds and colours, ancient cities and soaring skyscrapers I will take you to visit throughout this book.

Of course – as Churchill said – we also shape our buildings. And this doesn't stop when a space is officially constructed or renovated. We continue to shape our surroundings with daily use, adaptation, and the people and things we invite into them. Through public space, housing, workspaces, healthcare environments, and cities, I will uncover how space mediates community, creativity, and identity. The experiences of people with different personalities, nationalities, and abilities. The impact of time and wear.

Our streets and cities function like wolf tracks or hermit crab shells – imprints of our lives and the lives of those before us. We follow in them, diverge from them, and run deeper ruts in them.

With the knowledge of how our environments affect us, we gain the power to build the world we want to be defined by.

CHAPTER 1

The *Woonerf*, the Stoplight, and the Roundabout

The Laweiplein paradox and the petrified wood principle

I n the first year of our new century, a Dutch traffic engineer
named Hans Monderman gave an obscure intersection
in Friesland a radical makeover. He removed the stoplights,
lanes, traffic islands, even the curbs and some of the crosswalks.
The entire intersection was flattened to become one 'shared space'.

Laweiplein is not a small intersection – approximately 22,000
vehicles move through it daily. If you're imagining a quaint Dutch
street lined with tapered canal houses and bike parking, think
again. Laweiplein looked a lot like any multi-lane intersection
you might drive through in the US. There was something a bit
more European about the shape of the office buildings and the
wide sidewalks. But it was essentially a vast expanse of road
already, just a very cluttered one.

Monderman put a landscaped traffic circle in the middle.
But he didn't post any signs about who to yield to, how fast to
drive, or which way to circle. There is a subtle paving difference
between the central asphalt section and the brick-paved outer
areas, but no clear lines dividing cars, bicycles, and pedestrians.
People thought he was crazy.

11

The Laweiplein intersection, before
© Knowledge Center Shared Space

The Laweiplein intersection, after
© Knowledge Center Shared Space

But the result was groundbreaking. Not only were Frieslanders able to make their way safely through the intersection, accident rates actually *declined*. The new Laweiplein was also more efficient. Both vehicles and pedestrians experienced shorter delays.[1] By clearing the road of lanes and signals, Monderman forced drivers to pay attention to what was happening in the space before them the way you might on a ballroom dance floor. He made them look at each other, and this made them behave more responsibly.

Humans are social animals. We are strongly influenced by those around us. We adapt to what we perceive as *normal* behaviour in an environment – the *social norms*. And this is especially important to our behaviour in public space.

Imagine that you are in a national park in Arizona – the Petrified Forest National Park, to be precise. But this park looks more like the surface of Mars than a forest because the trees are no longer standing. Approximately 218 million years ago, these plateaus and lowlands contained a great river system, forested by conifers, tree ferns, and gingkoes. When the trees died they floated downstream, collected in logjams, and were eventually buried under earth and volcanic ash, where they became petrified. Today, this barren landscape is covered with formations of brilliantly coloured minerals, preserved in the form of logs and stumps.

So imagine your walk through these so-called forests: Jasper, Crystal, Black, Blue, and most spectacular, Rainbow. There are so few people around, and so many petrified wood chips, and you start to wonder if it would be so terrible if you took one of these little rainbow gems home with you. But then you see a sign: 'Your heritage is being vandalised every day by theft losses of petrified wood of fourteen tons a year, mostly a small piece at a time.' Would this make you less likely to take the wood chip?

Unfortunately not, according to Robert Cialdini of Arizona State University and his colleagues. In fact, it may even make you more likely to steal. This sign delivers logical statistics about a social problem: lots of woodchips are being stolen. But it also sends another very powerful message: *everybody's doing it!* The sign assumes we are rational creatures who follow directions and make careful, information-based decisions. The problem is, we aren't, and we don't.

Cialdini and his team spent five weeks scurrying around this Martian landscape placing different signs in the different coloured forests, to test visitors' reactions. When the sign said simply, 'Please don't remove the petrified wood chips', less than two per cent of the wood chips were stolen. But when signs read, 'Many past visitors have removed the petrified wood from the park, changing the state of the petrified forest', eight per cent were taken – over four times as much.

The first sign delivers what is called an *injunctive norm*. It tells us what the rules are, how we *should* behave. But just like when we're told we should stop smoking, eat vegetables, or abide by the speed limit, we often do not do what we should do. The second sign communicates what's normal in terms of what people are actually doing, which is called a *descriptive norm*. Let's call them *should norms* and *do norms*. Do norms are very powerful. But unfortunately, this sign makes it sound quite normal to steal a wood chip. It might as well say, 'Get yours before it's too late!' It normalises the very behaviour it is trying to prevent. What happened in Laweiplein works on the same principle. A sign displaying a speed limit tells us what we should do. But if the environment invites us to look around and gauge our speed limit based on the other road users, we focus more on what others do.

Monderman had one central goal: to reduce traffic speed to the level at which people can make eye contact. When drivers move slowly enough to communicate visually with pedestrians and bicyclists, a fundamental change happens. They start to look at each other, to wave and nod, to drive more carefully. In Laweiplein people even began using hand signals to indicate turning. Monderman was known to walk backwards into traffic. This was the 'crucial test' he used to demonstrate the success of his intersections.

This critical speed threshold for making eye contact is around 20 mph. It's no coincidence that this is close to the maximum running speed for humans. It also marks a major threshold for the severity of collisions. When cars crash at speeds faster than 20 mph, the propensity for human injury skyrockets. It's a human speed, a human scale. The pace of life that we were built for.

Traffic engineers are trained to think like structural and water engineers. They design roads to accommodate the maximum load they will need to bear, like the Black Friday shopping rush. But roads are different from water pipes because they involve conscious actors. And this is what made Monderman's approach so radical – he designed a space trusting people to interact with each other instead of trying to orchestrate their every move.

So are signs and rules and curbs the root of all our social ills? If we took away the guard rails of public life, would everyone act more responsibly? Not exactly, but guiding behaviour through subtle design cues may well be more effective than banging us over the head with a list of rules. As a society, we act a bit like teenagers. If our parents are unreasonably strict, it makes us all the more rebellious. Conversely, a total lack of structure or positive role models can also produce wayward teens. Designing public space is a subtle balancing act between these two extremes. And like different parents, each country has its own style.

I had never thought much about public drinking laws until I met Barbara Ophoff – a tall, lean German with jet-black hair and a matching lean, black dog named Spoon.

'I can't take my dog to the park, I can't have a beer in the park – what is this with these American parks?'

We were in a room full of tigers. Growling wood-carved tigers, sleeping china tigers, and tiny toy tigers, inhabiting an archipelago of potted palms. We were at the offices of Paper Tiger TV, a New York City media collective that has been broadcasting on public access television since 1981. I had come to meet Barbara and some other tigers (as collective members are called), who wanted to make a documentary about public space.

Barbara had moved to New York from Berlin with her husband Ingo, who was working as a translator. Like many Europeans, she was mystified by the long list of rules found in New York City parks:

Park rules prohibit
- Littering and glass bottles
- Bicycles, roller skates, scooters, and skateboards
- Pets
- Using illegal drugs, alcohol, and smoking
- Amplifying sound, except by permit
- Disorderly conduct

- Feeding birds and squirrels
- Standing on swings
- Rummaging through trash receptacles
- Engaging in commercial activity, except by permit
- Performing and rallying, except by permit
- Barbecuing and open fires
- Bare feet

New York may have a particularly authoritarian streak. I'm pretty sure most city parks in California allow dogs and bicycles . . . not sure about standing on the swings. In New York, the space itself is hard, rigid. You find small triangles of pavement surrounded by walls, which are called parks.

The public drinking ban, however, is pervasive throughout the US today. Some analysts estimate it is now outlawed in ninety-seven per cent of American communities.[2] We may be known for our puritan roots, but public drinking was widespread in America both before and after Prohibition. It wasn't until the 1950s and 1960s that laws against the simple act of sipping a beer in public as opposed to 'public drunkenness' came in. It's a long story involving various states and Supreme Court cases. But more importantly, these 'open container' laws weren't even fully enforced in many places until the 1990s.

What happened in the '90s? A new style of police enforcement came into fashion, sweeping the nation from New York to New Mexico. It was based on an idea called the 'Broken Windows' theory, which was first introduced by James Q. Wilson and George L. Kelling in 1982. Wilson and Kelling proposed that superficial signs of disorder such as broken windows, litter, and public drinking communicate a general tolerance for lawlessness.

This sparks further disorder and petty crimes like theft and vandalism, spiralling into more serious offences like murder and drug-dealing. If these broken windows were promptly repaired, they believed, theft and murder rates would decline as well.

Kelling started working with the NYC Transit Police to tackle graffiti in New York City subways in the mid-1980s. But it was in the 1990s that Mayor Rudy Giuliani and Police Commissioner Bill Bratton put Kelling's theory fully into play through what they called the 'quality of life' reforms. The NYPD cracked down on minor offences such as fare-dodging, public drinking, and public urination. And over the course of the decade, crime rates in New York dropped. Wonderful! said Kelling and other commentators. The Broken Windows theory had worked. Or had it?

The problem with the Broken Windows theory is that it was just that – a theory. When Kelling and Wilson introduced their theory in *The Atlantic Monthly* in 1982, no substantial empirical research had been conducted to back it up. But in 2008 a group of researchers led by Kees Keizer at the University of Groningen in the Netherlands decided to test the theory through a series of experiments.

Keizer and his colleagues had a head start because Robert Cialdini, back in Arizona, had already done some research, about littering in particular. Cialdini had discovered that people were more likely to litter in a heavily littered environment than a clean one. And, in litter-strewn spaces, people were even more likely to throw a flyer on the ground when they saw another person litter. Like the petrified wood story, this research supports the Broken Windows theory at the most basic level: litter is likely to encourage more litter and graffiti invites more graffiti.

But Keizer and his colleagues Siegwart Lindenberg and Linda Steg wanted to take the experiment to the next level. Would the impact of a broken window extend to *other* disorderly behaviours? Would a graffitied space make people more likely to litter, or even to steal?

Groningen, where Keizer conducted the experiments, is a Dutch city coincidentally not far from Monderman's famous Laweiplein intersection. So, like most of the Netherlands, the streets are filled with handsome Dutch bicycles gliding, ambling, and waiting around for their masters to collect them. The researchers found a popular bike parking spot, against a wall with a sign forbidding graffiti. They attached a flyer from an imaginary sports store to the handle of each bike, and then waited in secret to watch what happened when the masters came to collect their trusty steeds. On some days the wall behind was covered with graffiti and on others it was painted black. The impact was extremely significant. With no graffiti, only thirty-three per cent of cyclists dropped the flyer on the ground. With graffiti, sixty-nine per cent littered – over twice as many.

Keizer and colleagues kept experimenting with variations on this theme and consistently found that evidence of minor infractions made people more likely to commit other minor acts of deviance. This held true for rules set by the police and private companies, like signs forbidding locking bikes to a particular fence. They even found that people were more likely to litter when they heard fireworks set off – illegal at that time of year in the Netherlands.

But finally, they wanted to test whether evidence of a minor infraction like graffiti would encourage a more serious offence like stealing. To do this they placed an envelope with a €5 note (visible through the address window) hanging out of a mailbox. Once again, they watched unobserved, changing slight factors in the scene. In a clean mailbox without litter or graffiti, thirteen per cent of subjects stole the envelope. But when they staged the scene with litter on the ground or graffiti on the mailbox, as many as twenty-seven per cent stole the €5.

This tells us some very interesting things. But it doesn't actually tell us much about the situation the Broken Windows theory was applied to in New York City. It tells us that superficial cracks in the order of our environment can weaken our conformance to social norms; norms against the mild infraction of littering, and the slightly more serious offence of petty theft. But can we really put swiping five euros on a continuum with armed robbery? Or even homicide? Perhaps the Dutch hold a stronger social norm against petty theft than Brits or Americans do. Based on my own highly anecdotal sample experience of a semester studying abroad at the University of Amsterdam, the Dutch have quite a high tolerance for petty theft. Everyone in Amsterdam has at least one bike, and for each bike you must have at least two locks. But this doesn't matter, they will tell you. Your bike will be stolen within a matter of months.

In Amsterdam bicycles function almost as a form of currency. Upon arriving, I found I had two choices: either spend €120 on a new bike or spend €5 on a 'junkie bike'. Junkie bikes were certainly stolen – possibly by junkies – and could be easily obtained from shaggy characters hissing '*fiets*' (Dutch for bicycle) on dark street corners. There was a sense that it was bad bike karma to buy a junkie bike before yours was stolen, but after you'd lost your first it was a bit more like collecting a bicycle from the bike-share docking station. For the record, I managed to buy a shabby second-hand bike and it was never stolen – although it did end up becoming mangled beyond repair in someone's attempt to wrench off the lock. But more importantly, how does this hold up against the Broken Windows theory? I would have said that Amsterdam was incredibly safe, but as of 2009 it had the highest rate of violent crime of any city in western Europe.[3]

It's very tempting to look at statistics like these and draw the same conclusions as Kelling and Wilson. But sociologists Robert J. Sampson and Stephen W. Raudenbush have demonstrated that these links are far more complicated. They tested the Broken Windows theory by examining the relationship between signs of physical and social disorder and crime rates in over twenty-three thousand streets in nearly two hundred Chicago neighbourhoods. They found that neither litter nor public drinking were good predictors of violent crime. In fact, there was no strong connection between homicide and disorderly environments or behaviour. Robbery was the only criminal activity examined that was directly linked to disorderly environments.

The best predictor of crime rates, they discovered, was the level of poverty in a neighbourhood. But socio-economic disadvantage was mediated by a critical factor that they called 'collective efficacy': the level of trust, cohesion, and informal social control in an area. Do people know their neighbours? Would they stop to help a stranger whose car has broken down? Would they step in to resolve a conflict between children in the street? These are signs of strong collective efficacy. When collective efficacy was high, violent crime was low, regardless of socio-demographic factors and broken windows. So while crime and disorder might have similar roots in structural factors like poverty, to say that disorder causes crime is sweeping the true problem under the rug. This is especially true in the case of violent crime.[4]

What the Groningen experiments do demonstrate is how susceptible we are to the subtle cues and social norms an environment communicates. And this tells us a lot about how shared spaces like Laweiplein work. But Monderman's ideas for Laweiplein also didn't come from out of the blue. They were born out of another Dutch curiosity called the *woonerf*.

Woonerfs (or *woonerven*, the Dutch plural) were pioneered in Delft in the late 1960s. A group of neighbours decided they had had enough. Cars were constantly cutting through their residential streets, making them unpleasant and unsafe for children. So they got together and dug up their brick streets and rebuilt them as swerving paths with trees and play areas. To redefine them as the living space between homes rather than the driving distance between cars, they called them 'residential yards' or 'living yards': *woonerven*. By 1976 the *woonerf* had been officially added to the toolbox of Dutch traffic regulation strategies, and there are now more than 6,500 around this tiny nation.[5]

A *woonerf* differs from the broader concept of a shared space street in that it is specifically residential. In a normal street, the needs of cars take priority over the needs of people. In a *woonerf*, the needs of children playing and neighbours socialising are given priority over driving and parking. And like larger shared streets, the cars, children, and cats have to negotiate more spontaneously.

What makes *woonerven* work? According to the great urban designer Donald Appleyard, the design communicates that the street is a place for people. The car is a guest invited in to visit. Rather than ordering drivers to slow down, design the environment to make them feel it's normal to drive slowly. Think of a wide, straight road defined by curbs and yellow lines, stretching out before you. It looks a bit like a lane in a bowling alley. It screams, 'I'm yours to zoom down!' One study by Peter Swift and his colleagues in Colorado found that accident rates increase not proportionally, but *exponentially* as the width of a street grows. In a *woonerf*, the driving space is narrowed and the curbs are levelled. The street is often curved, bent, or bottlenecked to further narrow drivers' line of sight. Instead of curbs and lines, pedestrian space is defined by seating and play structures, trees and flowers, or bollards and varied paving materials.

Physically, this obstacle course makes it more difficult to speed down the street. But, like the graffiti on the mailbox, it also sends a message about social norms in the space. The benches and play structures invite children to play in the street, to leave their bikes and balls there. Old people bring their chairs out to sit in the sun. They start spending more time tending their tulip gardens. The street users negotiate a new set of social norms about how to use the space. And this means drivers tend to slow down to around 10 mph in these *woonerven*.

Even before Monderman expanded upon this concept to tame his Friesian intersections, the *woonerf* had started spreading to neighbouring European nations like Germany, Denmark, and Sweden. And after Laweiplein, news of Monderman's wonders spread quickly. Biking advocates and progressive transport planners from Edinburgh to Oregon were desperate to get a shared space of their own.

England was an early adopter. In 1999, fourteen 'home zones', modelled after the Dutch *woonerfs*, were piloted across the nation. Legislation was changed, curbs were flattened, and the government invested thirty million pounds in sixty-one home zones across the country. Surveying a selection of English projects to date in 2010, urban designer Mike Biddulph found they had reduced traffic speeds, lowered accident rates, and were safer for children.[6] Municipalities and agencies quickly moved on to make full-on shared spaces in the image of Laweiplein at larger intersections like Poynton in Cheshire, the Ashford Ring Road in Kent, and Exhibition Road in London. Reports of reduced accident and injury rates and increased cycling and pedestrian traffic abounded. The English shared space initiative seemed to be a great success.

But over the past few years there has been a considerable backlash. There has always been criticism from groups concerned about vulnerable road users and drivers who say the streets feel dangerous. But a 2014 study from Simon Moody and Steve Melia at the University of the West of England has challenged whether shared spaces serve pedestrians and cyclists as well as they promise to. They point out that while proponents cite pedestrian benefits, the evidence tends to focus on driver behaviour, traffic flows, and accident rates. Looking at Elwick Square in Ashford, Kent, they found that most pedestrians had to yield to vehicles and weren't able to follow their *desire lines* — the most convenient paths across the intersection. The majority of pedestrians said they felt safer before the transformation.

Moody and Melia claim that in transposing shared space more widely in the UK, British advocates wildly expanded its objectives from Monderman's simple aim of 20-mph speeds. They envisioned it as a way to promote other paragons of Dutch virtue. Shared spaces could make people bike and walk more, beautify the public realm, and increase health and well-being. Even enhancing social and economic capital was added to the list.

This was certainly the sense in New York when I started working on the NYC Streets Renaissance Campaign in 2007. Biking advocates were importing Dutch cargo bikes, Danish architects, and continental traffic-calming. There was a definite feeling in the air that if we could change the form of the streets, the culture as well as the function would follow. But would a *woonerf* born out of the Dutch culture of tolerance work in the New York context of stoplights, open container laws, and no standing on the swings?

The Dutch are well known for their tolerant attitudes on issues like sex-work and drug use. They are proud of their long history of *gedoogcultuur*, which translates roughly as culture of tolerance or permissiveness. As part of my orientation at the University of Amsterdam, we were indoctrinated with history lessons and field trips to water processing facilities, where we learned about the long battle to 'reclaim the land from the sea'. It was the need to unite against the sea, they said, that fostered tolerance and the related notion of the *poldermodel* – the effort to reach broad consensus on critical issues. A *polder* is a low-lying piece of land protected from the sea by dikes. And in *polders*, it was crucial for everyone to compromise – to tolerate each other, to ensure they didn't end up under water. In New York, wonky transport planners and hip, fixed-gear cycle-riders idolised the *woonerf*. But they were even more excited about another Dutch innovation aiming to separate road users rather than mix them together.

A 'physically separated bike lane' protects bikers by segregating them from cars – simply achieved by switching the bike lane with the parking lane, so the parked cars form a protective wall from moving traffic. In 2007, 365 cyclists were killed or seriously injured in New York.[7] So while the *woonerf* was a wonderful ideal, it couldn't easily be transplanted to the car-dominated grid structure of Manhattan. The grid system was not an American creation, but it has excelled in the so-called 'land of opportunity'. Many early settlements like Boston and Nieuw Amsterdam in lower Manhattan were more haphazard. The grid has been favoured as a tool for colonial expansion and rapid development since before the Roman Empire but was applied at a new scale and pace in the US. Varying grid plans were soon employed in cities ranging from Savannah to New Orleans and Chicago, and taken to new extremes in New York. Historian John Reps has described the entire west of the US as developed through a 'giant gridiron imposed upon the natural landscape' by the 1785 Land Ordinance, which divided new territories into neat square-mile packages to be sold off to the highest bidder.[8]

The grid continued to spread across the US as the railroad system expanded and development boomed in the second half of the nineteenth century. Some cities were laid out in perfect squares, while others were shaped around long thin rectangles. Some were broken into smaller pieces than others – one Sacramento, California block is over twice the size of a Portland, Oregon block. But across the nation, the grid generated similar conditions: continuous through-streets meeting at right-angle intersections, often without any natural hierarchy.[9]

It's a system that physically creates more confrontation – more points at which drivers and walkers must negotiate who goes first – than the meandering medieval network of many European cities, where narrower side streets feed naturally into major arteries. And setting loose the new addition of the automobile put the grid system to test.

Early traffic control was conducted by a policeman posted in the middle of an intersection. This proved not to be very healthy for the policemen or for municipal budgets, however. So American officials brought in the 'sleeping policeman': a lighted signpost instructing drivers to circle right around it. Unfortunately, the sleeping policeman was knocked down even more often than his waking counterpart. But Americans continued to develop this general idea, creating traffic circles and then rotary systems to direct traffic circularly around a central island. Rotaries were flawed – primarily because they gave priority to incoming vehicles, which blocked up the whole system. But they continued to be widely used up to World War II, especially in states like New Jersey.[10]

During the war, road construction was put on hold. While commanding the Allied forces in Europe, General Eisenhower was impressed by the German autobahn. The German network of super-highways was the most advanced road system in the world at the time and had been instrumental in speedy troop deployment. After returning to the US and becoming president, Eisenhower championed the construction of the interstate highway system. American transportation planning in this period was led by the goal of accommodating the automobile. Rotaries, replaced with stoplights, disappeared from highway design guidance standards.[11] In American cities like Detroit and Los Angeles, as much as 75 to 80 per cent of all urban land was committed to moving and storing automobiles.[12] In addition to new roads, the highway system 'improved' many existing streets, changing their form and function to better serve cars. Streets were widened and made unidirectional for greater efficiency. As the number of cars, collisions, and pedestrian injuries increased, authorities assumed the antidote was greater segregation and control. More stoplights, speed limits, and speed bumps.

Meanwhile, in the UK, British traffic engineers were busy improving upon the traffic circle and rotary to create the round-about. The Bath Circus, built in 1754, is considered the oldest traffic circle in the world. Roundabouts came into wider use in the early twentieth century, working on the same principle as American rotaries. As automobile use grew after the war, British circular systems buckled under the increased pressure. The 1950s saw a 'lock-up' crisis: circles backed up past entrances, bringing throughput to a grinding halt.

There was only one hope for the roundabout – an experimental innovation called the yield sign. Highway staff deployed these triangular novelties at roundabout entrances, reversing the priority to vehicles already in the circle. They feared the worst. But instead of casualties and chaos, vehicle delay times dropped by forty per cent, capacity increased ten per cent, and crashes resulting in injury dropped forty per cent. The modern British roundabout was born.[13]

Why did Britain persevere in perfecting the format abandoned by their American cousins? The US had greater availability of cheap land, and a stronger post-war economy to fund highway construction. But roundabout historian Edmund Waddell attributes this divergence to another important distinction: the British government paid for hospital bills as well as highway construction!

A standard intersection between a pair of two-way streets provides thirty-two vehicle-to-vehicle conflict points and twenty-four vehicle-to-person conflict points. A roundabout in the same space presents only eight points for vehicles to collide and eight between people and vehicles. Statistically, the average

INTERSECTION VERSUS ROUNDABOUT

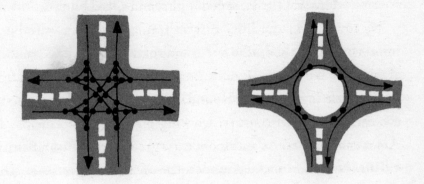

Comparison of possible vehicle conflict points
Source: NCHRP Report 672 Exhibit 5-2

roundabout in England is much safer than an American stoplight-controlled intersection.[14]

After having spent a year making a documentary about the political importance of public space with Barbara and the other tigers, I ironically left New York just as the Occupy Wall Street movement took off. But not before witnessing one of its first mass arrests – a peaceful protest marching from Zuccotti Park towards Union Square – taking place at the base of my very own apartment building. Between frantic suitcase stuffing and refrigerator scrubbing, I tried to film the strange scene unfolding feet below my window, which looked somewhat like an awkward dress rehearsal. Cops in blue penned the crowd in with a long red net, moving slowly to engulf them like an amoeba – a quintessentially American authoritarian approach to social control.

There was no sign of the Occupy movement when I arrived at the quiet campus of the University of Surrey. But when I made my way to the Occupy London camp at St Paul's cathedral a few months later, I was struck by the comparative lack of police presence and interference. The St Paul's site was one of the longest-standing Occupy encampments worldwide, ending only with a long court battle.[15]

On a spectrum from Dutch tolerance to American discipline, the British model of social control must fall somewhere midway. Public drinking is permitted, but marijuana is criminalised. Police officers are largely unarmed outside of Northern Ireland. From littering fines to criminal sentencing, punishment is generally much less severe than the US. I was impressed by what seemed to be a more communal approach to the public realm in Britain. Like the *poldermodel*, you feel you're yielding to the common flow, the greater good.

But trying to cycle around a London roundabout was terrifying. And then there were the one-way systems – a British term for one-way streets that seems to embody an entirely different idea of your relationship to the space. One-way systems are used not just for cars, but for people at festivals like Glastonbury and in city centres. One gets a sense of being herded like a cow in these packed paths between barriers where you are carried along by the crowd. Imbued with the logic of segregating and directing, British traffic engineering doesn't trust people to interact with each other much more than the American approach. British streets are a jungle of lines and posts containing species including zebra, pelican, puffin, and toucan crossings – though the avian members of this family bear little resemblance to their tropical namesakes.

While roundabouts are safer, less confrontational – more collective in a sense – they aren't particularly lovely places. The British roundabout has been constantly, intensively engineered to create an experience that feels more like going through a vacuum cleaner than a public space. You can easily see why the idea of making them more like shared spaces was so appealing. When surveyed, most shared spaces users have rated them as visually improved.[16] Part of the problem with roundabouts, according to urban designer Fin McNab, is scale. 'It's the huge, gyratory, split-level roundabouts – for example at the M32 in Bristol – which is where they become very challenging for pedestrians, for humans in general,' says McNab. In its most extreme expression we have the Magic Roundabout at Swindon, a monstrous roundabout of roundabouts.

Many shared spaces, such as Laweiplein, include some kind of circle in the middle. But do they offer more than aesthetic advantages over a comparably sized roundabout? In 2016, Benjamin Wargo and Norman Garrick at the University of Connecticut conducted a study comparing six shared spaces in five different countries. While the spaces have different levels of 'sharedness', they are all found at intersections between standard two-lane, two-way streets. The researchers compared video footage of the spaces with computer-modelled data on how they would perform if managed through more conventional, signalised intersection or roundabout strategies. The ostensible paradox of Laweiplein, they found, holds true: shared space frees pedestrian movement, while also making intersections more efficient. Shared spaces cause shorter delays for both vehicles and pedestrians. And, importantly, the more truly shared a space is, the slower the speeds are. In those with the fewest segregating elements and most interactions observed between user types, cars drive the slowest. Shared spaces are also found to enhance 'sense of place' while maintaining safety levels of traditional intersections.

So why didn't the transplantation process always go smoothly when British enthusiasts set about grafting the *woonerf* onto their own roads? Moody and Melia suggest that British shared spaces like Ashford haven't accommodated pedestrians as well as the original *woonerven* did. Elwick Square has none of the landscaping and street furniture that helps define safe space for pedestrians. And of course, Britain lacks the cultural context of *woonerven* that most Nederlanders are familiar with. In moderately trafficked parts of many Dutch cities, shared space strategies are employed to varying degrees throughout the entire area.

The problem with some shared spaces may be that they have gone too far in the other direction, focusing on the ideal of a completely naked street rather than carefully heeding the needs of the place and people in question. Before we invented curbs and traffic lights, all streets were shared spaces. But that doesn't mean this philosophy will work for all of them now.

In the US, there are still very few examples of Laweiplein-style shared space. As of 2016, Wargo and Garrick were only able to find one US example of a shared space intersection matching their comparative criteria. Uptown Circle in Normal, Illinois is a yield-controlled circle with a grassy, tree-lined central park. Wargo gives it his lowest sharedness rating – some might say it's actually a roundabout. But it looks like a nice place. A place you would want to sit and read a book.

And for all the excitement about shared space in New York, this concept has been difficult to translate to the mega-grid of

Manhattan. Gansevoort Plaza in the Meatpacking District is a notable specimen. This wide, cobblestoned intersection was successfully pedestrianised with a handful of gum-drop shaped bollards and planters in 2008. This is a sort of 'naturally occurring' shared space. But most America intersections aren't magically going to be transformed into Italian plazas just by flattening the curbs. Most of the inspiring transformations of public space in New York over the past eight years have been more about claiming car space back for people and bikes than mixing them all together.

Rather than copying the form of shared space, the trick is to translate the underlying principles with context sensitivity – principles such as creating a better sense of place, enabling pedestrians to move freely, reducing vehicle dominance, increasing safety, and ensuring transport needs are still met. And maybe most importantly: less is more. The most effective social control is the kind where people keep each other in check. And this sort of informal social control in public space is one of the keystones of collective efficacy, according to Sampson and Raudenbush.

Public spaces need to guide us to a certain extent. They should provide litter bins and should not be so secluded that we feel unsafe. But we also need space to negotiate and interact. Public space should inspire us to be good citizens – to be respectful of each other and our community. And the best public spaces encourage us to be creative. To push the boundaries a bit as well.

As with the Broken Windows theory, we can't say that roundabouts brought about the British nanny state or that the grid system makes Americans more authoritarian and confrontational. What is likely is that the same root causes, developing over centuries, have produced both these symptoms. Large numbers of Americans have come to believe it is morally wrong to step off your front porch with a glass of wine. But there has been little change in rates of alcoholism since Broken Windows policies came in. And as we have seen with the tragic deaths of people like Eric Garner, this type of social control has unacceptably unjust consequences. The block where Garner suffocated in a police chokehold for the inconsequential misdemeanour of selling loose cigarettes in 2014 is now reported to be rife with crime and violence.[17]

What we learned from the Groningen experiments is that subtle environmental features impact our moment-to-moment actions, even our values and attitudes, below our awareness. This means that a setting like a *woonerf* continues to reinforce the cultural values that generated it. It means that changing a street's design can impact our behaviour and our social norms. But it won't change our entire culture overnight. And if we don't examine the underlying problems, we may simply be pushing them deeper down – only to see them erupt again.

But before we move on from the *woonerf*, there is one more important point to make. The critics say people report *feeling* unsafe in shared spaces. They say this is proof that they don't work. But I also felt less safe at British roundabouts initially, simply because I was used to American intersections. We don't always have a good sense of what is good for us. Or of how space shapes our actions.

The strangest turn in the Petrified Forest story is that the park authorities ultimately decided not to change their signage. Cialdini presented his compelling research to the park administrators. Despite this evidence, park rangers interviewed some park visitors who claimed the knowledge that fourteen tons of petrified chips were stolen each year would deter them from stealing. And based on this information, administrators decided to keep the counter-productive signs. We have a strong desire to believe we can control behaviour through logic and information, even when we're shown we can't.

How do we understand these intricate relationships between an environment, the people in it, their identity, and behaviour? This is the complex web of dynamics that I will unravel over the next chapters of this book.

CHAPTER 2

The Defeat of the Ninja-Proof Seat

The Hawthorne effect, personal space bubbles,
and the open-plan office

When I try to explain environmental psychology to someone new, they always say the same three things:

'So you ask trees about how they feel?'

This, they clearly think, is a very witty comment that I have never heard before. Mine is a vast, murky, unknown topic to most people. So I explain to them how I apply environmental psychology research to create better workspaces. This clicks immediately. And they say, 'Oh, my office is *terrible*! We should get you in.' And then they almost always say, 'Can you make us a Google office?'

If you work in an office, or a factory, or even a school, you probably feel the same way. Only fifty-three per cent of workers surveyed by the Leesman Index (the largest independent database of workplace effectiveness data) say that their workplace enables them to work productively. Many of us have become used to spending the majority of our waking hours in dull, grey boxes with slightly fuzzy movable walls. But when you take a step back, it seems quite strange that all these buildings dedicated specifically to getting work done don't work as well as they could for that purpose.

Researchers and businesses have been trying to figure out how to make workers more productive for a long time. It began in 1924 at a manufacturing plant outside Chicago. The Hawthorne Works was a flat, grey factory with twin chimneys billowing smoke out into the flat, grey Midwestern sky. Inside, twelve thousand workers were working on assembly lines, winding coils to manufacture a hot high-tech device called the telephone. The company, Western Electric, wanted to find out if they could make the workers work a little faster by shining a bit more light in this grey box they worked in.

A group of researchers led by a man named Elton Mayo started running some tests. They shone more and less light at certain times on different assembly lines. And like all good researchers they also had a control group, whose lighting levels stayed constant. The workers with more light did work faster. But strangely, the control group workers were more productive as well. Next, they tried lowering the lights, and the workers were able to maintain production levels even when lighting was reduced by seventy per cent. Finally, they pretended to raise the lighting while actually keeping it constant. Not only did productivity increase but the workers also told them how happy they were with the improved lighting!

At least, that is how the story goes. The Hawthorne Effect, as it came to be known, is highly debated. It has an almost mythical status in the worlds of occupational psychology and human relations. The original studies themselves were never formally published, but were recounted and reinterpreted by many subsequent researchers, a little like a ghost story. More recent scrutiny has uncovered major statistical and methodological flaws.

But the impact the Hawthorne Effect has had on workspaces is difficult to overstate. Researchers concluded that the presence and attention of the research team and the novelty of change had made the workers more productive. And this led many people to believe that environmental factors like lighting were less important to productivity than social factors like supervision. The Hawthorne studies helped give birth to the human relations movement, which you now find embodied in your company's HR department. It led businesses to focus on management, social relations, and motivation rather than the workspace itself. It led researchers away from looking at factors like layout, noise, and light quality – how the shape of a table might make us more collaborative, or the height of the ceiling might make us more creative. Or how not being able to make the space our own in some way might make us want to spend as little time there as we can.

On some level we know these things affect us. I once worked in an office full of software engineers who were obsessed with what they called ninja-proof seats. A ninja-proof seat is one with its back to the wall so you can be sure no ninjas can sneak up from behind. Setting aside questions of whether ninjas can fly or climb walls, your computer screen can't be seen without your knowledge. Our original office was an industrial conversion in New York's West Village, although it wasn't really converted for office use. It was a small sail-making factory that a flamboyant man named Franz had fitted out with Grecian columns and internal balconies, before running off to Berlin and subletting it to our organisation. This meant there were many internal walls and small spaces. In the largest room the software developers had arranged their desks in a large U so that everyone could have a ninja-proof seat.

As the organisation grew, we needed to move to a larger, more professional office. The new space was lovely, with outstanding amenities like a living green wall, well-stocked kitchen, and expansive views. The company was vying to attract top engineering grads, wooing them with a workplace they would never want to leave. But as you often find with these Google-esque offices, lots of energy had been put into these eye-catching extras, and much less into the workstations themselves. It was essentially a large open-plan office with long rows of desks down the centre.

And this meant there were no ninja-proof seats! Not a single one. The developers' complaints were dismissed as irrelevant – except for the most fearsome socks-under-Birkenstocks-wearing coder, who was mysteriously allowed to claim a broom closet for his sole use. (He may possibly have had a reputation for being more productive than all of the other developers combined.) The HR team was convinced that ninja-proof seats were mainly good for getting away with playing video games at work.

The term 'ninja-proof seat' may only be used by those fluent in Python and JavaScript, but you will find people who are adamant about their need for one in any office you go to. This is because they provide what geographer Jay Appleton calls *refuge and prospect*. If you imagine a time when we were being chased by lions and men with swords, certain places would be much safer than others. Climbing up a hilltop would allow a good *prospect* of approaching threats. Building a fort against a mountain face would be even better as it would provide *refuge*, and limit the directions these lions or pirates might attack you from. Our preference for ninja-proof seats works on the same principle. Many people feel most comfortable and at ease when they have their back to the wall rather than an open room or door.

More importantly, we actually concentrate better on our work and demonstrate increased cognitive performance in ninja-proof seats.[1] Then again, some people aren't bothered about where they sit or what type of lighting their office has. Certain personality types, like introverts, may be much more strongly impacted by issues like noise. And others may report that it doesn't bother them, but their performance is nevertheless impaired.

So how did we come to find ourselves in these monotonous boxes called offices?

Before the industrial revolution, many people's work happened in and around their homes: farming adjacent lands, running a shop downstairs, or even weaving in the kitchen. The industrial revolution brought many people's work out of their homes, collecting them together in big boxes called factories. The form and location of early factories were typically determined by sources of power and light. Mills required fast-flowing water power, so they were often built near hilly streams, removed from low-lying coastal commercial centres. Waterwheel technology worked by turning a long shaft, which powered machinery inside the mill. Reliance on natural light required a narrow building no more than 60 feet (18 metres) wide. So mill factories were shaped as long narrow boxes.[2]

Iron, structural steel, and concrete revolutionised the scale and form of factories, and then offices. But our concept of productivity has continued to be defined by a factory-based notion of workers as cogs in a machine striving to obtain perfect efficiency. The foundations for this concept of productivity were laid by a man named Frederick Winslow Taylor. Studying industrial efficiency in factories, he developed an approach called 'scientific management', or Taylorism, and pioneered the

practice of management consulting. Productivity has traditionally been defined as the ratio of output to inputs, including
things like materials, labour, and capital. In the factory model,
you put these in one end, and get telephones, rubber ducks, or
some other widget out the other end. Similarly to the design of
our streets, the concept of productivity comes from an engineering framework, aiming to achieve the maximum output possible
for a production process, given a set level of input. But trying to
achieve supreme technical efficiency may not always make economic sense.

Assigning each worker to their own box of space was a key
strategy in the design of traditional offices and management
systems. With everyone in their proper place, materials, productivity, and output could easily be accounted for. But the rise of
information and communication technologies has caused what
employment studies expert Alan Felstead calls a 'weakening of
the spatial fixity of the workplace, with workers increasingly
detached from their personal cubes of space.'[3]

Now, rather than being stationed in a set desk or cubicle
for forty hours a week, office workers are told the key to
productivity is to plug themselves into different 'hot desks', roam
from workstations to soft-seating break-out pods, and vary their
work location between home, office, and cafés on a daily basis.
Companies are even beginning to sublet desks within their own
offices through services like Deskcamping.

The parade of office design trends keeps marching on. But
it is important to differentiate innovations motivated by new
working patterns and research findings from the latest fad for
air-plant terrariums. Setting aside whatever you may have been
told about goat-hair carpets and living walls, what do we really

know about what we need to be effective at work?

■ ■ ■

Outside of the artificial lab environment, the office provides perhaps the best testing ground to consider the plethora of environmental factors influencing our mood and behaviour from moment to moment. Do you work more efficiently in complete silence or with mild background chatter? Is it easier to concentrate in a cubicle, or to collaborate in an open floorplan? We have inputs to consider like light, noise, layout, dimensions, and temperature. And we have outputs to consider like individual efficiency, creativity, collaboration, and the elusive metric of productivity.

In 2013, University of Sydney researchers Jungsoo Kim and Richard de Dear conducted a study to try to pinpoint exactly which indoor environmental qualities are most important to workers' overall happiness with their workspace. They looked at satisfaction with air quality, thermal comfort, lighting, layout, acoustic quality, cleanliness, and even furnishings. Reviewing over forty thousand survey responses from the University of California at Berkeley's Center for the Built Environment database, they found one crucial satisfaction factor that outranked all the others: the size of one's individual office space.[4]

Personal space is like an invisible bubble that we wear around ourselves wherever we go. When pigeons perch on telephone lines they tend to space themselves evenly apart, and people do the same thing. Think of how we stand in bus-stop queues.

Anthropologist Edward T. Hall was one of the first researchers to establish these basic dimensions of personal space – 'proxemics' – through a series of observational studies conducted in the 1960s. Hall discovered that people have four key sizes of personal space bubbles, which they inflate and deflate depending on where they are and who they're with. Proxemics are the spatial requirements of humans and animals. But Hall believed there was more to read into these dynamics than calculations of population density. He saw the space between people as a form of communication.

Working in the US State Department to train foreign service personnel for posts in disparate parts of the world, he encountered intercultural communication issues from Japan to Syria to Germany. He found that 'the way in which both time and space were handled constituted a form of communication which was responded to as if it were built into people and, therefore, universally valid.'[5] This 'silent language', he believed, functions as part of the DNA of the cultures it is rooted in.[6]

Hall studied various cultures, but particularly his own: middle-class Americans of northern European descent. We must remember that, in his day, the state of ethnic integration in the US was primeval. So while this may sound like an oddly specific definition today, it was relevant at the time. Even within the US, he found that different ethnic and socioeconomic groups had different personal space norms.

In the language of Hall's subculture, the most intimate level (0 to 1.5 feet) is reserved for romantic partners, comforting gestures, and special scenarios like sports and theatre seating. At the personal level (1.5 to 4 feet) we interact with close friends and pass by people in a shop or the office kitchen when necessary. For more formal and impersonal dynamics, we bring out our social distance bubble (4 to 8 feet). And for public settings – performing or speaking to an audience – we prefer a distance of more than 10 feet.[7]

These thresholds aren't completely arbitrary. They are defined

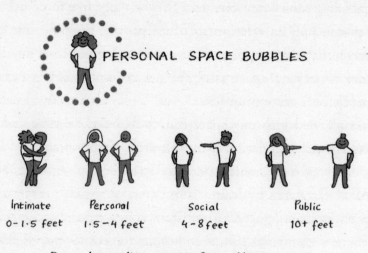

Personal space distances are influenced by situations,
relationships, and human dimensions.
Source: Adapted from Hall (1968)

by human scale in relation to cultural norms about acceptable interactions. In the personal zone, you are within reach: standing elbow to elbow or one arm's length away. The social zone tends to place you just out of reach. And at the public distance, you are roughly the length of two not very tall people apart. I tested this out a few times recently, and was surprised to find how accurate it was. Whether sitting or standing, I found myself reliably just out of reach from the informal acquaintances I was in conversation with.

While it is whimsical to imagine ourselves bobbing about our days in big pink bubbles, it is important to add that there are some limitations to this metaphor. Our space bubbles are not actually spherical, for one. We have a higher tolerance for the proximity of others behind us than in front of us.[8] Our bubbles also aren't like armour, protecting us from everything we interact with. They are permeable, allowing chairs, sandwiches, and even cats and babies into contact. They're more like force fields that operate only in relation to other people, bristling into action when they come into proximity with other humans. Finally, the idea of personal space as a bubble may emphasise protection too much over communication. And while architectural elements are allowed into our space, our bubbles do shrink and warp enormously in relation to our physical surroundings.

As rooms get smaller, personal space bubbles expand.[9] Men in particular seem to desire more personal space in environments with low ceilings.[10] Our comfort zones require more space in narrow rooms than square ones, in the corner rather than the centre of the room, when we're inside instead of outside, sitting down rather than standing up, and in more crowded spaces. As with the concepts of refuge and prospect, this may relate to basic survival instincts. In more constrained environments, we need more personal space to keep our flight and fight options open.[11]

The personal space bubble is the most basic dimension of people and space. But what happens to different people's bubbles when they come together in the space of an office? We are all familiar with the idea of territory, but how does it differ from personal space? While personal space is invisible and movable, territory is relatively fixed and visible. Territories also tend to be larger than personal spaces. They relate to the idea of ownership, and can extend past the individual to small and large groups of people.

Like many features of human behaviour, psychologists are split on whether territoriality is innate or learned – whether we are born with the instinct to put up fences around our properties or learn this custom during our upbringing. In the animal kingdom, mammals, insects, birds, and even fish define and defend territory in various ways. Territory functions as a way for these animals to control mating opportunities and access to resources such as food and shelter. Dispersing population ensures that a particular area doesn't become overpopulated, threatening the survival of the species as a whole.

Humans differ from other animals in that we have developed extensive physical and legal structures to mediate territorial relationships. And this means that we use physical conflict to defend individual territory less often than many of our animal counterparts – at least in recent history. We also invite people into our territories, which wildebeests and hyenas don't tend to do. And when we do battle for territory we like to do it in groups, whereas other animals tend to fight individually. Still, territory is critical to our sense of safety and survival. [12]

American researchers in the 1970s identified three main levels of territory, which we define and defend in different ways. A primary territory is a place we feel very strong ownership over, such as our home or an individual office. Even if we don't actually own our apartment or office, we feel a high degree of control over who can enter these areas and how they will be used or decorated. A secondary territory is a place that we feel a moderate sense of control over, such as a local pub, classroom, or community garden. Public territories are public spaces such as parks, streets, and sidewalks, which we have little control over. But even in these spaces, we may temporarily claim territory by parking in a parking spot or laying out a picnic blanket.

One of the main ways we define these territories is by personalising them. Personalisation is the purposeful decoration, rearrangement, or adaptation of an environment to reflect the identity of those who occupy it. It is estimated that seventy to ninety per cent of working Americans personalise their workplace in some way, though women are more likely to personalise their desks than men, and use more plants and social items like photos. Studies indicate that personalisation has many benefits, such as greater satisfaction with work, increased well-being, higher morale, and lower staff turnover. [13] These positive psychological benefits are understood to be a result of support for the expression of identity and distinctiveness. But bureaucracies and corporations have often unfortunately resisted personalisation in the workplace.

Personal space, territory, and personalisation all relate intimately to privacy. Social and environmental psychologist Irwin Altman believed that they were all smaller pieces of the bigger issue of how we control our privacy. Altman suggested that privacy is not just the state of being in private; it is the ability to selectively control access to yourself. Like personal space, privacy is just as much about communication as it is about separation. We often find that more private spaces are more personalised. Compare a private office to one shared with others, for instance.

The only private office I have ever worked in was at my first job at the Gotham Center for New York City History. As part of the City University of New York Graduate Center, it was housed within a behemoth of a building filling the entire block at the corner of Thirty-Fourth Street and Fifth Avenue in Manhattan – right across the street from the Empire State Building. The cafeteria on the top floor had a glass ceiling, through which you could peer up at the Empire State at an uncomfortably close angle. The Italianate structure had been a luxurious department store, called B. Altman & Company. Many years before, my grandmother had spent Saturdays perusing the same floors, when they were stocked with small leather goods, neckwear, and a blouse bazaar. But the building had been largely gutted in renovation, so only a few traces of this history remained – the windowsills, a railing in a back stairway where I would steal away to glimpse the sun.

By my time, the building was a maze of long interlocking corridors with identical grey doors. My office was a little windowless cube off a windowless hall. Sometimes I was joined by another woman named Melinda who talked a lot about her cats. But mostly I was alone in a small dark room. I spent a lot of time imagining myself on a spaceship. It was not the most stimulating environment – I found myself getting very sleepy. So I never had any desire to close my door. I kept it open to watch academic superstars like geographer David Harvey passing by.

The saving grace of this solitary space was that I could control certain key elements. I played the radio and adjusted the furniture. But more importantly, I never used the harsh overhead light, which made me feel like my brain was in a microwave. Using a few lamps with a softer quality of light made a huge difference to my happiness. Working away at thrilling tasks like filling in Excel spreadsheets with the names of New York City public school teachers, I yearned for the stimulation of engaging co-workers. The Gotham-themed prank calls I received ('Hello, this is the Joker, can I speak to the Batman?') became the social interaction highlight of my day. But with more people comes less control. And if I hadn't had control of these few little factors, I was certain my performance would have suffered.

When people get in touch with my consultancy today, it is

usually because they have decided that an open-plan office is the answer to their problems. Typically, there is some other motivating factor. The company is expanding, the lease is up, or they have raised funds to give their tired digs a facelift. They want it to be sustainable, creative, productive! And they have also heard that this open-plan, hot-desk thing is the thing to do. But somewhere along the way, problems start to appear – often when they are well into the process of working with an interior designer or fit-out company. Initial plans have been drawn up and the finance team is enraged! Why have they all been shoved into one windowless corner? Or perhaps it is the reclusive research unit who are concerned about being placed directly next to the chatty recruitment team.

The modern open-plan ideal was popularised in the late 1950s with the 'bull pen' format, where desks are laid out in straight rows without partitions.[14] Office landscaping, or *Burolandschaft*, a German concept introduced to the US in 1964, divides a space with interlocking shoulder-height partitions, filing cabinets, and potted plants. These innovations were expected to be more efficient for teamwork, facilitate easier supervision, and reduce renovation expenses. This trend was taken a step further with the 'non-territorial office', in which employees have no assigned desk. Non-territorial working began to appear as early as the 1980s, but is now known more commonly as hot-desking. In non-territorial offices design, the bias against personalisation is essentially built in.[15]

Max Weber, a pioneer in the study of bureaucracy, alleged that work systems were increasingly efficient as the work itself was more depersonalised. Particularly when brought out of the private office, personalisation has been discouraged as 'blight' on the clear expanse of desks. This is unfortunate because the assumption that physical neatness is connected to organisational efficiency has not been supported with empirical evidence.[16]

The move to open-plan offices has been motivated by both economic and ideological objectives. In an open-plan office you can fit more people into a smaller space. Less space is taken up by walls and doors. And you can more easily reconfigure space to accommodate organisational change. The economic advantages have been well demonstrated.[17] And with hot-desking, the savings can be even greater. Ten employees can typically be served with only seven workspaces, correlating to enormous savings on an expense which is second only to staff for most companies.[18] Citi has recently been able to accommodate two hundred workers with only 150 desks in their New York office.[19]

This all sounds wonderfully open and flexible. Open-plan proponents envision these offices as dynamic collaborative places, where conversations take place in the open, knowledge is shared freely, and people can spontaneously collaborate. They have argued that open-plan offices improve individual and organisational productivity by promoting greater communication and collaboration. These are lovely ideas. But unfortunately, the evidence does not corroborate these claims. In fact, it suggests the opposite.

There is quite an extensive body of research in this area, with researchers generally finding that open-plan layouts have a negative impact on people's happiness with their offices. The move from closed to open offices makes many people feel they can't do their work as well, and has been linked to slumping job satisfaction and productivity.[20] Research over the past four decades has consistently identified two main problems with open offices: privacy and noise.[21] If you work in an office, you probably know the worst type of noise – your co-worker a few feet away telling the thrilling story of how their Chihuahua choked on a chicken bone over the weekend. Loud and clear, irrelevant but intelligible speech makes it very difficult to work.

A group of Finnish researchers led by Annu Haapakangas found that nearly twice as much working time is needed due to noise in open offices.[22] This type of noise interferes especially with individual work requiring higher cognitive processing and complex verbal processes.[23] Noise may specifically reduce productivity by making workers less motivated. What's ironic is that we have known about these problems with open-plan offices for quite a long time. As far back as 1982, Alan Hedge at the University of Aston found that open-plan office workers were less happy with their offices due to the same two issues: decreasing privacy and increasing disturbances. Hedge's systematic study found the work itself as well as the workers' well-being was affected. While the open plan did allow for more flexible space use, Hedge found almost no evidence to suggest the flexibility was actually taken advantage of at the organisational or personal level.

In environmental psychology, 'sociopetal' space describes environments that facilitate interaction and communication, whereas 'sociofugal' space does the opposite. The seating you typically see in airports and theatres, for instance, is sociofugal. Long rows of seats facing the backs of other seats don't orient people towards interacting with each other. The spacing of seating is one component of sociopetal space – people seated outside Hall's social distance are less likely to interact. But seating geometry is also key. As with our four personal space bubbles, we use four key seating geometries for different social dynamics. And when we have to fit ourselves into these formats, they cue us to take on those stances as well.

The first one is obvious. When you come into a room to play a card game or enter a tense business negotiation, where do you sit? Across from your opponent.[24] But what about when we meet a friend to catch up over coffee? Do we sit across from them as well? Or perhaps side by side, as benches and couches invite us to do? This is what personal space researcher Robert Sommer expected to find. But he discovered that people actually tend to sit corner to corner when conversing: a 90-degree orientation. While we tend to think that sofas are a good place to get together for a chat, side-by-side or 180-degree orientation can actually be detrimental to conversation. In cooperative situations people tend to sit adjacent, as this facilitates looking at the same material. But what about sharing a table with someone you don't know in a library or crowded café? When people want to ignore each other they tend to sit diagonally – 'catty corner' as we call it in the US.

Much of this comes down to eye contact. Sitting directly across from someone allows direct eye contact – an ideal oppositional position, which can be too intense for more friendly situations. Similarly, strangers sit diagonally to gain greater distance from each other, but also because it allows them to avoid eye contact.

Extend these concepts to broader office layout and you can start to see how an entire workspace can function sociopetally or sociofugally. Are people spaced close together or far apart? Facing in towards each other, or outwards? Office design trends have reflected changes in the nature of our work, as well as notions of how cooperative or independent our work should be. Sociofugal cubicles isolated paper-pushing white-collar workers, while shared hot desks are intended to foster creative collaboration for

SEATING GEOMETRIES

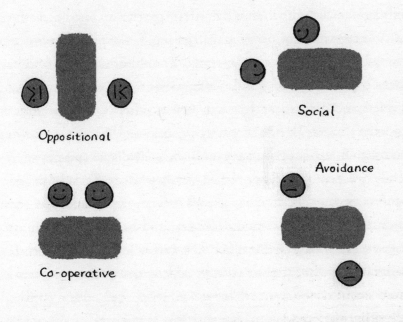

Oppositional

Social

Co-operative

Avoidance

today's multi-tasking knowledge workers.

But let's get back to Alan Hedge. His 1982 study found that open-plan offices were successfully sociopetal, but more socialising did not help workers do their jobs better. No evidence for the idea of open-plan offices improving productivity was discovered.[25] Of course, many things have changed since Hedge conducted his research. Many more people now work from home at least one day a week. Could this provide the critical balance of private space? And to many workers today – especially younger ones – the idea of ever having a private office may sound as fantastical as having a private jet. Have changing expectations changed perception of open-plan environments?

The 2013 study by Kim and de Dear mentioned earlier re-examined some of Hedge's findings, specifically comparing workers' satisfaction with various indoor environmental factors depending on different office layouts: private and shared enclosed offices, cubicles with high and low-level partitions, and open offices with little or no enclosure. Unsurprisingly, the private office was favoured, followed by semi-private. The different types of open-plan offices received similar scores. But one thing was clear: cubicles were the most detested. Across office types, the amount of individual working and storage space was the most important factor in how happy workers were with their workspace.

Interestingly, the importance of other factors varied considerably between office types. Visual privacy was ranked as least important to those in private offices, and became more important the less enclosed the office was. Noise level was also seen as more important by those in open offices, but sound privacy was even more important than noise level and visual privacy. Partitions were found to help with visual privacy, but not sound. What can we take from this? One conclusion is that factors are often considered 'less important' when they are working well. People enjoying the benefits of their own office may say visual privacy isn't that important, because they don't know what it's like to have colleagues constantly peering over their shoulder.

Even in the private office, satisfaction with sound privacy is much lower than satisfaction with visual privacy – probably due to the use of flimsy lightweight partition materials, which don't adequately block sound. And much in line with my own experience, lighting levels were also seen as more important in private offices.

All in all, people are deeply dissatisfied with sound privacy. But this doesn't have as much impact on overall office satisfaction as the amount of space they have. This may tell us as much about what people expect from their offices as it does about productivity. While noise may be more annoying, not having enough space feels like more of a slap in the face.

And as for collaboration, open-plan workers were no more satisfied with how easily they could interact with colleagues than those in private offices. Further, insufficient interaction was not a major source of discontent for anyone. Some researchers have even suggested that open-plan offices may be detrimental to communication because they provide few opportunities for confidential tête-à-têtes.

The supposed sociopetal benefits of open-plan offices do not seem to outweigh their noise and privacy deficits. And yet, we already have quite a lot of open-plan offices on our hands. So what can we do to make them work better?

Companies looking at smarter strategies for open plans and hot-desking have a lot to learn from co-working spaces such as the Impact HUB network. Impact HUB is an international network of over eighty co-working spaces at the forefront of thinking and design for the twenty-first-century model of work. The organisation was founded to nurture the social innovation sector by providing professional workspace facilities, business incubation support, and a community network. A social enterprise itself, Impact HUB operates on a 'federated' model (a friendlier and more open sort of franchise) and has grown to serve over thirteen thousand members in cities ranging from Milan to Kuala Lumpur and Harare. But it all began in London.

Serviced offices like Regus have been around for some time. But the current craze for co-working spaces is a fairly recent phenomenon. The very first Impact HUB opened its doors in 2005 in Islington, with the Kings Cross office coming soon after as the first purpose-built HUB. In 2008, everyone was getting excited about this new concept of 'co-working'. So they built a perfect space for that purpose: collaborating, meeting, and coming together. A space for a diverse community of freelancers and social enterprises to cross-pollinate ideas and projects.

It's a stunning space in an old warehouse building across the street from Kings Cross station. The structure was renovated by Architecture 00 to maintain much of the original stonework and wooden beams, while opening up the space through a central atrium beneath a giant peaked skylight. Meetings are held in glass cubes that seem to hang in the air between the two main floors. And the entire ground floor can be transformed into an event space through Tinkertoy-style furniture, which comes apart to hang on the wall. With such a beautiful space, what could possibly go wrong?

Five years after opening, Impact HUB Kings Cross (IHKC) were experiencing some growing pains. They asked us to take stock of how their space was performing, and how it could better support the many functions and people coming together there. We spent a few weeks studying what was happening in the space. We talked to people and asked them to fill out a survey. But we also analysed their behaviour objectively. At set intervals on different days, we noted how people were using different parts of the space, how full it was, and what the noise levels were.

We found that they were very happy with the look and feel of the space. 'We love the wooden beams and historic texture of the space,' they said. 'The natural light is an amazing asset!' But when we asked people what type of work was most important to their time at the HUB, a different picture emerged. Forty-eight per cent of members said that individual work was the most important function for their HUB time. This was followed by phone and video calls at thirty-one per cent, and meetings at only thirteen per cent. Our observations confirmed that people did spend the majority of their time working alone – fifty-eight per cent of the time on average. But looking at how well the space met these needs, we found it didn't align with their priorities. Members said the space worked much better for meetings than it did for individual work or phone calls.

In all the excitement about collaborative work, less space had been reserved for solitary activities like focused work and phone calls. The need for spaces supporting quieter and louder work had been underestimated. There really wasn't any adequate place to politely pop away from your desk to take a long noisy call. This meant that volume levels were high throughout the space at peak times, impacting many people's ability to focus. You could almost see a domino effect rippling around the room, as each person's decibel level rose a little higher than their neighbours'. Heavy-duty headphones were pulled out and spiteful glares darted at the worst offenders.

Sound levels in the space told a similar story. The ground floor area included a café and was generally regarded as the noisy area. Our research confirmed this. But it also told us a bit more. The upstairs is a doughnut-shaped space divided into two working areas by an open atrium. The back area had by far the lowest noise disturbance levels, while the front area fell right in the middle for noise levels.

Working with the IHKC team and an innovative Dutch furniture company called PROOFF, we developed a design strategy accommodating more specialised and secluded space for phone calls in part of the front upper area. It was not a very easy space to add features into. Many subsequent Impact HUBs, such as the Berkeley, California, branch were equipped with built-in phone booths – tiny rooms just big enough for one or two people. Many furniture companies now offer a host of pods and banquette booths promising to provide the precious asset of sound privacy. But the unique layout of the IHKC space wouldn't accommodate any of these options. The ground floor had to remain completely flexible for event use. And the hollow first floor plan was further complicated by lovely collections of wooden boxes hanging from the exposed brick walls to provide library and storage lockers.

One of the other things our space audit identified, however, was under-utilised areas. One of the front corners was being used as break-out space, filled with big bean bags and some other shabby chairs. I was a fan of the bean bags myself – perfect for sneaky napping! But I had to admit that very few people used them. The break-out area utilisation stood at thirty-five per cent. The space needed something that could function as a phone booth or a meeting room, and PROOFF had the perfect solution. If evil aliens captured a classic wing chair and subjected it to cyborg and genetic mutations, it would probably look a lot like their EarChair. These oversized, angular armchairs have grown even more oversized 'ear' wings. In addition to making you feel like you're on a space station, these ears have been carefully engineered to avoid sound leaking. Placing two chairs facing each other creates a sort of whispering gallery.

Introducing three of these creatures into the King's Cross break-out space was an interesting experiment. But the EarChairs quickly became such popular phone booths that the space managers had to ask people to limit their calls to one hour so everyone could have a chance! They were set up sociofugally – facing towards the wall to enhance privacy – but could easily be arranged more sociopetally if desired. With the addition of two fuzzy wall-mounted phone boxes, five sound-mitigating enclaves had been added to the space.

But more importantly, creating specialised space for noisy calls helped to change the social norms in the other areas of the upstairs space. With appropriate amenities for calls elsewhere, people started being more considerate. The decibel domino effect subsided. The EarChairs helped create a mid-volume level space in the front upstairs area, while the back upstairs area was used for quiet activities.

Impact HUB Kings Cross faced many of the same problems

PROOFF'S EarChairs at Impact HUB Kings Cross.

we find in generic open-plan and hot-desking offices. But a big part of the problem was the imbalance between function – workers' needs – and form. So while we know open-plan offices can be problematic, much can be mitigated by getting the right fit between people, purpose, and place.

The tendency towards one-size-fits-all solutions is a problem that has plagued workspaces across decades and design trends. With the latest craze for Google-style AstroTurf and ball pits, we're still failing to ask what would work best for the people and purpose of specific spaces.

Of course there are a number of factors we know are important to supporting well-being and productivity at work across the board. According to Jacqueline Vischer, an environmental psychologist at the University of Montreal, these factors impact us on three levels: physically, functionally, and psychologically. Issues like good air quality, moderate temperature, and cleanliness impact our well-being on a basic physical level – traditionally given the icky-sounding description of 'hygiene factors'. In addition, layout and space allocation affect our performance on a functional level, as we saw at Impact HUB Kings Cross. But we must also consider the loftier psychological level: the look and feel of the space, the colours and textures, light quality, and dimensions.

Curved forms, for instance, make us feel calmer than angular ones.[26] The presence of plants in an office can reduce blood pressure and increase attentiveness and reaction time by twelve per cent for people performing stressful tasks on a computer.[27] And while an adequate level of lighting is a functional factor for

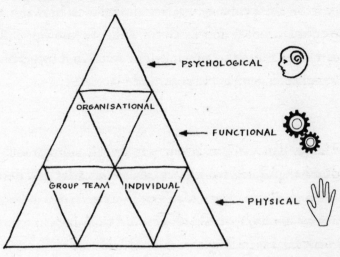

Environmental factors impact well-being on multiple levels and scales.
Source: Adapted from Vischer (2008)

the tasks at hand, lighting quality affects us more deeply. Having larger windows and sitting closer to them has been linked to higher productivity. Having a good view and blinds to control glare has a positive impact also.[28]

Many studies may not account for these psychological factors because they don't ask about them. And even if they did, people might not realise how much these factors impact them subtly. Vischer has questioned the overwhelming focus on satisfaction as a metric of successful offices. Satisfied is a funny term. It brings up an image of a fat, grinning cat. Is that what we are looking for our workspaces to inspire? As we have seen before, people don't always have a good sense of how things affect them. Or what they may be missing.

Over the years of working in offices I've developed a checklist that brings the best of this research together with today's most pressing workspace issues. I call it the BALANCED Space checklist because it provides a framework to balance the needs of people and purpose with the constraints of space and budget. To balance what's already working well with what could be better. And, of course, because it forms a handy acronym:

B   Biophilia: natural elements, materials, views, and patterns

A   Atmosphere: light quality, air quality, temperature, and smell

L   Layout: space utilisation and allocation, wayfinding, and circulation

A   Amenities: supporting good nutrition, fitness, ergonomics, and rest

N   Noise: avoiding disturbing noise levels, friction points, and design flaws

C   Cohesion: community, communication, and control

E   Energy: reducing use of energy, resources, and waste

D   Design: colour, shape, material, proportions, detail, and style

It's a framework to identify needs and patterns specific to space, organisation, and people. Layout and Noise may be assessed objectively, as we saw at Impact HUB. Biophilia and Cohesion may be assessed through interview and observation. And this all comes together to inform design strategy and priorities.

We hear a lot of things about the wonders of standing desks, living green walls, and meditation rooms. So how do you know which of these novelties are most important to invest in? And what do you do if you can't afford any of these things? So much of what we hear about offices is reserved for the upper echelons. What can you do with a basic office space on a minimal budget?

This was the exciting challenge I had in working with Happy City, a Bristol-based well-being charity who also run a co-working space out of their office. Working to move and expand their office on a very low (as in virtually non-existent) budget required some resourceful creativity. Like my New York workspace with its ninja-proof seats, the old Happy City was an unconventional office space. With hardwood floors and two walls of light, airy windows overlooking colourful street art by Banksy and others in Bristol's hip Stokes Croft district, it didn't really feel like an office.

The new space was a characterless 1960s unit with the tired bluish carpets and suspended ceilings typical of the era. Everything about the place said 'dull, grey office', so we knew we had a lot of work to do to recreate the character and culture of the old space. First on our checklist was Biophilia. The wooden floors and plentiful natural light in the old space were major benefits we couldn't transfer to the new space. To counterbalance the sterile nature of the new space, we filled it with plants and made use of as many natural materials as we could. A DIY approach – involving co-working members in creating the office and using reclaimed materials – was key.

We started by populating the office with cheap and hearty dragon plants, and asked everyone to bring in one plant of their own for variety. We worked with local furniture recyclers and resellers to source bookshelves, desks, and chairs, and got donations from other offices closing down. Co-workers helped us re-paint the furniture and walls, brightening up the grey space with a palette of bright green, white, and natural wood tones, and Happy City's signature colour: hot pink.

Clever layout choices are another way to make a big difference on a small budget. Before moving in, we used string to map out where the major pieces of furniture would go. We used bookshelves with plants on top of them to define the space and create smaller territories, including a lounge where people could eat lunch, peruse the Happy City library, or take a nap in the bean-bag pile – amenities supporting healthy eating habits and rest are key to well-being at work.

There was no budget for fancy phone booths or sit/stand desks, so we created our own DIY solution. We employed a carpenter to transform an old, wooden door into two café-style bars with window views – one in the lounge and one further into the office. With the addition of some freshly repainted bar stools, these lovely spaces overlooking a tree-lined street have become the pride of the office. Some people use them as impromptu standing desks, while others just like to break up the day by moving to different spots depending on what they're doing – a rising trend in office design now known as 'activity-based working'. The bar seating in the lounge is particularly popular for people to slip away to when they want some privacy for phone calls. The lounge area doubles as a casual breakout meeting space outside of lunch hours, in addition to the formal meeting room we had built.

Lastly, we thought very carefully about how to lay out the actual workspaces in the office, and who would sit where. Happy City co-founder Mike Zeidler had previously helped found the Bristol Hub – one of the first Impact HUB network spaces outside of London. While the Bristol Hub ultimately branched off on its own, Happy City had inherited three of their signature petal tables: a trio of different sized, tear-shaped desks branching out from a central point, which can be fanned out to suit the shape of the room. These petals – also made from reclaimed wood – were much heavier than their name suggests, so it was important to get the layout right. We experimented with different formations using string laid out on the carpet to get a sense of how the spacing and circulation would feel. And in positioning the petals, we made sure not to forget about those sneaky ninjas!

While we all might ideally like an office seat optimising refuge and prospect, these can be hard to come by. Working across different offices, I've found many people have a strong preference for one or the other – they can be divided into 'refugers' and 'prospectors'. We've discussed 'people factors' in the workspace in terms of the nature of people's work and how much they work with others. But some preferences just come down to individual personality. The size of our personal space bubbles, our penchant for personalisation, and desire for order are all influenced by personality.

We've all heard of introverts and extroverts, but this is just one aspect of personality. The Five Factor Model (FFM), or 'big five', is considered the most scientifically robust tool for measuring personality. Through many years of research, psychologists have come to define people's personality in terms of their ranking on five key traits: openness, conscientiousness, extraversion, agreeableness, and neuroticism. These traits can impact our built environment preferences and can even be communicated by the spaces we inhabit, as personality psychologist Sam Gosling at the University of Texas has demonstrated.

People high in introversion, low in agreeableness, or high in neuroticism may more often be refugers, for instance. While we are all instinctively drawn to spaces with refuge and prospect, a need for more personal space is linked to introversion and higher rates of anxiety.[29] Introverts are overwhelmed by excess stimulation and draw their energy from solitary pursuits. You'll often find them sequestered away in their own little fortress at the back of the office, where they can survey the room. Sitting on the periphery can also be a sign that you are low in agreeableness: the tendency to be helpful, cooperative, and sympathetic. But refugers certainly shouldn't get a bad rap: introverts can be highly inventive and productive types who need their own fortress to flourish.

Extraverts, on the other hand, are excitement seekers and get easily bored without stimulation. The intriguing potential of a prospect position helps reduce boredom, which may attract the extravert.[30] These cluttered, chaotic, and colourful types like to surround themselves with knick-knacks related to their many activities and warm, saturated colours like red.[31] They have a high need for social interaction and less need for personal space, so you may also find their desk at the circulation crossroads where they can catch people passing by. Notice a welcoming extra chair, or biscuits to share? These features invite people in to stop and chat. But with their days so busy, extraverts often don't have enough time to tidy up![32] While you might think that a cluttered workspace would scare people away, a controlled amount of clutter is actually more inviting than either a sparse space or an overstuffed one.

Highly open people – who are creative, intellectual, and amenable to new experiences – may also prefer prospect-oriented window seats for enhanced inspiration and creativity. Open people tend to be artistic and imaginative, so you may find artwork or remnants of creative projects at their desks. A highly personalised office can signal either openness or extraversion, but the workspace of an open person is distinguished by being stylish, unique, and versatile – reading material and music collections betray their insatiable appetite for diverse genres. Personalisers are more likely to have greater job satisfaction, psychological well-being, and even physical health, so personalised workspaces have benefits for both employees and employers.[33]

An extremely tidy and organised workspace tells people that you are conscientious: orderly, disciplined, and cautious. You'll find these minimalists' desks stacked with organised files, sharpened pencils, and calendars planning for 2019. Conscientious people tend to be hard-working, reliable, focused, and achievement-oriented – they like to make plans and follow routines. And while such desks may be lauded by anti-clutter guru Marie Kondo, these may also not be the most creative or innovative folks around.

Finally, anyone who has worked in a hot-desking office or co-working space is familiar with the expander. Every day, their portion of the desk seems to grow a little bit bigger with a new stack of files or that kettle they bought and haven't managed to take home yet. You pop out for lunch and return to find your spot occupied by their half-finished sandwich! Highly territorial behaviour may signal that a person is more dominant and aggressive, or less sensitive to others around them. You may find the expander in the centre of the room, as central-seaters tend to be more dominant and defensive of their space than those around the edges.[34] But it's also important to point out that scarcity of space and uncertain ownership make people more territorial. Today's highly shared workspaces can bring out the expander in anyone if not carefully designed and managed in consideration of human needs.

Most offices are likely to have a mix of people with different personality traits. But certain industries do seem to attract certain personality profiles. Tech workers tend to have high rates of introversion and low rates of agreeableness, which may lead to a greater need for ninja-proof seats, as we saw with the software developers in my New York office.[35]

But whatever type of office you're in, the key to making it a productive and healthy workspace is to make sure it fits the needs of the people working there, and the purpose of their work. Back at Happy City, we used an office-wide survey and conducted interviews with members of different teams to understand people's needs and preferences. We placed the refugers in ninja-proof seats, and gave the prospectors window views. And we also planned seating according to noise levels and working needs. These are quite simple steps. So simple, that they might be considered irrelevant, when they are actually some of the easiest and least expensive ways to make an office better fit for purpose. The layout of Impact HUB Berkeley (pictured here) provides a particularly nice example of how to optimise refuge and prospect needs in a small space, arranged quite similarly to Happy City.

One last key lesson from the Happy City office is that it was very much a work in progress. Their team and members have experimented with different positions for desks and bookshelves, upgraded furniture as more suitable pieces became available, and encouraged co-workers to make their own mark on the space. Happy City have taken time to let the space grow and develop, softening the hard edges over time.

Of course, this DIY approach wouldn't work for everyone. But corporates may have more to learn from this model than they realise. Like shared streets, co-working spaces present a model

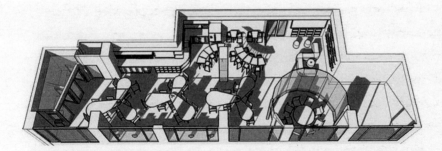

Original layout of Impact HUB Berkeley, arranged similarly
to the Happy City space. © Impact HUB Berkeley

for managing space that is often more fluid and flexible than the engineering-driven, Taylorist, top-down model of efficiency and productivity. And they create places that people are attracted to. Spaces that feel like places instead of fuzzy grey boxes. We will delve further into the impact of biophilia, light quality, and specific design features later on. But perhaps the most important point of all is cohesion – how the place comes together in relation to people and purpose. The cohesion element on my checklist brings together the related issues of control, communication, and community.

Researchers at the Centre for Facilities Management Development at Sheffield Hallam University have found that effective communication can have a huge impact on how happy workers are with a hot-desking transition. Working with a blue-chip company called FinanceCo, they discovered that workers engaged in various communication strategies were more satisfied with the final hot-desking arrangement. The end results were the same across FinanceCo's buildings: approximately five desks per six full-time employees, shared on a team-zoned basis. Communication made the key difference in how happy workers were with their new, non-territorial office.

And by communication, I don't mean one-way communication from the management to the general staff. A feeling that feedback was heeded was key to satisfaction, as were quality and frequency of communication in the FinanceCo study. Research has also found that even the negative effects of noise exposure can be reduced if people can control the noise to some extent.[36] The dynamics of control, communication, and community are inextricably intertwined with the culture the space has grown out of.

On a recent trip to New York, I had the opportunity to visit Google's famed Manhattan office myself. And I had to admit, it was pretty impressive. Exploring the endless succession of Lego playrooms, treehouses, green-walled eateries, and break-out areas resembling Sherlock Holmes's study was like progressing through increasingly fantastical levels in a video game. So given choices between working in a vintage train car café, a library study stocked with comic books, or an indoor AstroTurf garden with deckchairs overlooking the Manhattan skyline, what's the best thing about the Google office?

'Honestly it's more the food, and the juice and gym, and the game room,' one employee named Chris told me. 'I think it's more about having all the different wacky features, going to a different part of the building and being surprised.' Exporting any one of these possibly gimmicky, certainly expensive elements on its own isn't likely to have the same impact as their combined effect. The variation of environments gives employees choice, control, and flexibility. 'People make the jump from thinking it's these cool office features that lead to Google's success,' Chris said, 'but it's really the company culture that underlies them.'

Rather than fancy football tables and slides, we may just need a few good ninja-proof seats.

CHAPTER 3

Why We Dream about Houses and Cry about Wind Farms

NIMBYism, the high-rise, and the housing crisis

If you type #housingcrisis into Twitter, you will see stories about cities like Auckland, Bengaluru, and Vancouver. But you will be certain to read about two places in particular: London and San Francisco:

'California housing crisis spreads to the middle class.'

'Teachers are having their own housing crisis because they can't afford to live where they work.'

'Housing crisis forces disabled couple and daughter, four, into motorway services.'

You will also find stories about people fighting passionately against new developments:

'Mission protestors fight for housing by fighting against it.'

'Campaigners fight to save London skyline from 230 more skyscrapers!'

'Tech companies and workers are vilified while long time homeowners who fight high-density growth continue to profit from rising rents and property values.'

Why would these people feel so strongly compelled to oppose new housing in the face of such great need? You may have heard the term NIMBY (Not In My Back Yard) used to describe such people. And when we call people NIMBYs, we usually accuse them of being selfish, ignorant, and territorial. As a 2015 *Daily Mail* article put it:

'Housing experts have accused older homeowners of preventing their children from ever getting on the housing ladder by guarding the "pristine" land around their properties. They said that, despite the nation's housing shortage reaching "emergency proportions", there was still more land dedicated to horses in Britain than to homes. Older generations are selfishly blocking new developments and "drawing up the drawbridge behind them"'.[1]

But this isn't the whole story. Researchers such as Patrick Devine-Wright at the University of Exeter have spent decades studying how people react to developments like wind farms, tidal energy converters, and power stations. Their research has busted some core myths about NIMBYs.

Myth #1: NIMBYs only care about developments in their own backyard – close to home. Surprisingly, someone living three miles away from a proposed power station isn't likely to object any more strongly to it than someone who lives six to twelve miles away. In fact, those who live further from opposed developments are sometimes the biggest naysayers.

Myth #2: NIMBYs are ignorant and irrational. If only they knew how important this new high-rise was they would support it. This one has got to be thrown out as well because research has shown that NIMBYs tend to be very well-informed about the issues, technologies, and areas they speak out about. And some of their objections might be based in concerns that are very important to well-being in housing. Issues like the restorative benefits a few trees in an empty site can bring to a neighbourhood. How a tall building could transform a sunny street into a dark wind-tunnel. And whether the increased traffic on that street might make you less likely to know your neighbours. This is not to say that one person's need for housing is less important than another person's need for grass and sunlight. But to dismiss any opposition as 'irrational' misses the point.[2]

Many of the above concerns are situation specific. But Devine-Wright and others have found one factor that explains NIMBYism across time and context: identity. More specifically, place identity. The notion that the home is a foundation for identity isn't new. Ancient mystics and Freudian psychoanalysts alike say the house represents the self in our dreams. Dream interpretation dictionaries are full of pearls of wisdom such as:

'House: dreaming about a house symbolises the many facets of the self, with different rooms relating to the different characteristics of an individual's personality.
Bathroom: This could either symbolise emotional relief or that you have to use the bathroom.'

Environmental psychologists were surprised to discover that our emotional attachment to our homes can be almost as strong as our emotional attachment to other people. Home environments are key in defining who we are, so much so that we almost feel they are part of us. When they are threatened, we feel our own identity is threatened.

In the introductory week for my Masters at University of Surrey, one lecturer told us a story about an experiment she had taken part in many years before. There she was, a young mother with her beautiful one-year-old baby Flora, bravely volunteering the two of them as lab rats to further the progress of scientific discovery.

She came into a lab filled with bright toys, expecting to be observed while little Flora played. This was how it began. But then a strange woman came into the room, and said she would watch the baby while Mummy left the room for a few minutes. Leave her baby! She closed the door and little Flora predictably began to scream. 'I was a new mother,' she said, 'I was absolutely besotted with my baby.' Unable to bear the terrible tone of her baby's cries, she rushed back into the room. And when mother and baby were happily reunited, Flora stopped crying.

This is a classic study, known by the ominous name of the 'Strange Situation'. It was through experiments like these that psychologists came to understand the process of attachment between babies and mothers. They found it was natural and important for babies to become primarily attached to a caregiver, to be deeply upset when separated from them, and comforted upon being reunited.

Like goslings that imprint upon their mother goose, it is important for infants to form a deep and lasting emotional bond to a parent figure. Attachment is an incredibly strong bond, enduring across space and time. This process of attachment between babies and parents happens in the same way all around the globe. And while attachment is usually a two-way connection between child and parent, it doesn't have to be. A child can be attached to a caregiver who is not attached to them. And this helps us understand how we might be able to develop similar feelings of attachment to a place, even though places can't love us back in quite the same way.

Goderich, Ontario is a small town on the shore of Lake Huron whose motto is 'Canada's prettiest town'. It was known for its historic wood-frame houses, picturesque beaches, and Courthouse Square: a unique octagonal traffic circle in the very centre of the town. This octagonal 'square' was the heart of the community. A tree-filled green space around the courthouse surrounded by the library, town hall, post office, chamber of commerce, shops, and restaurants.

But in August, 2011, the pretty face of Goderich was changed forever when a tornado swept off Lake Huron at 174 mph, right through Courthouse Square. Thirty-seven people were injured, hundreds of homes and businesses destroyed, tens of thousands of trees uprooted, and one person killed. A total of $130 million-worth of damage was caused. Courthouse Square took the worst of it, including the devastation of two hundred trees.

The damage was very unevenly distributed, however. Some areas of the town emerged largely untouched. The town has now been almost fully rebuilt, thanks to generous local and national donations. But the loss of trees left a deep scar on the landscape. The community unified and reacted swiftly, forming volunteer groups to plant new trees. Bakeries reopened and tourists returned to the town the following year. But these new little trees don't quite fill the shoes of their full majestic forebears. And the young buildings don't look quite like the old ones.

The community experienced a universal sense of loss and sorrow. And interestingly, the level of these feelings was extremely consistent across the town. Residents experienced deep grief, shock, and loss even if they faced no personal injury or damage, according to researchers at the University of Waterloo, Ontario. Other studies have suggested that proximity to physical damage can have a bigger impact on suffering than individual loss in situations such as these. The residents' home town had been injured and they felt injured themselves.[3]

People say when someone you love dies, a part of you dies. And when a place we love disappears, we feel a part of ourselves has disappeared. Even in war-torn situations where people have lost family and friends, they sometimes say the complete destruction of their home is as painful as the loss of the community that filled it. Even in very poor-quality living conditions, the feelings of grief people express when their home is destroyed are remarkably similar to those they express about the loss of a loved one. Just as babies become attached to parents, we become attached to places. Especially those we spent formative years in. And the places we are attached to also become a foundation for our identity. We strive to maintain a consistent sense of self as we develop throughout our lives. And the continuity of places from our past can be key to reminding us of who we are, who we were, or who we want to be.

I was born in the Mission district of San Francisco: the epicentre of the housing crisis currently raging across the Bay Area. My parents rented a small apartment on San Jose Avenue, where they made the brave choice to bring a baby into the world right in their very own bedroom. I suppose you could say they were that very first phase of gentrification – the artistic types who move to an area with low rent, paving the way for others with more lucrative jobs. Like many cities at that time, San Francisco was cheap when my parents arrived there in the '70s. My father was a poet, as were many of their friends. My mother worked at a movie theatre. My father had a job dispensing pencils at a school. And on these meagre salaries, they were able to afford their rent in a neighbourhood where a one-bedroom now goes for more than $3,410 (£2,647) a month. And they had two bedrooms. 'We would never have bought a cup of coffee,' my mother says. 'You wouldn't just go out and buy a sandwich.' I envy them living in that San Francisco. A misty, black-and-white place, full of glowing, art-deco movie theatres.

In the '80s my father got a job at a company with a big new idea – an idea that was part of the end of that San Francisco. What if we had stores where people could buy computers? It was called ComputerLand. They had TV adverts where two guys in suits got sucked into a computer and became cartoons. And when I was young, I imagined my father actually went to work in some sort of cartoon ComputerLand every day.

When I was a year old, we moved across the bay to Berkeley, where my parents bought their first home. It was a two-bedroom stucco house, typifying the 'Berkeley Bungalow' style. Berkeley considers itself a city or a college town rather than a suburb. But it is more suburban than San Francisco in the sense that many people live in detached single-family homes with trees and backyards. This is a storyline that many middle-class Britons and Americans may be familiar with from their own families. Their parents lived in more urban areas in their twenties, then moved on to more suburban settings and bought homes around the time they got married and had children. This was the idealised housing ladder story. A housing ladder whose steps were associated with crucial life stages: leaving home, getting a job, marriage, children, and retirement. But as the press is constantly telling us, this story is changing for my generation.

Partly because our lifestyles have changed. But also because it is so much harder to buy a home.[4]

I am not going to explain the economics of the housing crisis. But I am going to explain why our reactions and decisions around housing may seem so illogical and strange. What strategies certain cities are using to address their housing crises. And what some of these different places have to learn from each other.

Why should we care about place attachment in relation to the housing crisis? Well first, because it helps explain so many things about how we act and think in relation to housing. But second, because we also know that when people feel attached to the place and community they live in, they also tend to have higher rates of overall well-being.[5]

A big issue in both the London and San Francisco area housing crises is that the most efficient way to provide more housing without sprawling into green space seems to be to build up. But many people are vehemently opposed to high-rise buildings. When I started doing research about denser development in downtown Berkeley, I was convinced that these people must be wrong. Those NIMBYs! How silly. But as I learned more, I started to question the pros and cons of the high-rise myself.

How high does a high-rise have to rise? There are various definitions, but US fire regulations define a high-rise as any building over 75 feet (23 metres), or roughly seven storeys. With the exception of certain places like the Yemeni city of Shibam, the mud-brick 'Manhattan of the desert', few cultures were able to safely build housing higher than seven storeys before the advent of steel-frame construction in the 1860s.[6] And perhaps not so coincidentally, this happens to align with the threshold of meaningful human communication for most able-sighted people. Beyond 60 to 80 feet (20 to 25 metres), we lose the ability to discern each other's moods and feelings.[7]

The modern idea of the high-rise was partly popularised by the Swiss-French architect Le Corbusier, who boldly stated, 'A house is a machine for living'. Born Charles-Édouard Jeanneret-Gris in 1887, he renamed himself, which was a fashionable thing to do in his time. Le Corbusier believed that houses should function purely and mechanically. An aeroplane is a machine for flying, a car is a machine for driving, and a house should be a machine for living.

What came to be called the functionalist movement in architecture was based on the idea that buildings should be efficient. Much like the traffic engineering approach to designing our public street spaces, the functionalist approach to building prioritises the cost-effective and methodical arrangement of people. Housing should be productive, hygienic, and functional. Aesthetic ornamentation not essential to the structure's function was seen as frivolous. The forms associated with house and home were outdated. Le Corbusier had a vision for what he called *Le Ville Contemporaine*, the Contemporary City. Imagine a geometric plane of green rectangular parks and streets. Cruciform sixty-storey sky-scrapers rise monumentally in the centre, housing the elite classes and their offices. Smaller apartment blocks set in smaller green squares house the working classes around the periphery. People and vehicles would be segregated in elevated and subterranean expressways, transporting residents between dwellings, workspaces, and leisure areas in efficient automobiles. 'Machinery is the result of

Le Corbusier's unrealised Contemporary City plan for Paris
© FLC/ADAGP, Paris and DACS, London 2017

geometry,' said Le Corbusier. 'The age in which we live is therefore essentially a geometric one.'[8]

At heart, Le Corbusier had some very good intentions. His tall towers would provide access to sunlight, fresh air, and magnificent views, removing the masses from the dark, dirt, noise, and stench of city streets. And by housing people more densely and efficiently, they would all have better access to the plentiful green space surrounding the towers. A number of living spaces he designed are considered to be quite successful. These include some little geometric houses standing on stilts in the woods. And a fleet of seventeen-storey apartment blocks deployed around France and Berlin, modelled on the concept of the ocean liner, complete with porthole windows and roof-deck swimming pools. He called his living machine *Unité d'Habitation*, which sounds like it has some lofty aims of unity, but in fact translates as 'housing unit'.

Regardless of whether you would like to live in one of these housing units yourself, Le Corbusier's influence extended far beyond the scope of his own designs. His visions inspired municipalities to expand and remake themselves in the image of his Contemporary City in places ranging from New York, London, and Chicago to the Soviet Union, Brazil, and Peru – sometimes filling war-torn patches of city, or tearing down lower-rise 'slums' and replacing them with graceful towers. High-rises were especially popular forms of public housing.

So were these 'towers in the park' a success? It is difficult to completely separate the impact of living in a high-rise building from related factors like socioeconomic status, neighbourhood quality, and lack of choice in living situation. But even accounting for these concerns, Robert Gifford's 2007 review of over a hundred studies suggests that people living in high-rises are less satisfied with their housing and suffer a range of negative impacts. Social relationships in high-rises tend to be more impersonal. People tend to help and trust each other less. Crime rates are higher. They are not ideal environments to raise children in. And they may even directly contribute to higher suicide rates.[9]

Much of the early correlational research was flawed because related issues like socioeconomic status were not accounted for. It is especially difficult to get really objective, experimental data about housing because dwellings are often longer-term commitments than, say, workplaces or hospital rooms. And maybe the difficulty of experimenting in this area tells us something important. Housing is more deeply intertwined with our sense of self, community, and safety.

■ ■ ■

Due to these difficulties, some of the earliest theories about living in dense populations came from studying other animals. Particularly a seemingly urban animal: the rat. In 1947, a man named John B. Calhoun asked his neighbour if he could construct a rat enclosure in the woodlands behind his Maryland home. But what he had in mind was more than just a few hutches. He created a quarter-acre (thousand-square-metre) 'rat city', which he populated with five pregnant females.

Calhoun had a hypothesis. He thought that, given ample food, water, and habitats, his rat city would swell to a thriving population of five thousand. The rats initially went happily along mating and procreating in their rat kingdom. But strange things started to happen once the group grew over one hundred and fifty: population growth plateaued. In over two years of tending his rat city, its population never surpassed two hundred. Calhoun had originally started studying rats in search of ways to control Baltimore's rodent population. But his compelling research into the relationship between space and population caught the interest of the US army, leading him to continue his research at the National Institute for Mental Health (NIMH) with both rats and mice.

Calhoun continued to build upon his rat city experiments, to create a more complex indoor habitat called 'rat universe'. Rat universe was actually smaller than rat city: a 10-by-14-foot (3-by-4.3-metre) space segmented into four quadrants. Each area was linked to those on either side by ramps the rats could climb up and over – except for quadrants 1 and 4, which had no ramp between them. This created two different types of habitats within the rat universe: the outer boroughs, which had only one entrance each, and the inner boroughs, which could be entered from two different directions. And within these boroughs, the rats even had their own high-rises – multilevel nesting areas, complete with cramped, winding staircases.

Under normal conditions, rats are quite conventional creatures, taking on the traditional gender roles we are led to believe ancient cavemen and women played. The average male rat goes around wooing a number of different lady rats to establish a little harem for himself. And, of course, his lady rats and their rat babies will need somewhere to live, so he also establishes a territory. His main concerns in life are mating with his harem and defending their territory – though they're really not belligerent fellows and don't like to fight too much. The female rats are traditional homemaker types – all about building nests and raising their rat babies, which are called pups. And while the whole rat social structure is polygamous, they are quite uptight about getting together with any rats outside their established harem. This is the normal social order of the Norway breed of rats.

Calhoun's rat universe played out much like a rat parallel to *High-Rise*, the recent movie adapted from J. G. Ballard's 1975 novel. These social norms and structures disintegrated and new destructive patterns of behaviour emerged, leading his rats to the point of virtual extinction! The rat population grew steadily, as in his initial experiment. But cramped in smaller quarters, they soon began to act strangely. Aggressive packs of male rats roamed the city raping and attacking females, who were unable to fend off their advances. Other males became hyperactive and hyper-sexual, making forceful advances to any rat they came across. The most deviant rats became cannibalistic.

Rat infant mortality rose as high as ninety-six per cent. The study marked a low point in rat history, with fifty per cent of females dying off due to disease and violence. Those who did survive and bear young were no longer psychologically and physically able to care for them. The rat population essentially stopped functioning reproductively. Crucially, theses disastrous impacts were much more severe in the inner quadrants, where overcrowding was at its worst. In the outer boroughs, infant mortality rates rose only to fifty per cent. This would not be a promising figure in any population, but reproduction was still possible. In the less crowded areas, male and female rats continued to fulfil their social roles, even if not very successfully. Strangely, the inner-borough rats tended to gather together, trembling in a great huddled mass – a phenomenon Calhoun called the 'behavioural sink'. Many reacted by seeming to withdraw psychologically, engaging with others as little as possible, even in the huddle. And even after their habitat became less cramped, the rats remained psychologically damaged and were unable to successfully reproduce.

Calhoun's rats became famous. His influential findings were published in *Scientific American* at a time when concerns about urban squalor and overpopulation were on the rise. The story of these socially deviant rats – poster animals for urban filth and disease – was too perfect a metaphor for the concerns surrounding human degeneration in increasingly densely packed urban slums. The popular press ran with the image of human cities as behavioural sinks. Calhoun's experiments were held up as evidence that dense living caused 'social ills' ranging from gang violence to deviance from heterosexual norms. Novels and movies depicting futuristic societies growing high into the sky and losing their humanity in the process abounded. In the *Judge Dredd* comic universe, whose creators have cited Calhoun's work as an influence, Earth's post-apocalyptic, drug-addled population lives in enormous city block towers housing over sixty thousand people each in sprawling numbered Mega-Cities.[10]

Early researchers assumed that high-density housing would also have a consistently negative impact on humans. While ants and rabbits may be more comfortable living on top of each other than we are, each species has an optimal density level it seeks to maintain. Calhoun believed there was a cap on the number of significant social interactions different species could cope with before a stress reaction set in − a maximum group size. And he believed this number was the same for rats and humans: twelve. When crowded past species-specific comfort levels, the consequences for most animals are severe.[11]

But for humans, the relationship between population density and urban form is complex − often more so than meets the eye. One important distinction is the contrast between social density and spatial density. Let's say you live in a small, three-bedroom flat. And, as is the case for quite a lot of us these days, it's just about big enough for you and your two flatmates. If three more people suddenly move in whom you don't all fancy sharing your beds with, you would probably feel the social density was two high. Alternatively, perhaps you and your two flatmates wake up one day to find your flat has shrunk to half its former size! Your bed is precariously balanced atop your wardrobe because the furniture no longer fits in the room. Both scenarios would likely cause you some stress. But in the first case it's coming from having to interact with too many different people. The second case is about simply having too little space − however that may be defined. It's also important to distinguish between how density impacts us on the small and large scale: how many people live in a room versus how many people in a hectare or acre. Indoor density versus outdoor density.

It can be quite difficult to fully disentangle social and spatial density, however, because many high-rise buildings are in densely populated urban environments. So even if you live alone in a spacious apartment, you encounter bustling social density on the city streets every day. As well as in the elevator. High-density situations generally tend to impact humans in a few predictable ways: first, there is an immediate impact on how we behave. Second, we develop a number of coping mechanisms to deal with the situation. And lastly, our psychological state continues to be affected even when we are no longer in these environments.

Both high social and high spatial density situations can have an immediate impact on our physiological stress levels, as well as how quickly we can solve puzzles and how we interact with the people standing next to us. On the physical level, even spending a few hours in a cramped room versus a spacious one means your heart rate and blood pressure are likely to be higher.[12] When socially or spatially cramped, our performance on cognitive tasks also declines. A group of researchers at the University of Texas at Arlington found that both high spatial and social density situations made it more difficult for people to solve maze problems. But the damage to their performance was worst when they had too many people around them.

As social and spatial density rise, our affinity for those around us declines. Eight men who don't know each other tend to be friendlier when spending an hour confined to an adequately sized room than a cramped one.[13] Even the expectation of being crowded can make us more aggressive and unfriendly. But much like Calhoun's rats, male people seem to be driven to greater behavioural extremes by density-induced stress. One study found men's cortisol levels to be higher after spending an afternoon at a shopping mall than those spending the same time on a university campus – an effect that did not hold true for women. This might seem to have as much to do with women's higher tolerance for shopping as their higher tolerance for high density. But researchers suspect these widely recognised gender differences may relate to women's smaller personal space bubbles and social norms encouraging camaraderie over competition.[14]

In 'human universe', however, living at high density can be highly desirable. The downsides of the high-rise seem to depend on whether the setting inspires sensations of crowding, over-stimulation, and lack of control. High-rises are often built for very high or low earners, who may have very different experiences of this building form. Someone living in a luxury, fifty-storey apartment building in New York or Hong Kong might have a great amount of personal space and control, so they don't feel crowded. Living far from the ground is highly sought after in places like these, and in many cases, it has worked quite well.

London and San Francisco inevitably look to New York as both a model and a cautionary tale in addressing urban housing. High-rise critics have been warning of the impending doom-filled 'Manhattanisation' of their cities for decades. New York has had a housing crisis for so long that it's not really news. But having campaigned on the 'Tale of Two Cities' platform, highlighting wealth disparity, Mayor Bill de Blasio's administration has put the issues of housing affordability and supply front and centre.

'I look at the city as a success,' Anusha Venkataraman, of the New York City Department of Housing, Preservation, and Development, told me. 'We have so many jobs and so many people who want to live here that we don't have enough housing for all those people.'

Packing in ever more dwelling units at greater density is the main strategy on the table for increasing housing supply in New York at this point – no one is talking about eco-towns or garden villages. Densification is happening through re-zoning various areas of the city, as well as more innovative models like micro-units and 'co-living'. The micro-unit model, approved under previous Mayor Michael Bloomberg's reign, has effectively decreased minimum size standards. Previously, developers were not permitted to create properties entirely composed of such small studios. Inventive features like expanding tables and contracting beds are meant to make these minuscule spaces more liveable.

Co-living ventures like WeLive and Common have arrived at a similar housing model via the concept of extending the success of the co-working model to meet living needs. WeLive, the new arm of co-working giant WeWork, offers fashionable living spaces on flexible month-to-month terms, sometimes directly attached to their workspaces. In line with the co-working format, co-living is based on a membership model. Members can book a bedroom for a few nights or more permanent residence, and share communal amenities like fancy kitchens and hot tubs, some of which can also be booked for private use. Co-living ventures such as The Collective have already opened in London as well, with WeLive and others on the way.

'They're actually really nice', Venkatatarman said about the New York micro-units she had taken a sneak peek at.

Too nice, perhaps.

When I heard about micro-units, I naively assumed they would be less expensive than apartments where you don't have to fold your bed into the wall like you're living in a sleeper train carriage. A spot at Ollie, New York's first micro-unit development in Kips Bay, will cost you $2,920 (£2,267) a month for 360 square feet (33 square metres). At WeLive's flagship Wall Street location, units range from $2,000 (£1,552) a month for a private, 450-square-foot (42-square-metre) studio to $1,375 (£1,067) for a spot in a 1,000-square-foot (93-square-metre), four-bedroom unit.[15] The *New York Post* ran some calculations comparing an Ollie pad to an 808-square-foot (75-square-metre), 'Billionaire's Row' one-bedroom. How do they line up? Ollie costs you $97 (£75) per square foot per year, while Billionaire's Row is only $54 (£42). Plus you can live on the fifty-ninth floor, if that's your kind of thing.[16]

Both Ollie and WeLive market themselves as ready-made communities with 'friends included'. One gets a distinctly creepy sense that the model-esque tech-employed robots lured to live in these pods are not programmed with the ability to buy toilet paper or participate in social interactions not facilitated by an iPhone app.

In extremely over-inflated housing markets like New York and San Francisco these rents may be below median. There is certainly something to be said for simply increasing housing supply to quell the crisis. But it would be hard to call them 'affordable'. Asking housing professionals in these cities about radical, new, community-driven tactics to create more housing, I found myself met with some blank stares. It's hard to innovate when space is so scarce and pricey.

While I spent almost four years living in a high-rise building in New York, I never thought of it in those terms. This was partly because we lived on the first floor. Partly because it was in Manhattan, where seventeen storeys doesn't seem that high. And partly because it was a place I had known before I knew the concept of a high-rise, or most other things for that matter. It was my grandparents' home. My father's home.

It was a substantial brick building – the prototypical New York City apartment building. 'I always felt like I was the third little pig that lived in the brick house,' my father says. 'The wolf could huff and puff but he couldn't blow my house down.' My grandparents moved into this high-rise in 1953, when my father was five. And, since it was rent-controlled, they went along living there happily and securely for decades without any particular ambitions of home-ownership. Everyone my father knew in New York lived in an apartment building, and everyone he knew rented. His parents had a nodding relationship with the neighbours. But most wouldn't go so far as saying, 'Hello', or inviting each other in. There were no block parties. They weren't as friendly with their neighbours as my parents are now with the people on their slightly urban Berkeley street of detached, single-family homes.

One criticism of Calhoun's research is that his findings may say as much about territory as they do about density. The outer quadrant rats were better able to define and defend their own territory, which was part of why they were not as overcrowded. As we might expect, high-rise residents tend to encounter many other people in their building, and may know more people by sight than those in low rises. But overall, it is more difficult to manage the volume of social interactions. Taller buildings mean less territory under personal control. This can lead people to withdraw – as we saw with a subset of Calhoun's rats. And this, in turn, can weaken overall community cohesion. Research has consistently found that people tend to help each other less in high-rises than other building forms.[17]

But my father remembers an idyllic childhood in his big building. He had a dog named Lucky, a best friend who lived in the apartment above, and together they would all run downstairs outside and play a fantasy game called Jim and Bob. Jim and Bob were cowboys who rode their bicycle horses around the sidewalks of the wild west, getting into all kinds of cowboy ambushes and snafus. 'Sidewalks weren't so crowded then,' he says. 'We could horse around on them. We could ride around the block ourselves at age eight.' As children in the 1950s, it didn't seem so different from the TV shows in which little suburban boys lived next door to their best friends and played cowboys outside. But of course, he lived on the first floor. You felt very close to the street there. You could see and hear and smell the street. One floor above in his friend's apartment, the street felt far below. There is some evidence to suggest that there may be what is called a curvilinear relationship between building height and resident satisfaction. People living on the lower floors value easy access to the street, and people living up top benefit from a sense of superiority and expansive views. But people in the middle floors are least satisfied because they feel cramped and claustrophobic. They can't get out easily, but also don't have the sense of living in the sky.

Generally, however, evidence suggests that children are adversely impacted by the combination of being cooped up indoors more at a younger age, and subsequently less supervised in areas with more potential risk factors once they are allowed out. This has a

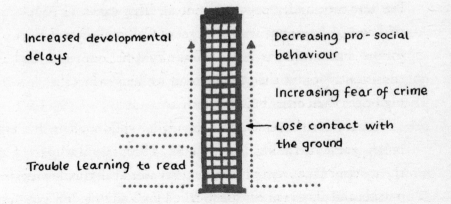

number of negative knock-on effects in terms of developing motor skills, amount of time spent watching TV, and even toilet training. One Japanese study found that developmental delays in infants increased above the fifth floor.[18] At the other end of the building, children on lower floors closer to traffic noise can experience greater trouble learning to read.[19]

When high-rise housing goes wrong, the greatest victims are families, especially those with small children. Mothers on higher floors experience more stress due to the particular difficulties of raising children far from the ground.[20] Apartment-dwelling men have been found to have higher rates of 'psychiatric impairment' and worse relationships with children, including physical abuse, even when controlling for age, education, and job type.[21] Building height in its purest essence does not predict psychological stress, but it certainly doesn't seem to temper it. And for those living on low incomes or in public housing, the high-rise also does not appear to make life much easier. Low- and mid-rise public housing has been linked to greater well-being.[22] But much public housing built in the post-war years was based on a model inspired by Le Corbusier's Contemporary City ideal.

'We have these giant towers which are very imposing,' says Anish Patel of Lantern Community Services, which provides supportive housing services to New Yorkers impacted by homelessness. 'No one feels comfortable walking around them. They're huge. Then there's all this open space, and even that has been a controversial idea.'

As Jane Jacobs described in her classic, *The Death and Life of Great American Cities*, the 'parks' that Corbusian towers were set in often became unsafe areas due to the lack of activity and 'eyes on the street', the ability for people to look out for each other. Planners assumed that more green space would have a wholesome influence on the 'huddled urban masses', but it often had the opposite effect. This was the case in Pruitt-Igoe, a famously failed high-rise development in St Louis, Missouri. Built according to Le Corbusier's planning principles, Pruitt-Igoe looked a little like a community of giant radiators. Achieving only a moderate density, the eleven-storey buildings were intended to keep the common grounds free for communal activities.

Pruitt-Igoe was a big hit when it first opened in 1954. But the buildings soon fell into disrepair and crime escalated so severely that the development was demolished less than three decades after the first residents moved in.[23] Apartment blocks in this immense complex lacked semi-private areas, which architect Oscar Newman dubbed 'defensible space'. He believed that the high density of people served by common areas like stairways, rubbish facilities, and green space prevented residents from identifying with these territories – from seeing them as part of their home. His theory was supported by striking contrasts within the development itself. Certain areas, where only two families shared a landing, tended to be well-maintained. But corridors shared by twenty families and lobbies serving 150 families were piled with rubbish and rife with crime.[24] Bigger buildings tend to be less well looked after by residents and less personalised – even within personal living areas. In public housing, people often don't have much choice over where they live and are less able to personalise their space. This constriction of agency, expression, and customisation hampers place attachment – the foundation of home.[25]

Research has been nearly unanimous in finding that pro-social behaviour like helping others is less common in high-rise buildings. Would you mail a stamped envelope found in the hallway? Could you ask a simple favour of your neighbours? These pro-social behaviours and a general sense of community decline as the building climbs higher.[26] The collective efficacy researchers in Chicago found that this special quality was harder to achieve in high-density places, which may help explain the tragedy of Pruitt-Igoe. Greater anonymity in the high-rise warren of interior, unsurveilled areas failed to foster the social cohesion and helping behaviours needed for informal social control. Larger and taller buildings seem to be associated with increased exposure to, and fear of, crime relative to residents' socio-economic status.[27]

The total collapse of Pruitt-Igoe was probably not due solely to the buildings' height, however, but to the compounded factors of being built too big, too quickly, and too uniformly. It lacked what Jane Jacobs called 'organised complexity': the almost organic variation in height, style, and texture of the tall buildings we find in New York.

In human universe, living in a dense city can come with great public resources and amenities not found in rat universe.

Pruitt – Igoe, St. Louis, Missouri
© Bettmann/Getty Images

We benefit from shared culture, opportunities, and common resources like great libraries and subway systems, which crowded rodents and rabbits don't enjoy. Sadly, the more optimistic elements of Calhoun's research never drew as much interest as the pessimistic vision of 'rat-manity' painted by his most famous experiment. He spent a great deal of time designing environments to inspire intelligence and creativity in his rats and mice, attempting to breed rodents better able to deal with the difficulties of high-density life. One socially withdrawn group of rats pioneered a new burrowing method – rolling out balls of dirt – a break-through Calhoun likened to humans inventing the wheel. While largely ignored by grown-up news outlets, these findings did inspire the children's book and subsequent movie, *Mrs Frisby and the Rats of NIMH*, leading countless American children to believe that the National Institute of Mental Health was breeding a highly intelligent species of super rats.

Despite all the supposed setbacks, people identify deeply with high-density housing in many parts of New York. 'In a lot of parts of the Bronx people are like, "Give me density. I want even more! Build towers, as long as that means that more of it will be affordable,"' Venkataraman said.

In New York, high-rise generally fits in with place identity, so we don't see the same opposition to it that we see in cities like London and San Francisco. Pioneering projects like the award-winning Via Verde development in the Bronx are working to combine the benefits of dense urban life with new forms of vertical density. This low-income development uses balconies and 'set-backs' (a planning term for tiers) to craft a dynamic structure with plentiful light, enticing residents up to green roofs where they can grow their own vegetables and work out in the gym. This development also stands out for taking an innovative approach by combining low-income rentals, home ownership, and health clinics in one facility.

'Via Verde works *because* of the density,' says urban planner Alice Shay. 'You can have a balcony and overlook the green roofs. It's shaped to have an interior courtyard so there is a sense of community amongst the many people in the complex. Those types of amenities couldn't work without the density.'

In parts of New York less well served by public transport, however, some people seem to identify as much with their cars as their houses. 'In Staten Island, which is a very different part of New York, they're like, "Just don't take our cars away!" says

Venkataraman. 'Same thing in Queens. Anything that reduces parking options, there's a lot of opposition to.'

The differing reactions to densification demonstrate that NIMBY responses to high-density development are tied to place identity. New York is a thriving place, a unique place, a coherent place. A place people are excited to call home. And density is integral to this.

Looking to London, the housing crisis is generally discussed as a national issue spreading far beyond the capital. Whether accurate or not, it's difficult to understand the psychology of the housing crisis without considering place identity on a broader level in England. When Americans imagine England, we tend to think of the countryside: rolling green hills dotted with sheep, hedgerows, and country lanes. We think of scenes you might find in the work of Jane Austen and Beatrix Potter, because this is largely the way England has been presented. This image of England as a green and undeveloped place is one that is dear to many British people as well. But this image is very far from the reality of everyday life, and has been for a long time.

England is believed to have been the first culture in the world whose people began to live primarily in urban environments. The twin forces of imperialism and the industrial revolution combined to draw the English people in to live closer together. By the early 1900s, approximately seventy-five per cent of the population were already living in cities and towns, at a time when most Americans were still living in cornfields.[28] Only twenty-eight per cent of Americans lived in metropolitan areas in 1910.[29]

England's early urbanisation evolved into large-scale suburban-isation, continuing throughout the post-war era and particularly in the 1980s and 1990s. By some definitions eighty per cent of the English population now lives in suburbs, though the official rural/urban classification statistics define eighty-two per cent as living in urban areas.[30] This statistical confusion is reflected in a landscape where 'urban' and 'suburban' can be difficult to distinguish. And neither look much like their counterparts in America, where 'suburb' refers to bedroom communities, found outside of a city as opposed to the British understanding of sub-urbs as residential districts within cities.

Despite, or perhaps because of this, the image of the country-side has historically played a particularly important role in English place identity. In terms of popular literature, cultural critic Raymond Williams has observed:

> 'English attitudes to the country, and to ideas of rural life, persisted with extraordinary power, so that even after the society was predominantly urban its literature, for a generation, was still predominantly rural; and even in the twentieth century, in an urban and industrial land, forms of the older ideas and experiences remarkably persist.'[31]

The English have indeed done their best to hold on to a bit of country in the city. Eighty-four per cent of dwellings have some type of private outdoor plot and fifteen per cent have a shared plot, meaning that only one per cent do not include an outdoor space.[32] But personally, I was confused to find the long narrow strips of grass and concrete behind English houses called gardens. Where were the rose bushes and vegetable patches? In America, it's just a yard until you grow a garden in it.

The idea of the garden city was dreamt up back in 1898 by a man named Ebenezer Howard. Much like Le Corbusier, Sir Ebenezer had a vision for a better way to house the urban hordes. But it was a very different vision. Inspired by the history of the English country town, he proposed the garden city as a way to relieve the pressures of cramped and sooty towns. The provision of 'wholesome housing' was at the core of Ebenezer's vision. And for housing to be wholesome, he believed, it should be very green. The community would be organised around a central garden, with parks and greenery running throughout. In order to avoid the evils associated with high-density cities, he believed the ideal population of such communities should be no more than 32,000. The garden city would be encircled by a green belt in which no development would take place. His diagrams depict the garden city surrounded by an idyllic succession of fruit farms, cow pastures, allotments, and forests. These small communities would be connected by railway lines to central cities.

Influenced by Howard's ideas, the British policy of establishing green belts around cities has curbed the spread of American-style suburban sprawl, seeming to keep the countryside within reach. But green belts have also played a big role in densifying urban municipalities, while ironically making their broader commuting catchment areas less compact. England is the third most densely populated country in the EU, and even little Wales takes eighth place.[33]

In simple terms, population density tells us the average number of people over a total area. But there's a lot it doesn't tell us. Consider the dwelling density: how tightly are dwellings distributed in the built-up regions? And further, how much space per person do these dwellings provide in square metres and number of rooms? The UK as a whole is densely populated by almost all these measures. The average new dwelling in the UK is smaller than in any other EU nation except Italy.[34] But oddly, the central areas of major cities such as London have traditionally bucked this trend, with surprisingly low dwelling density. Cities like Paris and Berlin are far more densely populated, although they are set within countries that are much less dense overall.[35] Why would the British be so much more averse to compact city-centre living than their European cousins?

One answer is that the overall density of built-up areas and small dwellings leaves Brits feeling perpetually cramped. You have the feeling of never being able to get away from people. It looks so green outside the city. But it's so hard to escape the sad, constant whirr of the motorway. Another explanation for continental Europeans' higher tolerance for high-density urban apartment living is that many maintain family connections in villages and other bucolic locations that they can easily escape to. This, in a sense, was the case for my father growing up in New York City as well. As part of my grandparents' work in microbiology, they spent their summers at a research centre in rural Long Island called Cold Spring Harbor. Like urban Greeks and Spaniards retreating from the summer heat to rustic islands and hill towns, my father had the benefit of spending barefoot summers in this science village. They lived in a rickety white cabin, immersed in grass, swimming, and microscopes. And this annual, summer-long getaway from the hot, stinking city was key to making high-rise life not only bearable, but appealing.

Of course, the British are no strangers to high-rise living either. British high-rises seem to pop out of nowhere, mainly in the form of post-war council housing. The British were busy building Le Corbusian public housing on a much greater scale than the Americans in those decades, largely with similar implications for well-being. Along with roundabouts and NHS facilities, the post-war government constructed public housing on a scale unimaginable in America. Accounting for over thirty per cent of tenancy at its peak in 1980, the proportion of English people living in social housing has since decreased to seventeen per cent – a figure that is still quite large by US standards, where public housing accounts for a minimal piece of the pie.[36]

The irony of the towers-in-a-park model is that big buildings like the British council estates and Pruitt-Igoe often don't achieve vibrant density dynamics. The British terraced house or American 'town house' is a deceptively compact building form, which can achieve the same densities we find in high-rises. The handsome four-storey terraced Georgians in Kensington and Chelsea comfortably arrange their occupants in the highest population density formations found anywhere in the UK.[37]

More recently, 'compact city' policies have further encouraged dense development on existing urban brownfield sites and discouraged greenfield development, especially surrounding cities. In reaction to the sprawling, car-dependent trends of the post-war era, these policies have aimed to reduce energy use by zoning for denser urban forms. Higher density was intended to bring about benefits such as urban resurgence, social sustainability, and greater productivity.[38] But ever-increasing density takes a toll. British homes today are half the size they were in the 1920s, and fewer are being built with gardens.[39]

So we have a densely populated nation that doesn't quite embrace this identity. A predominantly urban nation, with aspirations for the seemingly non-urban form of detached homes with gardens. And we have a society living in spatially and socially cramped quarters. Even the coveted village cottages are cramped! There seems to be an ongoing push and pull between the desire to preserve the countryside and the desire to be in the countryside. There's a bit of an identity crisis about what the country is like, and what it should be like. In the current housing crisis, this is played out in the debate over whether to densify further or to create new garden cities and garden villages.

Garden City: it sounds like the best of both worlds. Some of the early examples, like Letchworth Garden City, developed to implement Ebenezer Howard's ideas in the early 1900s, seem to have created quite successful residential communities – regardless of whether Letchworth lives up to being either a garden or a city. Letchworth even has the distinction of having been home to the first British roundabout! But post-war new towns like Milton Keynes, which sought to rehash garden city ideals, don't seem to have stood the test of time as well.

'In many ways Milton Keynes is a phenomenal success story', urban designer Charles Clarke told me. Halfway between England's two largest urban centres, London and Birmingham, Milton Keynes has seen steady population growth since its creation. 'The "garden" title is used to sell the concept of development, to give the impression that it's a lower density, rural thing. It was meant to have the benefits of both garden and city, but ends up being a bit of contradiction in terms.'

Planners adopted a landscape-led approach in which no building was to be higher than the highest tree. Milton Keynes would be a 'city in the forest', with trees planted along all the roadways. Remnants of the farming landscape would be reclaimed to form the basis of urban parks. Residents would play boules in their spacious green spaces. And all of this would be combined with the latest model of traffic-planning efficiency based on the US grid system! With British roundabouts at the intersections. And three-lane roads inspired by the Champs Elysées. And, of course, a big shopping mall in the centre. They took inspiration from many places. And the combination of these disparate ideas bears as much resemblance to an organic, cohesive place as a crazy golf course does.

'It lacks dynamism because it's so low density', says Clarke, 'And it loses a sense of place identity because of the sameness of the grid system.' Despite its success, Milton Keynes doesn't exactly have a reputation as a great place. As with Le Corbusier's Contemporary City, the garden city ideal seems to tick all the items on the list that should make for good housing: greenery, light, air, shopping opportunities, wholesome houses, and safe roads. This is no coincidence. Le Corbusier was directly inspired by Ebenezer Howard, calling his Unité d'Habitation high-rises 'vertical garden cities'. But creating places that people feel attached to and identify with is more complicated than putting together the ingredients for a cake. You also have to bake the cake.

This brings us back to the issue of home.

When people talk about home they could be talking about their house. But they could also be talking about their neighbourhood, their town or city, or even their country. This is why it's important to think about place identity when it comes to housing. If we don't create houses and neighbourhoods that feel like homes, they aren't likely to work well. We may even end up soon having to tear them down, as we saw with Pruitt-Igoe in St Louis. This is why many British housing experts think it's better to focus our energies on the many existing settlements that already have the bone structure of a successful place, but which need investment in housing stock, the public realm, and amenities like transportation – as well as people and jobs – to breathe life back into them.

Still, building upon existing places is no piece of cake either. If we bring new housing that clashes with local place identity into an existing area, people are likely to object to it. This is what I found speaking with NIMBYs in my hometown about why they oppose high-rise development. Downtown Berkeley is an interesting case study within the broader San Francisco Bay Area housing crisis. This small business district has not historically contained much housing, so residential displacement is not the major sticking point. It was never a thriving place in my youth. Typical of neglected American city centres in the '90s, it was mainly populated by parking spots, frozen yogurt shops, and mobile phone stores. Most Berkeleyans I spoke to in 2012 agreed that it was ripe for change of some sort. But many people still object to high-density development in downtown Berkeley because it doesn't look like it's meant to be a home for anyone. It's transient housing, competing with San Francisco's luxury housing. A place for students or young professionals to perch for a few years before, most likely, moving out to the suburbs with their two cars and two kids.

As Andre, a 26-year-old working downtown who sees himself as the kind of 'young professional' these buildings should be targeting, explained, 'These apartments cost roughly half a million dollars for a studio that's . . . basically a closet and that offends me so much. Who are you building this for? It's certainly not for me because I can't afford that.'

Further, much new development wasn't seen to build upon the distinctiveness of Berkeley's place identity – either socially or aesthetically. People often maintain a sense of individuality through asserting the uniqueness of a place they identify with: Berkeley is diverse. Goderich is pretty! In Goderich, Courthouse Square was key to the town's distinctiveness – its identity as Canada's prettiest town – which is why its destruction was so crushing.

We use places with which we identify – from the micro scale of the desk or bedroom to the macro scale of the neighbourhood and landscape – to support a strong and positive sense of identity. A large body of research on what is called 'identity process theory' has identified a number of props we use to support our identities, such as sense of continuity over time, positive distinctiveness, self-efficacy, self-esteem, and belonging. In a groundbreaking 1996 study on London's Rotherhithe docklands area – rapidly changing with the development of Canary Wharf – Clare Twigger-Ross and David Uzzell demonstrated that people anchored their identities in physical manifestations of these props.

Feel upset that an old building is being demolished? Perhaps it makes you feel a bit old and ready for demolition yourself. A glance at your overgrown garden or littered street may strengthen your sneaking suspicion that you are a terrible gardener . . . and your life is a mess. And when your favourite local shop is replaced by a multi-national chain, you feel indistinctive and disconnected yourself. Studies of NIMBY behaviour have often found that those who are more strongly attached to a place are more resistant to any physical change.

But we can also use these same features of place identity to better integrate new additions. One of Patrick Devine-Wright's studies found that a tidal energy converter project was positively received in Northern Ireland because it was perceived as strengthening the 'positive distinctiveness' of the area, both by 'visually fitting' its character (looking like a lighthouse), and by distinguishing the area as the first to have a sustainable energy innovation. Residents who felt more strongly attached to the place were more likely to support the change.[40]

Yes, of course, most people wouldn't want a big building put up next to their house that blocks the view and sunlight or stands on top of where they used to walk their dog. But when it matches what people understand to be the special distinctiveness of that place, they tend to be much more receptive.

Density can make for very vibrant and successful places. But the concentrated vertical density of the high-rise is a hard space to foster collective efficacy – especially for low-income groups dealing with a variety of stressors and challenges. And as we see clearly in the UK, we don't have to build high-rises in order to live at high densities. If we densify moderately, in line with local place identity, we can grow more organically. The high-rise itself is not a failure. But the idea of the house as a machine for living has been.

Coming from the Bay Area, I'm excited about the idea of more people living there. Having lived in denser places like New York and the UK, I wouldn't mind a bit more buzz in a place where it's hard to find a meal after 9:30 p.m. – along with amenities such as the public transport infrastructure this could help support. And, of course, we desperately need more housing.

But I would like to see this happen in a way that will provide real homes. And in a way that won't make my home look like it could be anywhere else in the rapidly developing world of high-rise luxury condos. I know that's not easy to do. But if we don't want to repeat the mistakes of the past, it is important to do.

More than just building housing, we need to create homes.

CHAPTER 4

A *Truman Show* for Dementia Patients

Savannahs, snakes, and the mystery novel model

Not long ago, I got an excited email from a friend of my parents who had reached his 60s and had fears of dementia on his mind: 'In the US, they put you in a locked floor of a nursing home. But this new facility in the Netherlands has you living in a house designed to look like the era when your short-term memory ended! This place is like an un-televised *Truman Show*. You walk around a specially built town, mad as a hatter, and people make sure you don't hurt yourself or anyone else while you do normal stuff. I'm signing up!'

He was talking about Hogeweyk ('dementia village'), a dementia-care facility in the Dutch town of Weesp. Here, with characteristic Netherlands genius, the Dutch are pioneering an approach to residential care based on trusting people to follow their instincts. Residents can buy groceries, walk tree-lined lanes, and dine out in a café-restaurant. The groceries have no price tags and the streets have no cars. But that's not so far from reality in the land of *woonerven*. The staff dress in everyday clothes, and villagers take part in household chores like making meals. Creator Yvonne van Amerongen calls it a 'neighbourhood' for people with dementia.[1] Care-taking environments are typically designed to keep people safe, clean, and medically attended. But environmental psychology research has revealed that traditional care facilities can be extremely disorienting and frightening for dementia sufferers. As memory and context slip away, patients come to rely more heavily on the script of their immediate environment.

For much of his career, architect and environmental psychologist Romedi Passini has been researching how people with dementia find their way around. He and his colleagues have observed that even people with very advanced Alzheimer's can eventually find the water fountain. But they do this in a very different way than you or I would. They are not capable of plotting an overall wayfinding plan or making decisions based on memory and inference. They rely entirely on easily accessible environmental information, allowing them to move from one decision point to the next. This means that monotonous, undifferentiated environments – long, bland corridors with identical doors, for instance – are a nightmare.[2]

Hogeweyk couldn't be more different. Brick and stucco apartment blocks form a natural perimeter, sculpted around an inner network of gardens, terraces, and walkways. The pathway structure is fairly simple. Most squares have only one entrance except those that are actually expansions around the central ring path. But each space is distinguished by shape and design. The Mediterranean *winkel centrum* (shop centre) is lined with mosaic benches and planters, while the *stadsplein* (town square) offers boules and giant chess games beneath trellised vines. Dementia patients are prone to wandering, which they can do freely here. Exploration is key to their ability for wayfinding.

People with dementia are an extreme case of cognitive deficit. But in some ways, they are simply more sensitive to subtleties of the immediate environment that affect us all – the intimate connections between nature and human nature.

As a teenager, Roger Ulrich spent a lot of time in hospitals. He suffered from a painful condition called nephritis, a form of kidney disease. Bouts of infection confined him to bed, both at home and in the hospital. At home, he spent hours gazing out the window at a stately pine tree in the backyard. The worst periods of illness sent him into the hostile, sterile world of white coats and bright lights. And he found it ironic that such small comforts as his favourite tree were lost at the moments he most needed them.

Years later, Ulrich tested the difference one tree could make, in what went on to become the most frequently cited study in environmental psychology. It was a perfect natural experiment: a gallbladder surgery recovery ward with two nearly identical rooms, served by the same nurses. But while one room had a view of some deciduous trees, the other looked out at a brick wall. Reviewing five years of hospital records, the researchers compared patients matched evenly for age, gender, health, and other factors. They found that patients with the tree view not only recovered more quickly, but also experienced less pain in the process. They requested far fewer doses of narcotic pain medications than the unlucky wall watchers next door.

How could a view of a few trees make such dramatic physical and psychological difference? To understand this, we need to take a few steps back.

■ ■ ■

Imagine an African savannah. A wide-open grassland, scattered with widely spaced acacia trees, large friendly mammals drinking from a shallow lake, and some distant hills. This is the environment that many evolutionary psychologists believe we evolved in. The environment that first moulded our biology and behaviour to form *Homo sapiens*. In the early twentieth century, fossils uncovered in southern and eastern Africa led anthropologists to believe that early hominids had migrated to savannah settings from more forested biomes. During the Pliocene period (5.3 to 2.6 million years ago), Earth's temperature dropped, causing Africa to become a drier continent. Savannahs and open woodlands expanded while tropical jungles shrank, driving our humanoid ancestors from cosy, tropical tree homes with plentiful fruit to the more treacherous savannah. In order to survive on the savannah, we had to adapt and evolve in certain ways, changing us to be the creatures we are today – or so it was believed.

The question of what makes us human has been closely tied to the mystery of the environmental forces that led us to become bipedal. But like many areas of scientific inquiry, theories of evolution are constantly evolving themselves. The critical step in our evolution from human-like apes to ape-like humans was a breakthrough that fossil records place at least 4.2 to 3.9 million years ago.[3] Was it moving from jungles down into savannahs that led us to walk on two feet? The original savannah hypothesis was based upon a macho ideal of male hunters chasing zebras around with spears. It is now believed that foraging for more sedentary food sources like roots and tubers may have first drawn us down from the forests, as they became increasingly less fruity. While this image of early humans hunting yams is not quite so heroic, they would certainly have been easier to catch.

Proponents of the waterside ape theory suggest that lakeshores and wetlands could have been a major source for these 'fall-back foods', progressing to a taste for aquatic snails and catfish. This close relationship to water could provide an explanation for some of the strange ways we differ from other primates, such as our lack of fur and subcutaneous layer of blubber-like fat.[4] Recent findings suggest that our ancestors may have evolved in a greater variety of environments than the savannah, including grasslands and forests.[5] A recent skeleton CAT scan of our infamous Australopithecus ancestor Lucy has indicated she died falling from a tree, implying a more arboreal lifestyle.[6]

While savannahs may not have been the exclusive environment of our speciation, we can be sure that our ancient ancestors lived in their vicinity.[7] And we find over and over again that people are drawn to the elements of the savannah – open fields, copses of trees, and water – and to specific arrangements of these elements.

We also know that the vast majority of our development as a species took place on the African continent. Some evidence indicates that our ape-like ancestors began moving from Africa to other continents close to two million years ago. But other clues suggest our common ancestors diverged more recently. Human genome research has revealed that we are a bit inbred as a species. If you compare the genes of two humans from disparate corners of the globe today – say Argentina and Mongolia – they will be more similar than the genes of two chimpanzees who live in neighbouring African chimp clans.[8] All modern humans seem to share a common ancestor dating back less than 200,000 years.[9] And after our hominid ancestors dispersed, they continued to live in more overwhelmingly natural settings than most of us do today.

Where do we draw the distinction between natural and unnatural? Was the first hut made by the first cave people natural? And if so, is a skyscraper, built by many people using technology invented by other people and materials extracted from the Earth, not still natural? This is a tricky point. The *New Oxford American English Dictionary* defines nature as: 'The phenomena of the physical world collectively, including plants, animals, the landscape, and other features and products of the earth, as opposed to humans and human creations.'[10] But if an eagle's nest or a termite mound is natural, then why should our cave people huts and skyscrapers not be natural as well? Until conspiracy theorists manage to substantiate their claims that the pyramids were landing docks for alien spaceships with some fossil evidence of their own, it is difficult to draw a fine line.

But while eagles and termites have largely kept building the same type of structures for the past twelve thousand years, we humans have moved from living in small communities of small dwellings to dense cities and sprawling suburbs, removing us from the plants, animals, and landscapes we spent our formative generations surrounded by. It's easy to see that most humans now live in very different environments from the ones we evolved to excel in.

The term 'biophilia' was popularised by biologist Edward O. Wilson in his 1984 book of the same name – and in the same year, coincidentally, that Ulrich published his ground-breaking findings on hospital window views. Drawn from Greek, biophilia translates as 'love of life': human attraction to nature, our love of the living world. In the scope of our evolution as a species, it is only very recently that we have begun to build and live in larger settlements and dwellings – we have been doing this for probably only one per cent of our total history.[11] Wilson suggested that biologically, we are still programmed to prefer the settings that would have supported our survival long ago. The same way we still find signs of fertility and physical prowess attractive in potential mates, even if we don't want to have children or need to protect them from lions.

Nature comes from the Latin *natura*, which means both birth and character: one's most basic or inherent qualities. And while we now know there to be 118 elements in the periodic table, ancient Greeks and Romans believed there were just four: earth, air, water, and fire. Like our elements, they believed everything on Earth was made up of some combination of these essential ingredients. This elemental worldview was the founding principle of science, philosophy, and even medicine for thousands of years. The Roman physician Galen linked the four elements with four 'humours' of the body, describing different physical and psychological temperaments. Sanguine people were thought to have ambitious, fiery characters due to the excess of blood in their systems, whereas watery phlegmatic people would be calm and apathetic. This framework – sharing tenets with ancient Islamic medicine and the Indian Ayurvedic system – dominated European medical practice until the nineteenth century.

While we no longer believe that melancholy temperament is caused by a mysterious substance called black bile, these ideas have survived to some extent in our contemporary understanding of fiery and melancholic personalities. Millions of modern people still read daily astrological horoscopes, an archaic system which the Greeks and Romans essentially used to talk about the influence of our environment – the flora, fauna, and feeling of the seasons, as measured by movements of the sun, moon, and planets – on our personality and behaviour. At their most basic level, these ancient four elements acknowledged the importance of these natural features to our physical and mental well-being. This understanding of a link between our psychological and physical health is something we lost somewhere along our path to building ever bigger cities and health facilities. The four elements tell us much about the needs most basic to our survival and well-being. And when it comes to questions of survival, our competing origin stories often come into play:

Air

Air is essential to our survival. Most people can live no more than a few minutes without oxygen.[12] While air is seemingly invisible, scent, temperature, flow, and subtle visual cues may betray important information about this essential element.[13] Research has shown that we prefer natural ventilation to the highly processed and controlled air we breathe from the heating, ventilation, and air-conditioning (known as HVAC) systems of gargantuan buildings. Greater variability in air flow and temperature – more similar to natural conditions – has been linked to greater well-being, concentration, and comfort.[14]

Water

After air, water is our most immediate need. You can survive without it only for a matter of days. And it is probably because of this that we are so deeply fascinated by places, views, and images containing water. Why is it that a house with an ocean view will fetch many thousands more than the house next door without a watery vista? Even when both houses have equal beach access, or are perched equally high atop a hillside, this price differential is unquestioned for otherwise identical dwellings. Access to water was essential for our ancestors. While streams and lakes provided drinking water, the sea could also signal a plentiful source of nourishment. More than fifty per cent of humans live on or near the coast today – differentiating us from our broader primate family, whose habitats are far inland.[15] Spending time in green environments generally has restorative benefits. But research has shown that when people exercise in green areas with water, their mood and self-esteem is even more improved.[16]

Fire

Fire is sometimes said to be what makes us human. Darwin himself believed human command of language and fire to be our greatest achievements as a species.[17] The legend of Prometheus tells how the Titan god created humans from earth and water. Or less flatteringly, mud. His brother, Epithemeus, had been tasked with creating animals, giving each one a gift such as wings, claws, or fins. But when it came time for Prometheus to give his mud people their special gift, they were all gone! So Prometheus stole a bit of Zeus's sacred fire, endowing his naked mud beings with the light and knowledge of fire to give them an advantage over the other animals. Fire represents our ability to use tools, extract energy more efficiently from food, and develop culture. As diurnal animals, we are stronger, safer, and better skilled in the light than the dark. The myths of societies like the Yokut Indians of California held that the sun itself was a ball of fire. Sunlight is an essential source of Vitamin D, supporting growth and musculoskeletal health and preventing conditions such as osteoporosis, type-one diabetes, and rheumatoid arthritis.[18] Insufficient exposure to natural light increases levels of a hormone called melatonin, which generally throws off our internal clock, making us lethargic and depressed, and leads to Seasonal Affective Disorder (SAD) in extreme cases. Unsurprisingly, natural light is consistently cited as a critical factor in our preference for hospitals, offices, schools, homes, and gardens.

Earth

And, lastly, we have earth, which we take to include the landscape itself, as well as the redwoods, roses, and rhubarbs growing from it. Our concept of mother nature dates back to deities like Gaia, the earth goddess of the Greeks. Mother Gaia gave birth to the hills, the sea, and Uranus of the heavens, with whom she then began to beget other godlings like Prometheus! But after this scandalous episode she went on to fulfil her motherly role, providing caves and trees to shelter us and bananas and coconuts to feed us. The calming and restorative impact that sensory involvement with the Earth's plant life, animals, and even rocks or mountaintops has upon us is called environmental restoration. But while we like mountains, butterflies, and baby otters, vegetation seems to hold a special restorative appeal.

Building on his groundbreaking discovery about the healing power of trees for hospital patients, Roger Ulrich set out to learn more about the workings of environmental restoration. He hypothesised that exposure to non-threatening natural elements could alleviate negative psychological states like stress and anxiety. He showed stressed people slides of various scenes and found they felt better after viewing natural environs than American urban environments lacking natural elements. Even comparing different urban scenes, people tend to prefer cityscapes including some form of vegetation – especially trees – or water.[19]

Why do natural scenes hold such great restorative power? One potential explanation is that the restorative and pleasing impact of natural scenes functions at a geometric level. Modern urban environments tend to be formed of harsh angular lines and blocky buildings. Curvature may calm because it reminds us of natural forms like eggs, plums, and puddles. Forests and cliffs are built with a different scale of detail and variety than the asphalt deserts and concrete canyons we find ourselves in today.

On a geometric level natural scenes contain more fractal geometry: repeating patterns of expanding symmetry, replicating the same form at different levels. We see fractals in coastlines and trees, which repeat self-similar forms on multiple levels. The anatomy of flames, waves, clouds, and trees can be simulated by computer programs using fractal mathematics. And because our visual perceptual system evolved to function in a more fractal world, it may simply be easier for us to process these forms.[20]

But strictly speaking, we do not love all elements of the natural world. Take, for instance, snakes and spiders. While these creatures pose less of a threat to most modern humans than car accidents or gun crime, most of us continue to react with visceral fear at the sight of them. Evolutionary psychologists believe that we have developed a toolbox of 'cognitive modules or programs'.[21] Each tool gives us a strategy that we have held onto because it helped us deal with a threat or problem that was key to our ancestors' survival. For example: snakes posed an ongoing threat to our survival due to their penchant for venomous biting and constricting. So even though many snakes are harmless, we tend to fall back on the general snake-situation tool in our toolbox, which directs us to scream and run away. At least that was what I did when I almost stepped on a rattlesnake when I was eight. I think we were told at school to back away slowly and quietly, but that's not what my snake-situation instincts told me to do. Personally, I am also terrified of driving – an evolutionary adaptation better matched to the perils of modern life, perhaps? Then again, I have a life record of *two* snake collisions (a garden snake once entangled itself in the wheels of my stroller) to zero car crashes. So I'm glad my snake-fear instincts have not been overwritten in relation to contemporary risk statistics.

An aversion to snakes or spiders is a 'biophobic' response. On the other hand we have positive, affiliative responses: attraction or love for vegetative elements. Environmental psychologist Yannick Joye at the University of Groningen uses the term 'phytophilic' – love of plants – to refer more specifically to our attraction to plant-based life. Our snake-alert system is triggered when we see non-threatening snakes, as well as snake-like vines and garden hoses. And as anyone who has seen the many YouTube videos involving cats and cucumbers can attest, we are not the only animals who seem to react this way. In the same way, our greenery-loving response may be triggered by trees and flowers that don't specifically offer us apples or the ability to climb out of harm's way.[22] And this may tell us something about why elements like trees, water, and flowers would have a calming influence on us as well.

After experiencing stress – those pesky lions always chasing us around – it is important to be able to calm down to a baseline level of arousal. Continuing to be on edge is detrimental to our health, can interfere with sleep, and means we will be less able to deal with the next threat that comes our way – a tiger or a bear this time! While various environmental restoration researchers differ in how they think this restorative process works, they generally agree that we have developed to prefer environments that would better support our survival, those linked with the goals of food, water, and shelter.

Acacia trees typical of the African savannah, which have low and wide-reaching branches perfect for people to climb, are often preferred over species such as oak, eucalyptus, palm and coniferous trees.[23] And beyond the acacia specifically, its general form has been found to have wide appeal. One cross-cultural study found people favoured trees with dense canopies and trunks bifurcating close to the ground.[24] Further research has identified a preference for the spreading form of this tree type over conical or rounded varieties.[25] These findings have sometimes been questioned because people's preference could be affected by the type of trees they are familiar with. We tend to like novelty as long as it doesn't trigger any of our threat-response patterns. But there does seem to be a preponderance of positive feelings for acacia-like trees, just as there are quite a lot of negative feelings for snakes.

Most species evolve to prefer the habitats they do best in. Research on primate populations indicates that environmental preferences are species-specific adaptations, likely to have at least some genetic basis.[26] The big difference with humans is that we have evolved to manipulate our own environments on such a big scale.

Take the giraffe. Natural selection has adapted giraffes over the eons to match the conditions of their environment, which also happens to be the African savannah. For generations, giraffes with longer and longer necks have survived better and multiplied further by their ability to reach up to the tippy-top leaves of the acacia trees when the zebras and elephants had munched up all the lower leaves. Their environment has also formed them to blend in to some extent with the tan-coloured savannah grasses, to be fit for dealing with the African heat, and to fraternise with other giraffes. If this giraffe were to relocate to England, it would find plenty of leaves to eat and it would no longer be chased by lions. Though it would probably develop a phobia of the many Red Lion and Three Lions pubs proudly displaying lion-like sigils. Ultimately, the giraffe would get terribly cold, encounter some nasty diseases it had no immunities to, and eventually starve in the winter when the leaves died, since it would be too afraid to go into any pubs. (As evolutionary evidence has demonstrated, this is the only way anyone in England manages to survive the winter.)

This is what Daniel E. Lieberman, chair of the Department of Human Evolutionary Biology at Harvard, calls an 'evolutionary mismatch'. In the eyes of evolutionary biologists and psychologists, we are essentially not very different from this giraffe. Our environment has been rapidly transformed since we began farming, as has the way we eat and spend our days. But our bodies and minds are still better matched to the Palaeolithic environment of our ancestors.[27] So do we, like this giraffe, possess some kind of inherent proclivity for the savannah landscape?

This is the savannah hypothesis, proposed by researchers such as biologist Gordon Orians and his colleague, environmental psychologist Judith Heerwagen. In 1982, two Oregonians by the name of John (Balling and Falk) decided to test this hypothesis.

Surveying a large and diverse US sample, Balling and Falk found that Americans' visual preference for this foreign environment was on a par with their ratings for the natural environments they were more familiar with: deciduous and coniferous forests. Americans of all ages preferred savannahs over deserts or tropical rainforests. And most significantly, they found that American children under twelve preferred the savannah over all other biomes. Balling and Falk felt their findings provided strong support for the savannah hypothesis. Younger children, they argued, revealed our innate preference for our species' native savannah environments. Over time, adults' cultural bias came to interfere with this inherent preference, providing an explanation for older Americans placing the quintessentially African scenes on a par with more American ones.

A typical savannah scene
© iStock

There has been much debate over how cultural bias may have skewed these findings. Familiarity and novelty both sway our preferences, clouding identification of the innate. But in 2010, Falk and Balling published another study extending their original research to test landscape preferences among Nigerian children and adults. The Nigerian sample overwhelmingly preferred savannah scenes. Crucially, the Nigerians sampled all lived in rainforest belt and delta areas, with the vast majority never having travelled outside these biomes. Like the Americans, most had no direct experience of the savannah. But they were also strongly drawn to its open grasslands and expansive acacias.

Of course, for those whose recent lineage is Asian, European, or American, our ancestors may have migrated out of Africa much longer ago than our hypothetical giraffe. Personally, I am not a big fan of savannah scenes – from a purely static aesthetic stand-point. I prefer the rolling English hills, the cloud forests of Peru, and the luscious creek-side crannies of northern California. But across these other continents, we often find that restorative green spaces have been shaped and pruned into forms mimicking the patterns of the savannah. And we see this with particular clarity in the English countryside. Imagine a classical English landscape painting. In the foreground you have a picturesque thatched cottage and stone mill opening onto a meadow. A peaceful river curves around the meadow, disappearing round the bend behind a line of trees. And in the background we have some hills, where our eye is drawn to a captivating castle. The English landscape was remoulded in this ideal by an eighteenth-century landscape architect called Capability Brown. Although christened Lancelot, he is rumoured to have earned his name from his tendency to advise his clients that their landed estates possessed great capability for improvement. It is estimated that he left his mark on the grounds of no fewer than 170 estates surrounding the grandest properties in England, rivalling Isambard Kingdom Brunel both for peculiarity of name and for impact on the face of the English landscape. Examples of Brown's work can be found at Blenheim Palace, Hampton Court Palace, and some remaining touches at Kew Gardens.

As geographer Jay Appleton has described, Brown simplified certain principles of landscape design pioneered by his predecessors. Under his influence,

The grounds of Wallington Hall, Northumberland, crafted by Capability Brown
© Duncan Davis/Getty Images

'The shapes of paths, avenues, and ornamental water-bodies became curvilinear and irregular. The groupings of trees and open spaces were designed to emphasise the natural lines of the landscape, where previously they would have been employed in an effort to efface them. This was an accommodation between art and nature in which each made the maximum concession to the other, and the result was a harmonious blend of those three components which flourish so felicitously under the English climate, trees (especially deciduous trees) grass and water. Among these were set occasional small structures such as bridges, gateways, temples perhaps, and of course the big house.'[28]

The core elements of this scene – the open meadow, the calm water source, combined with sheltering natural and built forms – are found in our favourite scenes and places time and again. Appleton was the first to intensively analyse this phenomenon in his 1975 book, *The Experience of Landscape*. Comparing landscape architecture to vernacular urbanism, paintings spanning the Renaissance to his own time, and garden design from Japan to the Americas, Appleton demonstrated the prevailing dominance of these patterns. Gordon Orians has gone on to show that Japanese horticulturalists have shaped their maples to more closely resemble savannah-like tree forms.

Since we lack the claws, fangs, wings, and shells that Epithemeus gave out to the other animals, a protective environment is critical to our survival. So critical, that we may be as strongly drawn to it as we are to sources of nourishment – depending on how hungry we are. We seek small protective sites of refuge, adjacent to wide open areas that give us a prospect of food and water sources, as well as early warning of potential predators. And ideally, we desire a balance of refuge and prospect. A refuge nest we can easily flee to from the prospect outlook. While deserts, tundra, and icy mountains are prospect-oriented landscapes, jungles and forests are refuge-oriented. Savannahs, with their open fields and climbable trees, provide the perfect mix. But refuge and prospect are not only about shelter and openness. They specifically relate to what Appleton calls the opportunity to 'see without being seen'. And this depends greatly on how light plays out over the forms and hollows of the scene. Our refuge should conceal us in shadow; the prospect reveals useful information with light.

Knowledge has long been associated with light. In an open meadow or savannah, sunlight provides a rich source of information, illuminating forms and movement through shadow and detail.[29] Like our fear of snakes, our fear of the dark is well founded. We have poor nocturnal vision. But we especially fear moving from the light into the dark because this allows us to be seen by things we can't see. Much of what we may perceive as 'natural' in the English countryside was shaped to serve these human desires by the helping hand of Capability Brown. His curving landscapes are in some ways just as artificial as the perfectly centred and angular French styles they departed from. But as the transformation of the English landscape passed from the hands of Brown to Brunel, the edges of the English world became more angular. And much of human experience has become steadily more straight and square as the factories and railroads of the industrial revolution reproduced themselves around the world.

■ ■ ■

Unfortunately, the environments we love most aren't square and orderly. We like streets that curve out of sight around the corner, leading us on with a tantalising hint of what lies beyond. We love mystery. The forest path, a tunnel of trees. The spiral staircase. Locked doors and secret gardens. Even scenes on a bigger scale. As Herman Melville once wrote, 'These mountains, somehow, they play at hide-and-seek, and all before one's eyes.'[30] We follow the promise of new environmental information like a bloodhound tracks a scent. But when I say mystery, I don't mean one that can't be solved. In the millions of murder mystery novels and *Law and Order* episodes devoured each year, how many don't unveil the murderer? We like environments that are mysterious enough to excite our curiosity, but also enable us to satiate it.

We owe much of our knowledge about environmental preference and wayfinding to a trailblazing husband and wife team named Rachel and Steven Kaplan. Having spent over half a century cultivating research and researchers at the University of Michigan, the Kaplans are the grandparents of this wing of environmental psychology. Analysing people's reactions to images of various natural and urban environments, they have built up a comprehensive picture of what we like, and some compelling theories to explain why. The Kaplans gave their theory a straightforward name: the Kaplan and Kaplan Model of Environmental Preference. But this name is a bit like a flat empty landscape – it doesn't make you curious to learn more. So let's call it the 'mystery novel model'. The mystery novel model relies on an idea similar to that of ninja-proof seats. But while the refuge and prospect concept focuses more on our weaknesses as a species, the mystery novel model emphasises our strengths.

As we know, all animals should be attracted to the sort of settings they do best in. The polar bears that wanted to lounge on the beach and rabbits that climbed into eagle nests died out eons ago. For humans, this means environments that provide the right balance of information – our special super power – and safety. We can't swim, fly, or smell very well, but we glide tactfully through skies and seas of information. Unlike the facts and data-bits we may now associate with the term, the information we thrive on is rich, deep, and contextual.

As with refuge and prospect, the Kaplans found that the most favoured environments balance mystery with legibility. An environment is 'legible' if it's easy to survey and to form a cognitive map of it. Depth of field is part of this – the ability to

MYSTERY NOVEL MODEL

Coherence

Complexity

Legibility

Mystery

Four factors we desire a balance of in our environments.
Source: Adapted from Kaplan (1987)

see the distance. But to be truly legible, there must be elements that help us find our way forward and back as we explore. Features like the clumps of trees we find in the savannah.[31]

Imagine a barren winter cornfield in Iowa, the flat horizon all around. Here we have prospect, but without distinctive landmarks and differentiated areas, the space isn't readable. And as witnessed in Cary Grant's famous *North by Northwest* scene, cornfields don't offer much refuge from modern predators like crop-dusting planes. Now think of the rolling farmlands of Devon, England. Add some curvature, drop in a few trees, define the landscape with some hedgerows – the scene is legible now. We like spaces that make it easy to plan our route out in search of new gems of information. And perhaps more importantly, to find our way back. What we like in a landscape is a lot like a mystery novel: a mystery that we can read. A challenge we know we can solve. And, like all good mystery novels, the mystery novel model has a number of layers.

Our perceptual system is designed to detect contrast, identify simple shapes and lines, and to seek an organising principle or focus point. Before we get drawn into the mystery of the scene, we may react more immediately to its coherence and complexity. A coherent abstract painting has a sense of focus and structure: repetition, symmetry, or textures that organise the scene. Looking back at our picturesque English landscape, the cottage and mill buildings would provide coherence. The textures of the meadow and river similarly help us understand the scene on a simpler level than that of legibility. We like coherent paintings, and complex ones too: scenes with a greater number and variety of features. A landscape could, for instance, be complex without being mysterious. A field full of sheep, cows and chickens would be much more complex than an empty field. But it's not particularly mysterious. It doesn't excite our curiosity the way the same field full of a winding network of festival tents might.

Generally, people tend to prefer scenes that are more complex – both natural scenes and urban ones. But only to a certain extent. Assessing natural landscapes, urban scenes, and abstract art, people tend to prefer those with an intermediate level of complexity. Perhaps because they are often less complex, complexity appears to play a particularly important role in our preference for urban scenes.[32]

Of course different people's landscape preferences do differ, according to culture, age, and even gender. Younger children tend to prefer less complex scenes than adults – the same way they like mild-tasting foods and cartoons with bold lines and bright colours. Complexity may also help explain why the children in Balling and Falk's study preferred savannahs, which may have a lower level of complexity than the forests the American adults had developed a taste for.

The mystery novel model gives us another avenue to understand our preference for savannah-like scenes. In addition to elucidating why we like natural scenes ticking these boxes, it also helps explain why we may prefer some urban scenes over others. The river curving beyond the bend, the path disappearing around the trees – these are what are called 'deflected vistas'. And we love deflected vistas in our city streets as well. Say you have a choice between three streets when wandering around a foreign city: one straight, one ending in a T junction, and one winding around the corner. All things being equal, most people will take the winding one. These curvy flirtatious street corners seduce us – they lead us on.[33] We crave the curiosity of not knowing what's around the bend. We like to be a little lost. But not too lost.

Cities laid out on a totally rectilinear grid like Manhattan make it easier to find our way around. But the monotony of the grid becomes oppressive. I remember envying my New York visitors after five years living there. The sense of mystery, wonder they still had in not knowing where they were and what they would find next. But this was a feeling I soon came to fear when I moved across the Atlantic and began trying to find my way around London without the aid of Google maps.

'London is too big,' my urban videographer colleague Clarence Eckerson said after a recent visit. As director of Streetfilms, Clarence has travelled the world chronicling sustainable transport and liveable street innovations from Oslo to Bogota, so he has some good grounds for comparison. 'I've never been as lost anywhere as I was in London'.

It's not just London's size, but the complete lack of legibility in its layout and street grid. And oh-so-many of those flirtatious street corners. Leading you on and on but never getting anywhere! After my second time hailing a cab for navigation rather than transportation, I had to admit it was time to join the twenty-first century and get a smartphone. Our big brains thrive on complex environments like London, and can grow even bigger when stimulated by them. London taxi drivers required to gain 'the knowledge' (a mental map of much of London's streets) have shown increased grey matter in their hippocampus.[34] Similarly, rats reared in more complex, information-rich environments develop larger brains with up to twenty per cent greater neural connectivity. These same rats then go on to demonstrate higher intelligence, superior performance in making their way through complex mazes, and greater training aptitude.[35]

While we like curvaceous streets and corners, too much mystery can be scary. We tend to remember both acute and obtuse corners as closer to right angles than they actually are. We imagine tangled streets into orderly parallel and perpendicular formations. We perceive buildings in the same 'area' to be closer to each other than those in a different neighbourhood, even when they're not. We strive to fit the complexity of reality into an orderly mental map we can make sense of. And when things don't fit, it can be very taxing, confusing and tiring. The environments we like most tend to strike a balance between mystery and legibility, complexity and coherence.

Seeing us as information-seeking creatures, the Kaplans theorised that the restorative impact of natural scenes and elements comes specifically from their ability to relax our minds. Or, in their words, to 'restore our capacity for directed attention'. To refresh us for the next informational quest.

And this brings us back again to the question of what makes us human.

Early evolutionary theorists imagined that our large brains had distinguished us from other primates early in our evolutionary journey. But this theory doesn't seem to tally with more recent fossil and nutritional evidence. As Daniel Lieberman says, 'It was not brains over brawn but brains plus brawn that made possible the hunter-gatherer way of life.'[36]

The human and chimpanzee family trees diverged around six or seven million years ago. Early hominids, and even our closer

Australopithecus ancestors like Lucy, had fairly small brains. We first started using stone tools around 2.6 million years ago. But it wasn't until after we began hunting, gathering, and cooking that our brains grew so unusually large. The human brain is an energy-guzzling organ. Simply sitting and having a chat with a friend will consume twenty to twenty-five per cent of your 'resting metabolic energy'. Our brains alone require about six hundred calories a day to run on. And while we have far too many readily available sources of high-calorie foods today, our big brains came at a high cost in the Paleolithic era.

What were the benefits of large brains then? Greater cognitive power allowed us to develop language, cooperation, division of labour, and collective memory – new forms of social interaction. This gave us many advantages – crucially, the ability to more efficiently gather fuel for our energy-hungry brains and lifestyles. It also enabled us to reproduce at a much higher rate than our chimpanzee cousins.[37] The question of what our ancestors ate to help grow these big brains is a heated debate. Were they slurping up zebra brains, catching catfish, or snacking on snails and water-lily popcorn – along with staples like the scarily named USOs (underground storage organs), which is actually just a fancy name for roots and tubers?[38] We may never know. And I'm not sure I even want to know any more about these brain-slurping, organ-digging relatives of ours.

But one thing we do know is that humans are especially well evolved to walk and run long distances. Hunter-gatherers tend to walk around 5 to 9 miles (9 to 15 kilometres) in a day. Compared to other animals we are not very fast or powerful. But we do have great endurance. We can't run short distances faster than antelopes, zebras, horses, or even dogs. But it is possible for us to outrun them over long distances – especially in hot temperatures.

What we consider quintessentially human characteristics like creativity and innovation developed hand-in-hand with intensive walking, running, climbing, digging, and possibly wading and swimming. Our cognitive capacity and physical prowess are intimately tied together. Like the bear who went over the mountain to see what he could see, our drive to explore the mysterious is linked to our physical skills and cognitive powers: our psychophysical speciation. Our preference for information-rich environments seems perfectly tuned to aid our survival during the long walks of these hunter-gatherer days. And our insatiable curiosity to see what's round the bend would seem to support one of our other specialities as a species: our knack for exploring and adapting to new landscapes. Our ancestors put these great walking and information-seeking skills to use, spreading out from Africa to the areas we now call China, Indonesia, and northern Europe.

Beyond big brains and bipedalism, we evolved culture, which has given us the ability to innovate – to adapt to different parts of the world in non-genetic ways. Evolution has by no means stopped since the Paleolithic period. But this cultural evolution has accelerated faster and faster, speeding far ahead of our physical adaptation, especially since the industrial revolution. Cultural evolution, like the advent and widespread use of agriculture, has in some cases expedited natural selection. The environments of our upbringing can also shift the expression of certain genes to an extent. People who spend their early years in hot climates develop more functional sweat glands than those in cold climates.[39]

It is believed that contemporary humans have higher levels of anxiety, depression, stress, short-sightedness and many other common disorders than our ancestors two millennia ago did. Genes play a role in all of these problems. But our environments have changed much more than our genes have over the last few thousand years. The prevalence of depression and type-two diabetes today has more to do with the interaction between these genes and our rapidly changing environments.[40]

Beginning around 10,000 BCE various societies moved from their roving hunter-gatherer ways to settle down and till the soil. Farming took division of labour a step further and enabled us to more efficiently extract energy from the earth. Farming was harder work and yielded a less nutritious diet. But it did produce more food, enabling still greater population growth. A novel phenomenon bloomed around the world: growing masses of people, newly tied to particular spots of land. Agriculture gave birth to the first cities, which are believed to have been built at least seven thousand years ago in the 'fertile crescent' area stretching from the eastern edge of the Mediterranean Sea to the Persian Gulf. We could now protect ourselves from lions and other foes with great walled fortresses. But coming together in these permanent encampments had unsavoury side effects: cesspools and other unsanitary conditions, unleashing plagues and other new diseases on an untold scale – a new survival challenge, which has ultimately led us to create the fortresses against illness we call hospitals.

The practice of scientific research and modern medicine evolved hand-in-hand with the industrial revolution, informing the way we measure people's health, treat them, and design hospitals. These developments have sought to control as many factors as possible through sterile, white, brightly lit labs and treatment rooms, where no contaminating influences get in or out. This made sense, coming out of an era with rampant disease and infection. But now, we seem to have inoculated ourselves in a maze of white walls, increasingly far away from the natural forces that make us feel whole.

As mathematician and architectural theorist Nikos A. Salingaros has pointed out, environments that deprive our senses of nurturing sensory stimulation mimic the experience of many illnesses. Spending time in drab, minimalist spaces lacking colour and legibility feels similar to the symptoms brought about by conditions such as stroke, macular degeneration, and visual agnosia. Sensory deprivation feels uncomfortable because it means we have no information about the threats or opportunities that may be around us. Sterile hospital environments make us feel anxious because they mimic the experience of neurophysiological breakdown.[41]

Somewhat surprisingly, there is a dearth of strong and broad evidence on the relationship between specific environmental colours, mood, and behaviour. [42] Studies in the 1970s suggesting that a special shade of 'drunk tank pink' could tranquillise naval brig and jail-cell occupants have not held up over time. Much of colour psychology appears to be culturally bound (though humans can distinguish more shades of green than any other colour – possibly going back to our need to distinguish those scary green snakes from all the other green leaves and grasses around us).[43] But there is strong evidence that contextual integration of colour, along with texture and pattern, has a positive psychological impact. Beyond fixating on pink or green, design that holistically employs colour to build upon our biophilic preferences is key.[44]

Our eyes and brains have evolved to discern intricate details, colour and contrast, symmetries and connections. The benefits of building features such as symmetry, detailing, ornamentation, and visual connection go beyond stylistic trends and conventions. Our perceptual system is designed to deal with these elements – the elements that have formed us, from our days in the savannah through to all traditional forms of architecture.

Despite long-standing evidence of the critical health benefits of biophilic design principles, most hospitals have yet to benefit from them. Being in the hospital is usually a stressful experience. Whether you have broken a leg, are visiting a sick relative, getting poked and zapped, or awaiting potentially frightening test results, it's not usually a walk in the park. Roger Ulrich discovered that conventional hospital environments were causing patients additional stress in a variety of ways. We're often denied privacy, control, and contact with family members. We are isolated in windowless rooms, cut off from natural light, breeze, and sights. Forced to stare into harsh ceiling lights, surrounded by the screeching sounds of gurney wheels, beeping equipment, and distress. Stress is a physical state as well as a psychological one, resulting in higher levels of cortisol and stress hormones like epinephrine that are hard on the heart and other organs. This physical state further decreases immune function, which slows recovery and weakens resistance to infection. Stress retards healing.[45]

But simply viewing a nature image or video can reduce cardiovascular stress within twenty seconds, as one group of researchers found using video footage of water.[46] Studies in natural and laboratory environments have consistently confirmed that nature views reduce stress within five minutes, as measured by heart activity, muscle tension, brain electrical activity, and blood pressure.[47] The patients in Ulrich's original study didn't just feel better and recover more swiftly, they also experienced less pain.

There are various theories about how this may work, including the idea that neural structures in the spinal cord moderate a sensory transition gateway to the brain. The negative emotions and stress related to conventional hospital environments may 'open the gate' to increase pain, whereas the positive feelings, stress reduction, and distracting mental stimulation of natural elements can close the gate.[48]

In a later study, Ulrich found that heart surgery patients who looked at pictures of savannah-like scenes experienced less anxiety and pain than those viewing abstract art or no art. These effective colour photographs had all the key elements – a well-lit view of an open area with trees and water – which seems to have been essential. Patients who looked at pictures of a dark and shadowy forest did not experience significant reductions in pain or anxiety.[49]

Some researchers, like Ulrich, believe that the restorative impact of natural scenes is a rapid, unconscious process while others, like the Kaplans, suggest it requires cognitive assessment. And still others believe that the make-up of natural scenes is simply easier for our minds to process, which makes them more relaxing to look at than the built environments we are not as well adapted to interpreting. This ease of interpretation requires fewer cognitive resources, resulting in a restorative effect. Whatever the mechanism is, we know it works.

Bringing the benefits of biophilia to healthcare environments can mean more than showing people tree pictures and water movies. And it should. Numerous studies have shown that intelligently designed hospital gardens hold great restorative power. In addition to reducing stress, gardens can increase physical activity and foster socialisation, all of which aid healing.[50] More generally, mild variation in light, temperature, airflow, and sound can gently fascinate and distract patients, creating a better environment for well-being than one in which these factors are held strictly constant like a refrigerator. And while many of us have come to shun the sun, older people exposed to moderate levels of UV light have been found to have fewer falls.

Artificial lighting differs from daylight not only in the quality of illumination – especially fluorescents and standard LEDs, which lack warmth and warp our perception of colour – but in its consistency.[51] Sunlight changes in intensity, colour, and direction throughout the course of the day and year. The blue-toned, uni-directional light sources we find shining intensely for many hours of the day and night in institutional settings can interfere with circadian rhythms.[52] Recent studies have found major benefits to well-being from varying the light spectrum throughout the day in hospitals, and MIT researchers are developing a new generation of super-efficient incandescent bulbs whose light better approximates that of the sun.[53] Both lamps and windows can deliver light in more naturalistic patterns of distribution, and from sources which we can easily control. Beyond bringing sunlight, air, views, and colour into sterile spaces, hospital windows can offer the variation of informational richness on which we thrive.

■ ■ ■

If you have a dog, you probably feed it some sensible dog food, designed to deliver the precise nutrients and vitamins needed for a shiny coat and long healthy life (in dog years). But when it comes to your own dinner, you slurp up a microwave meal full of delicious chemicals and preservatives, with far less nutritional value than our Paleolithic zebra-brain dish. Shouldn't we give as much attention to our own well-being as we give to our animal companions?

In between my first and second snake collision incidents, I managed to develop some more biophilic feelings towards savannah animals through frequent visits to the Oakland Zoo. And, during these years, the zoo environment evolved. The lions and elephants were upgraded from sculpted concrete enclosures to open hillsides on the outskirts of the zoo. As these regal savannah animals moved into an environment more similar to their native surroundings, the little sun bears moved up from little cages to the lions' old home.

Environmental and ecological psychologist Judith Heerwagen has charted how zoo design has developed in response to research on animal well-being. She cites one classic example, in which New York's Central Park Zoo sought the assistance of an animal psychologist. Their beloved polar bear was exhibiting strange, neurotic behaviour, endlessly swimming figure eights in his minuscule pool. After a few days the psychologist had a diagnosis: the polar bear was bored. He needed playthings, amenities, and a more complex environment to encourage play and exploration.[54] We learned that captive animals like bears and elephants need more naturalistic habitats to thrive. But we have left our hospital patients locked up like prisoners in the concrete lion cage. We followed our survival instincts to build farming systems, cities, and hospitals to better ensure our dominance as a species. But in the process of maximising our survival, we have compromised our well-being.

We have sought to maximise control and survival to unsustainably great extremes – from the design of hospitals to standards of scientific inquiry. Scientific method sticklers even criticised Ulrich's tree-view findings, because his study was not a randomised, controlled trial. But such stringent standards can be difficult and even unethical to adhere to when it comes to matters of life and death. As Ulrich himself has pointed out, there have been no randomised controlled trials for parachutes. Yet, we are still comfortable in our faith that parachutes are effective. We have come a long way from savannahs and acacia trees to finding our way around hospitals and city streets.

But let's come back to Hogeweyk.

Like the Dutch shared-space street design technique, Hogeweyk works because it trusts patients to follow their instincts. It gives them agency and treats them like humans. And as with the transformation we've seen in zoo design, it works because it's designed to nurture well-being rather than just maximising survival. It provides a naturalistic habitat – at least for the Dutch species of dementia sufferers. It provides an engaging balance of complexity and mystery, with a legible layout for wayfinding. And of course the key ingredients for environmental restoration are in place: trees, water, and open spaces.

Creating a serviced, naturalistic neighbourhood like Hogeweyk is not cheap. But instead of keeping dementia patients tranquillised and constrained, we can use simple layout choices and familiar settings to make them feel comfortable. Even a single tree like Ulrich's can make a big difference. Softening lighting and hard lines, warming colours, and loosening control to allow for variability in temperature and brightness can return some sense of sensory reality.

Our medical environments should take a cue from the everyday spaces that have supported our well-being throughout the ages. If we are mindful of the environments we are tuned to perform well in, we may be able to bring well-being back in line with the elements that first made us who we are. To rebuild the connection between nature and human nature.

CHAPTER 5

The Tale of Midwest and Yoredale

LEGO(s), frontier psychology, and
'acting basketball game'

When I moved to England, I knew that trucks were called 'lorries'. Many Americans are aware that elevators are 'lifts', the trunk is the 'boot', and the bathroom is the 'toilet'. But our knowledge of British English does not seem to have progressed since the time moustachioed men in World War II films were saying things like 'bloody', 'rather', and 'jolly good, old chap'.

When I arrived, I was fascinated by the mundane details. Favourite conversation topics included everyday facts, such as: you can buy clothes at Tesco? The crosswalk ('crossing') isn't on the corner? Math is called 'maths'. Sports are 'sport'. A scale is 'the scales'. And the fly on your pants ('trousers') is your 'flies'? When my first British boyfriend broke up with me he said I wasn't very interesting to talk to.

There seemed to be a different understanding of groups and individuals. Companies and governments become amorphous collective entities: 'The BBC are hiring', 'The government have cut costs'. After three years, I was shocked to discover that

British children refer to a pile of Legos by the singular 'Lego'. 'My new Lego is so smashing'? (Scratch 'smashing' as well.) But more importantly, 'Playmobils' are called 'Playmobil'! With Legos, I could sort of see it – all the little Legos built up to become one big Lego collective. But Playmobils don't even stick together. When the Playmobils of my childhood followed their fearless leader to colonise new coffee table and carpet territories they were definitely individuals.

Are these distinctions merely semantic, or do they indicate some deeper difference in the way our nations think about plural and singular, individual and collective – the small parts of the whole? While George Bernard Shaw may never precisely have said that Britain and America are two nations divided by a common language, these words resonate in our 'special relationship'.

People have been theorising about the ways in which geography and climate impact culture and personality since antiquity. Those same ancient thinkers who thought humours ruled our temperaments also believed these humours were influenced by climate, temperature, and moisture. Climate and geography can be difficult to separate because they are closely related. Mountains tend to have cooler weather than the lower lands around them.[1] If mountain-dwellers are calmer, we can't isolate whether it's the temperature, the clean air, or the lovely mountain views that pacify them. Or whether calmer people simply gravitate towards living in log cabins.

You might think studying how hedgerows and persistent rainfall shape Britons differently from Americans would be a key part of environmental psychology. But most researchers have steered clear of what is called geographical determinism because it is so difficult to isolate the variables – the potential causes

– of any interesting findings. What you can do is compare the patterns of connection – correlations – between people and the places they live. In-depth comparison of disparate places must be done carefully and methodically, which some of the earliest environmental psychologists pioneered in two places they called Midwest and Yoredale.

Midwest and Yoredale were both small towns surrounded by open fields. They had populations of around a thousand, removed from other settlements. But Midwest was in Kansas and Yoredale was in North Yorkshire. In 1954 a psychologist named Roger Barker and his team undertook an ambitious project to compare Midwest and Yoredale the way an ecologist would study frog populations in two different ponds. Like scientists exploring uncharted areas of the Arctic or the Amazon, they set up 'field stations' to dissect everyday life. They followed certain residents of these towns around, systematically scribbling down every activity they engaged in (e.g., 'Johnny crosses the street'), what type of settings they spent time in ('Johnny enters a bakery'), who was there, and what kind of interactions they had ('Johnny says "Hello" to Mrs Bramwinkle').

The first thing they found was that people's behaviour was overwhelmingly scripted by the setting. You may feel you act like yourself whether you're in a movie theatre or a post office. But Barker found that he could better predict a child's behaviour based on where he was than who he was. He called these 'human-sized units' of interaction 'behaviour settings'.[2] A behaviour setting is a small social ecosystem, embedded in the bigger ecosystems of town, region, and country. Settings like candy shops, band practice, and X-ray laboratories, where people come to do certain activities at certain times in certain groups.

Picture Midwest with its square streets and buildings, red bricks, and water towers. Picture Yoredale with its winding roads, steeple spires, and slate roofs. In Yoredale, people spent more time in settings oriented towards physical health and artistic pursuits. In Midwest, there were twice as many settings promoting public expression of emotion. Yoredalers had more spaces controlled by businesses, such as shops, while Midwesterners spent more time in educational and governmental spaces. But the most important difference was that Midwest had significantly more behaviour settings in proportion to its population. This meant that Midwesterners were expected to take on more positions of responsibility, especially in a voluntary capacity. For instance: 'Ms Evans-Williams of Yoredale might own and operate the local dress shop, teach an evening Scottish dancing class, and serve as a judge at the annual horticultural fair. Ms Sweeny of Midwest might be employed as a typist in an attorney's office, serve as president of the Eastern Star Lodge, sing at Presbyterian church choir rehearsals and worship services, be an attendant in a wedding, and work as a volunteer at the public library.'[3]

Ms Evans-Williams and Ms Sweeny both spent a similar amount of time working. But in her off time, Ms Sweeny was busy darting between the library, the church, and the Star Lodge (a Masonic organisation) to fulfil many other roles for the town.

Midwest, like the US as a whole, was what is called 'understaffed'. There were not quite enough people to go round for all the roles required of them. And in understaffed situations a few interesting things tend to happen. People define themselves and others in terms of the tasks they are responsible for. They accept lower performance levels. They also experience both success and failure more often. In Midwest and Yoredale, this fundamentally changed the way children functioned within the towns. With a shortage of adults to cast in all the roles, Midwestern children were expected to sing in the same choirs as adults, run bake sales, and volunteer in libraries. Midwestern children were involved in fourteen times as many 'public' adult settings as the Yoredale youngsters. They were encouraged to take on positions of leadership in the everyday spaces of their lives.

The children of Yoredale and Midwest probably didn't play with Lego or Legos because they were only invented in 1949. But you can imagine that these differences in settings and roles might reinforce certain personality traits, and certain ways of understanding one's role in society.

In an era when psychology was largely confined to laboratory experimentation, Barker looked beyond rooms and roads, to understand ecological systems of interaction between people and structures over space and time – along with the tractors, forks, and French fries essential to their functions.[4]

Writing and researching this book in 2016, I lived through the Brexit vote and the Trump election as a resident of each country. As someone who had a past there, and expected to have a future. In each place people would ask me about the other. Questions like, 'Why don't Americans like Hillary and her pantsuits?' 'Who is this Angela Merkel?' 'Is voting for Brexit the same as voting for Trump?' In the months between June in England and November in California, I explained to people in both my countries that these were very different situations. The pros and cons of EU membership were far more nuanced and complex than voting for a leader who claimed he could make Mexico pay to build a border wall. But ultimately, it seems, the nuances on either side were not what made the difference.

How have these two countries come to find ourselves in somewhat similar conundrums at the same time? The Brexit and Trump victories have clearly been propelled by similar underlying forces, in spite of differing contexts and dynamics.

People generally aspire to be free. We like to feel we are in control of our destinies – whether that destiny involves where we will live or what kind of sandwich to eat for lunch. When this feeling of freedom is threatened, we may feel endangered, depressed, and angry. Many of us will take drastic actions to combat this threat. Especially when we feel some freedom or space that is rightfully ours is being taken away. But the relentless pursuit of individual freedom comes at a cost. While some of us might like to own semi-automatic assault rifles, keep pet crocodiles in our gardens, or build swimming pools in the streets next to our homes, the freedom to pursue these individual desires may conflict with the collective good. And the closer we live to other people, the more critical it becomes to consider how our individual freedoms may trample on the rights of others. As Spock famously said in that great moral parable of the space-age frontier, *Star Trek II: The Wrath of Khan*, 'The needs of the many outweigh the needs of the few' – a point he makes dramatically in subjecting himself to fatal radiation poisoning to save his fellow crew members.

This balance between individualism and collectivism is by far the most heavily researched issue in cross-cultural psychology (according to social psychologist Lucian Gideon Conway III), revealing how critical this dynamic is, both to comprehending cultural differences, and to understanding the human condition itself. Individualistic cultures tend to prioritise personal freedom in this great balancing act, while we find collectivist cultures at the other end of the spectrum. And like the British conception of Lego, collectivist cultures also tend to place greater value on fitting into the greater whole of society – on group identity as part of the Lego whole over one's individual Lego piece identity.[5]

As a major immigration destination for four hundred years, the American frontier is assumed to have attracted settlers possessing a strong sense of independence, self-reliance, and an appetite for risk and personal gain, propelled by the mythology of Manifest Destiny. Individualists, it has been proposed, are more likely to seek out the opportunities and challenges of settling an unknown region. Mountains can be inhospitable environments, so we often find them on the outskirts of society. Inland areas tend to have more extreme temperatures than coasts, and have historically been further removed from maritime transportation and trade. These 'frontier terrains' can be harsh in terms of weather, conflict, and lack of resources – conditions which individualists are better fit to survive under, and which also reinforce these values. Places where self-preservation and promotion were essential.

Today, mountain-dwellers do tend to demonstrate an independent streak, according to Conway and his colleagues. More mountainous countries (especially those with more inland area) tend to enjoy greater political freedom and rank higher in individualism. This dynamic holds true when comparing frontier terrains within the US like Colorado and Montana with states like Louisiana and Maryland. People in western states are even more likely to give their babies more unconventional names, as are people in countries colonised by Europeans (like the US, Canada, and Australia) when compared to European nationals.[6]

Shinobu Kitayama and his colleagues have similarly found that residents of Japan's northernmost island are more individualistic than mainlanders. Colonised by ethnic Japanese in the late 1800s, Hokkaido's residents are almost as likely as white Americans to associate happiness with personal achievement today – a key expression of individualism. Kitayama argues that the history of 'voluntary settlement' has fostered the individualistic cultures of places like Hokkaido and the western US.[7]

This 'voluntary migration' approach may help explain frontier psychology. But many migration patterns have not been voluntary. One man's frontier has often been another man's front yard, as the Americas were for the native peoples whose land and lives were violently taken from them in this relentless course of westward imperial expansion. These involuntary migration patterns are also visible in our political geography today. Looking at a county-level map of the 2016 US election results, you will see a Democratic belt of blue running across deep south states from Alabama to South Carolina. This blue belt is actually called the 'black belt' after its rich, dark soil deposits, which trace a Cretaceous era coastline. This fertile crescent provided the most productive farming opportunities for crops like cotton, an industry based on the labour of black slaves forcefully relocated in great numbers to this region. Today, these counties tend to have a high proportion of African-American voters – typically fifty to eighty-five per cent – aligning with the voting patterns we see there.[8] The voluntary migration experience of white American settlers is only one of many perspectives. But as these white settlers often determined the laws and land-use policies we now live under, it may offer particular insights into American individualism.

What other forces can help explain the regional differences in personal and political temperament we frequently seem to see? Beyond the individualist/collectivist divide, we find that the history of climate, terrain, and agricultural opportunities affects the broad strokes of geographical personality patterns. Many psychologists believe that personality traits have an evolutionary basis – that humans have developed the ability to detect and take advantage of individual personality differences pertinent to reproduction and survival.[9]

Pathogens have posed a major survival threat to humans throughout our evolution. The selective force of infectious disease may be a key mechanism through which geography and climate have shaped regional character. In addition to immunological defences, we have developed psychological and behavioural defences to disease. Our fear of rats and distaste for physical signs of ill health may be among these. Pathogens are found all over. But many of these spikey, squirmy germs and protozoa thrive best in warm, wet, and humid places. So if you lived in a swampy place oozing with treacherous pathogens, you might have survived longer and multiplied further if you weren't inclined to run around socialising with your diseased friends and neighbours – if you were less extraverted. Highly open people with a penchant for sampling strange substances or deviating from social norms like those prohibiting promiscuity might also be wiped out. Factors like this may help explain why people in the Philippines report being relatively less extraverted than people in Norway do today. Geographic differences in openness and especially extraversion are closely linked to the historic prevalence of pathogens spread through human interaction.[10]

Broadly, the people of neighbouring countries like Danes and Swedes tend to have similar personality profiles, as do other regional neighbours like the French and Italians, Zimbabweans and South Africans, or Chinese and South Koreans.[11] Certain caricatures of national character seem to hit close to home. Citizens of central and south American countries tend to be more open, while those in Asian nations tend to be less extraverted. Southern and eastern European countries report lower levels of emotional stability (the inverse of neuroticism) than their western and northern European counterparts.[12]

There is evidence that these so-called Big Five personality traits (which you may remember from our exploration of desk personalities) have a significant genetic basis, and may be rooted in the biology of our hormones, neurotransmitters, and brain regions.[13] Many of our non-human animal relations have even been found to share similar patterns of these key traits with us, according to a review covering nineteen studies on a variety of animals. We find reliably extroverted and neurotic individuals among dogs, cats, pigs, chimpanzees, donkeys, octopuses, and guppies. Being agreeable does not seem to be a particularly important part of guppy and octopus life, but it was a clear trait for all the mammals studied.[14] And while a number of animals vary in components of openness like curiosity, conscientiousness appears to be limited to humans and chimpanzees.

Just as we saw at the micro-environment of one's desk, we often find ourselves in spaces that complement and reflect our personalities. In spiritual tales from Siddhartha Gautama to Muhammad, hermits and prophets retreat to mountains and forests for introspective meditation. Using an impressive variety of techniques, a group of researchers at the University of Washington have recently confirmed that mountain-lovers are indeed more introverted than ocean-lovers.[15] Like our workplace refugers, who seek a secluded ninja-proof seat, introverts seem to flourish in the mountains.

The shape of our cities, states, and counties is mediated by the crystallisation of political ideologies and infrastructure. Comparing regional data from across the UK and US Jason Rentfrow and his colleagues have found some compelling patterns of connection between geography, personality, and political orientation.[16] Both nations demonstrated the highest levels of openness in densely populated urban regions: the west coast and mid-Atlantic areas of America, and English cities like London, Bristol, Manchester, and Brighton. Individually, open people can be identified by the stylish, eclectic, and distinctive nature of their work and home spaces, which one could say scales up to the more varied and distinctive environments we find in cities. There is also evidence that assertive and excitement-seeking extraverts are more likely to migrate, and are less negatively impacted by moving.[17] And this means lots of these extraverts end up together in cities like London and Manchester!

Midwesterners are known for their warm apple pie and friendly nature, which also seems to hold true. The most agreeable people are found in the rural and spacious expanses of the Scottish Highlands, the north of England, and the south of the US as well as our Great Plains. On the individual level, agreeable people tend to be trusting, cooperative, sympathetic, and friendly. At the regional or state level, this trait appears to align with an orientation towards conventional values and community. The least agreeable British people are found in London and certain places throughout the east of England, suggesting the people in these areas are more – for lack of a better term – disagreeable: irritable, uncooperative, and argumentative. Social psychologist Stanley Milgram explained the unfriendliness country people often perceive from city people as a consequence of 'stimulation overload'. You cross the path of far too many people in the course of one day to smile and say 'Hello' to all of them as you might in a small town.

And then we have conscientiousness, a trait which is particularly interesting to consider in relation to the built environment because it reflects the desire for order and control, plans and schedules, fences and boundaries. We find particularly high levels of this trait throughout the south-east, south-west, and east of England – with the important exception of greater London, where it is especially low. In the US, conscientiousness is consistently low throughout the north-east, and high in many mid-west and south-west states.[18] This strong desire for order seems to align with the more politically conservative regions of both countries.

Of course, these traits vary from one neighbourhood to another and even house to house. While canvassing New York City suburbs for the highly unmemorable John Kerry campaign of 2004, I found even gardening styles gave me a good hunch about whether I would get a door slammed in my face. The houses with perfectly manicured square lawns were much more frequently associated with door slamming, while those with wild and colourful flower gardens were a good bet for at least a cordial conversation.

Overall, when people live in places where they need to be more self-sufficient, and benefit less from collective services like accessible public transport – places like Midwest and Yoredale – they often tend to express less support for social collectivist or 'welfare-state' policies. But the dynamics here are complex. It's not simply a case of individualist, underpopulated rural areas versus collectivist, densely populated urban centres and coasts. The high rates of agreeability – trust, altruism, and cooperation – found in rural areas are often accompanied by high rates of social capital and community cohesion. They are also often more ethnically homogenous than culturally diverse cities.

Lastly, social norms reinforce personality patterns formed by geography, climate, and migration. But as Barker and his colleagues discovered, these social norms are embedded in the settings of everyday spaces. A cold climate and mountainous terrain may set the scene, but the structures of our cities and villages write the scripts of the performances that unfold within them.

The America and England we see in Midwest and Yoredale were very different places from the America and England we see today. They were small, homogenous towns where people had good jobs. The gap in salaries between janitors and their bosses was probably small by today's standards. (In the US, for instance, CEO salaries grew from twenty times those of average workers in 1965 to nearly three hundred by 2013.[19]) They were probably exactly the type of places that many of those who want to 'make America great again' would like to return to.

In selecting Midwest and Yoredale, Barker and his team sought to choose specimens that were 'at least, not atypical' of

American and English towns at the time.[20] Both were rural, non-industrial centres of trade and local government. Both were small inland towns, smack dab in the middle of their countries. They were distinguishable geographical entities, similarly set apart from larger nearby cities, without being cultural backwaters. They were also almost exclusively white. (Midwest had thirty-seven African American residents.) Much has changed to make Midwest and Yoredale more similar and more different since then. But many of the cultural and behavioural differences these researchers meticulously catalogued over the course of two years separated by a decade (1954–55 and 1963–64) persist today.

Taking frequent train trips across the flat plains of Illinois, Barker had been impressed by the clustered distribution of human

'Midwest', Kansas today
Courtesy of Esri, USDA FSA

activity. How, he wondered, had people come to be organised in such similar, tightly spaced collections of activity (towns and cities) connected by roads and train tracks through vast expanses of cornfields? He first established the Midwest field station with the aim of studying how the order of these environments shaped children's behaviour. Using ecological research techniques identical to those used to study the dispersion of tree species over a series of islands or crabs across tide pools, he discovered that 'The laws that govern and regulate the operation of behaviour settings are altogether different from and incommensurate with the laws that govern individual behaviour.'[21] If we were to look down upon a city and pop open the roofs of all the buildings, we would overwhelmingly find people behaving according to the structure and conventions of each behaviour setting.

When five-year-old Maud was in the drug store (or pharmacy), for instance, she 'behaved drug store', as did her father. But when Maud and her father were watching a basketball game, they 'behaved basketball game', wildly cheering and hooting as they never would in a drug store, Barker's wife and collaborator, Louise Shedd Barker, explained.[22] Individual personality was insignificant compared to the prompts of the setting. These settings function like a secret script directing our actions. It's a script we play a part in writing by choosing where to work, who to socialise with, and how to decorate our homes. But like the actors in a play, we maintain the illusion that our actions are unscripted. Although this may sound obvious, it ran counter to the dominant assumptions of psychological research, which was focused on understanding behaviour and cognition at the individual level. The discovery of behaviour settings was hailed as a major breakthrough, likened to identifying the cell in biology.

Midwest and Yoredale did have some obvious differences. Midwest certainly couldn't be called a frontier in 1954, but it had been formed from the frontier mentality less than a century before the researchers arrived. Yoredale residents enjoyed not only a longer sense of history in place, but six hundred years of seeing Yorkshire as the pre-eminent county of their country. With 830 residents, Midwest's population was somewhat smaller than Yoredale's at 1,300. Given its smaller size, the researchers were surprised to discover that Midwest had not only a greater number of behaviour settings, but a greater variety of settings in relation to its size. To compare and quantify the variation of behaviour settings within and between the towns, they classified them according to larger categories they called 'genotypes'.

'Yoredale', North Yorkshire today
Courtesy of Esri, Digital Globe, Microsoft

Visitors between both towns would feel quite comfortable in genotypes such as libraries, scout meetings, and auction sales. Ice cream socials, chiropractors' offices, and piano recitals were found only in Midwest, however, whereas taxis, betting agents, and cricket games were found only in Yoredale. However, just as an American might have more trouble understanding the complex rules and variations of cricket than a Brit would have in making sense of baseball, the researchers observed that a Midwesterner visiting Yoredale would find more of the town's behaviour settings foreign.[23] Within the genotype of drinking establishments, one might find only the games of pool and darts in Kansas, for instance. But Yorkshire pubs are home to extensive ecosystems of green-felted playing boards and mushroom-shaped pegs, hosting a seemingly endless variety of games including skittles, snooker, bar billiards, darts, puff-and-dart, ringing the bull, toad in the hole, and Aunt Sally (a lesser known relation of the skittles family).

Despite the great British love of drinking in general and gin in particular, an American will find they have come to the wrong behaviour setting if they request a gin martini in a pub. These high-class beverages are found only in a separate and distinct genotype of the British environment known as cocktail bars. The broader category of American drinking establishments may offer a greater diversity of beverage types and interior design styles but far less complexity of local ciders and wooden skittles. More importantly, however, Yoredale contained fewer settings in which residents had high local autonomy.

'The quality of life for those who live in a community is influenced by the extent to which those people control the settings of the town,' wrote Phil Schoggen, a student and close collaborator of Barker.[24]

Keith Barbershop in Midwest is a fine example of a setting with high local autonomy. Barber Keith controls when it opens, whether to offer moustache trims, and how much to charge for them, among other things. The British Railways freight office, on the other hand, has quite a low level of local autonomy. Similarly, Yoredale's traffic ways were ruled by a vague and distant county council, whose authority hung over the town like a cloud that couldn't be bothered to move – a situation which rendered occupants more powerless and apathetic in this setting than their Midwest counterparts in their traffic ways. Transgressions on Midwest roads were ruled upon in Midwest. Some traffic laws were even matters of local decision. In 1964, these types of differences were a major distinction between the towns. Nearly fifty per cent of Midwest's behaviour settings had high local autonomy, while only twenty per cent of Yoredale's did. Thirty-seven per cent of Yoredale's settings were low-autonomy spaces like the freight office, while only nine per cent of Midwest's fell in this category.[25]

And just as the adults in Yoredale had less freedom and autonomy from the parental forces of far-off governing bodies, Yoredale children had less autonomy and freedom of their own. It has been said that in the US the children entertain adults, but in England it is the adults that entertain the children. And Barker's team found that child-rearing practices in these two seemingly similar countries were based in nearly opposite ideologies. Midwest employed what Barker called the 'melting pot system of child rearing'. While educational settings were valued and important, Midwesterners believed children should be socialised by participating in a wide range of town settings along with adults. There was a strong emphasis on taking on challenging tasks well beyond the child's capability. It was very important to 'do your part', even if you could not do your part very well. When one foreigner visiting a Midwest church service offered to remove and pacify a wailing infant, the mother indignantly replied, 'When do you think he will *learn* to behave in church if you take him out?!'[26]

Yoredale employed a contrasting approach, in which Barker saw strong parallels to England's role as a colonial overlord: the 'enlightened colonial system of child rearing'. Not content to segregate boys and girls and identify these little prisoners by school uniform, Yoredale treated its children like captive colonial subjects – seen as uncivilised creatures who must be segregated in specialised settings and trained by experts until deemed fit to be released into adult society. British adults exercised authority over children more often – scolding, giving orders, threatening physical punishment – and also seemed 'baffled by' and indifferent to their children more often.

How did this impact the relationship between children and adults in each country? US children gave their parents more kisses. In fact, American children displayed their affection for adults – hugging, kissing, and other expressions of devotion – in three times as many settings as English children. English children displayed indifference to adults – being inattentive, unaware, or unconcerned about them – in over seven times as many settings. Critically, Yoredale children were less free to move about different settings in their town. Midwest children were allowed in a greater proportion of spaces – an expression of territory which is commonly understood as a measure of power.[27]

It is through such different approaches to child rearing that researchers like Kitayama believe the frontier spirit of individualism and assertiveness is ingrained and re-enacted over generations, long after the reality of frontier conditions has faded into the past. American children were encouraged to take on more leadership roles in more versatile settings, just as American adults were.

Can the comparison of these two small, homogenous towns really reveal greater distinctions between these large, diverse cultures? All sub-fields of psychology research have favoured methodologies and sampling techniques which inevitably skew the nature of their findings to some extent. Over-reliance on undergraduate student subjects and disproportionate representation of highly developed global-north cultures are well-rehearsed weaknesses of more conventional approaches. Barker has been compared to Margaret Mead – both pioneered the study of humans in their natural habitats. But in addition to their disparate research techniques and locations, you have probably never heard of Barker. And it's easy to see why. Detailed records such as 'A Day in the Life of Mary Ennis', a Midwest eight-year-old who liked to play house and sing a song called 'Bunnies in the Store', are not quite as intriguing as Mead's titillating (yet potentially problematic) study of Samoan sexual practices. While the lives of these primarily white, small-town people cannot reflect the great diversity of British and American experience, they can provide a comparable sample for examination.

Barker's quantitative approach allowed his team to use some interesting techniques to test the generalisability of their findings, including the application of their behavioural ecology metrics to systematically sampled sections from a wide array of realistic literature from each country. Barker likened his research methods to a physician's diagnosis, which may require only a small specimen of tissue to identify a systemic condition; 'Some currents of national culture that affect behaviour flow strongly through even the smallest communities.'[28]

The Midwest-Yoredale findings are also largely in line with observations European visitors have made of the differences between their countries and the US for centuries. Writing of his famous 1835 visit to the US, Alexis de Tocqueville reported that American society was marked by a strikingly different organisation of people, money, and social status, which he saw as essentially classless. Democracy and the practice of dividing dwindling estates among all children created an unprecedentedly fluid culture, while at the same time driving those born into all levels of society to wild extremes of individualistic capitalism.

Barker and his colleagues believed the key force in the differing character of Americans was the lower density of their habitats. In studying the behaviour settings of Midwest and Yoredale, they identified the phenomenon of 'over-staffing', which they went on to research more widely around the US and beyond. As a community like a town, church, or school grew larger, the number of behaviour settings did not increase proportionately to the number of people. A very small high school (thirty-five students) in a small Kansas town might have a 1:1 ratio of students to settings, while a large high school (2,287 students) in Kansas city had a ratio of 8:1. To stay viable, a small school must enlist everyone into its activities. In the small school students were drawn to take on six times as many leadership positions. Large schools had more bystanders who were not as involved in playing baseball, writing for the yearbook, or singing in the glee club. These opportunities for leadership and teamwork have crucial developmental implications for young adults' personality, skills, and sense of self.

Allan Wicker, a student and colleague of Barker's, went on to find this same phenomenon present in communities of small and large American churches. Members of small church congregations not only participated in more church settings and took on more central roles in a greater variety of settings, they also attended church more often (sixty-four per cent versus forty-one per cent of the time), and contributed more money to the church.[29] Wicker hypothesised that all behaviour settings have an ideal adequately 'staffed' level: the level at which there are enough people to fill a good team. If there are not enough players to fill all the standard positions in a field hockey game for instance, you will find yourself darting between the defence and mid-field positions, scattering your energy by running to and fro, and not performing as well as you ought to in either position – that is, assuming you have the skills to perform these positions to begin with. I found out the hard way I did not have those skills when I volunteered to substitute on a friend's team in the UK. The street hockey played back at my California primary school did not involve wooden sticks that looked like lollipops or complicated rules about not hitting the ball (which I knew as a 'puck') with the back of the stick. But in volunteering for this miserable game, I had at least helped prevent the behaviour setting 'Bristol Women's West hockey in Swindon' from becoming dysfunctionally under-staffed.

In under-staffed settings, admissions standards are lowered. Superficial distinctions, including personality differences, tend to be ignored. People have to take on more roles and work harder than normally required. This explains the great variety of activities Midwesterners were called upon to take part in – why children were pressed into service as cobbler shop janitors and dairy barn helpers, positions which they were vastly unqualified for. Overall, this inclusion generates greater feelings of insecurity about the setting's success. People feel challenged. They often fail. But they also have the opportunity to gain a sense of competence – experience that is highly valued in the US. In over-staffed situations other types of problems arise. We find ways to control who is allowed in – to raise the standards for admission. We focus more on the superficial differences that were ignored when people were needed to fill out the team.

Yet even the nature of Barker's research may betray a particularly American worldview: our obsession with educational institutions and extracurricular athletic activities. Does the very idea of behaviour settings reveal a mentality prone to organising life into neat boxes?

'In the United States we use space as a way of classifying people and activities, whereas in England it is the social system that determines who you are,' Edward T. Hall described in his 1966 book, *The Hidden Dimension*.[30] Even lofty members of Parliament, he noted, 'often conduct their business on the terrace overlooking the Thames' as they are not afforded private offices.[31]

In Britain the world does not seem to fit so neatly and orderly into discrete boxes. There is a bewildering confusion about where London's boundaries begin and end. This strange fact makes more sense with the shocking discovery that London is not technically a city – beyond the City of London itself. The greater area referred to as London is technically a 'conurbation', a term describing a phenomenon that resembles a cancerous growth in its pattern of development as much as its name. Upon departing the Bethnal Green tube station on my first visit to London from Surrey, I asked a passer-by which way was north as I had often done to orient myself when exiting the New York City subway. And while always receiving a clear and sure answer in New York, it seemed that Londoners found this question quite bewildering. Americans, I realised, understand our lives to exist on gridded street structures aligned with the cardinal directions. Are we like the rats raised in simple environments who grow up to have less aptitude for navigating mazes and learning new tricks?[32] But what we lack in complexity, we may make up for in direction.

In America we like our lines drawn clear and firmly. Whatever one may think about how life on Staten Island compares to Manhattan or Brooklyn – however starkly its more conservative voting patterns may go against the other boroughs – there is no question that it is within the boundaries of New York City. These strong lines and boundaries may foster a more formal style of negotiation and business dealings, a more aggressive response to trespassing. But behind this rigidly structured American exterior, Barker's team found greater fragility.[33]

In over-staffed Yoredale, being expendable was a far more common experience. More people found themselves in a position not essential to the function and survival of the town – but the consequences were not all bad. Yoredalers tended to have higher adequate performance standards, and fewer responsibilities. They placed greater value on personal qualities. They were less versatile, but also more secure. And because they didn't work as hard, they also had more time to cultivate activities of leisure, which Barker believed was one source of the 'more prominent esthetic and muscular qualities of Yoredale behaviour.'[34] Yoredalers had more time for leisurely activities like gardening, countryside rambling, and long evenings in the local pub.

Barker's findings hold up against national comparisons between the US and UK, which have found Americans to be more extraverted, competitive, anxious, and to have a stronger work ethic than Brits.[35] But of course there are other influential factors – in the structure of these landscapes, the laws about who can go where, and the customs that have formed and been formed by them. In addition to having more free time to spend in pubs, Yoredalers' living spaces may have been too small for them to socialise in. And these smaller, more densely packed dwellings may in turn have meant many more Yoredalers could live within walking distance of shared resources, like shops and pubs. The Church of England may have frowned less upon its parishioners spending so many hours in the pub than the Methodist church in Midwest did. The Yorkshire moors may have attracted more rambling than the Kansas cornfields. And if you did attempt a ramble around a Kansas farmer's cornfield, he might very well come after you with his pitchfork. Or more likely, his rifle. The ancient rights of way that enable British ramblers to walk across privately owned farms and woodlands in Britain are almost unknown in the US.

Yet Midwesterners held more power over their environments than Yoredalers on two levels: a greater proportion of their everyday spaces were under local control, and in those settings they also held more leadership roles. And this meant that the 'value' of each Midwesterner was essentially greater than the value of each Yoredaler. If one Midwesterner was suddenly swept away in a tornado, the town's ability to function would be more greatly impaired than if one Yoredaler disappeared into a magical wardrobe. Given this greater value placed on individuals, you can see how Midwesterners and Yoredalers might think differently about society as a collective, or as a collection of individual pieces.

With Midwesterners' greater power, however, came greater weakness. Take the traffic ways in each town. Employed by the far-off county council, Yoredale's local traffic wardens had little power over the management of these spaces. Minimally represented on this distant council, no one in the town could exert much influence over their own streets. The Yoredalers stopped bothering to pester their traffic wardens about potholes and speed limits. When people continually find themselves in settings they can't control, they settle into a state of 'learned helplessness'. This syndrome, which is associated with high-density dwelling, reduces both motivation and cognitive activity.[36] In Midwest, the local officials had quite a lot of power over what went on in their streets. But this power meant that they were under constant pressure to fix potholes, change speed limits, and give out parking tickets – both directly from everyday Midwesterners and from the town council (which Midwestern civilians were also pestering with requests). And if those in power are unable to meet these constant and potentially conflicting requests, their leadership will be challenged.

'Their powerfulness reduces their security,' Barker observed. 'The greater but more fragile power of Midwest residents is an important factor in its greater habitat erosion and accretion.'[37]

New behaviour settings were emerging and receding at a faster rate in Midwest than in Yoredale. Midwest was founded in 1856, but in 1964 fifty-seven per cent of its behaviour settings had been established within the previous decade alone. The whole American behaviour setting ecosystem – both people and buildings – was more fragile, more susceptible to change. And, as Barker observed, 'It is sometimes easier to establish a new behaviour setting than it is to change the programme of the old one.'[38] Midwest was a young sapling, full of growth, but lacking the solidity of a mature specimen like Yoredale. To use another metaphor, it was a shifting and unstable geological landscape.

The behavioural ecologists didn't dwell on the physical structures of the towns. Were Midwest's traffic ways controlled by stoplights in 1954? Were Yoredalers lulled into complacency by roundabouts? We are left to wonder about the width of the streets and size of the houses. What of the orderly, angular arrangements of American buildings and blocks, the unruly rambling of the English roads and vine-grown walls? The grey Yorkshire clouds and stone walls? The red bricks and wide skies of main street America?

'Behaviour settings are the building blocks of society,' Barker said. And in America, these building blocks are very big – more like Duplos than Legos – from the packaging of the products we buy to the supermarkets they are stocked in and the refrigerators and homes we bring them back to. Older nations may not grasp the scale of the American landscape – the behaviour settings the country runs on – without seeing it first-hand.

'My wife and I got a car and drove across the US, and we felt we could really understand American culture, or at least white American culture,' British architect Alistair Parvin told me. 'This idea of the big sky, and the freedom to roam. This absolute independence.' Not only are these slices of life smaller in England, they also tend to be long and narrow. And as you may recall from our adventures in personal space, these imaginary pink bubbles ironically expand when we find ourselves in smaller, narrower, and lower-ceilinged spaces, as the British perpetually do. This constant constriction of personal space in train carriages and back gardens that are the width of many Americans' walk-in closets may help explain what Americans perceive as chilliness in British social norms.

Coming to the UK, I encountered wonderfully collective systems such as the NHS, public transport services covering much of the country, and the practice of buying a round of pints for people you have just met at the pub – accompanied by the special British method of tearing your crisp packet open into a single surface to share with your new friends. But like a little nation of Lego people, this greater sense of collectiveness comes with greater uniformity. For Lego to fit together, they must be made from the same mould. The culture that brought school uniforms to the world excels in uniformity. The rows of terraced houses, identical from town to town. The high streets stocked with clones of the same shops and restaurants. People talk about 'buying a kitchen' like the room is a new block to insert in their Lego home. Americans, by contrast, 'remodel' or 'fix up' their kitchens.

To the extent that people personalise their houses to reflect their interests and personality – communicating and confirming their identity as unique individuals – the British public have fewer opportunities for domestic individualisation than Americans. There is less variety in housing types, a smaller realm of changes one can make to them, and less room to make those changes in. The 'terraced house' is a foreign term in America, where such structures would be called 'row' or 'town' houses. But this translation loses the significance of the two-up, two-down setting where such a large part of British life takes place. Only eleven per cent of Americans live in row houses or semi-detached homes, which are called 'duplexes'.[39]

The British landscape and climate varies from the Cretaceous coast of Cornwall up to the misty highlands of Inverness. But this is hard to compare to the wild variation between the rainforests of Florida, the arid depths of Death Valley, and the snowy farmlands of Minnesota. Geographically, you can fit three Englands inside California. Whatever the impact of these impossible-to-isolate variables may be, there is certainly more variation in American geography and climate. As a smaller nation, people from different regions of the UK may be more likely to rub shoulders with people from disparate regions than in the US. As a smaller place, it feels more like one place. It's difficult to get away from people even if you want to. The British concept of a 'friendship group' translates roughly as 'friend group'. But like a friendship bracelet, there is something more collective and circular about this notion. The British friendship group grows like a snowball – its members may disperse but roll back again, accumulating 'mates' along the way. It is much harder to move so far away that you can't make it back for your mate's birthday, where you meet all their mates, and become mates with them too.

Americans scatter to pursue individualistic careers and opportunities. People make residential moves more frequently in the US than in almost any other nation. These higher rates of residential mobility require more individualism and make us more individualistic. Moving to a new state requires independent agency to operate without a network of family and friends or consistency of common support services and systems. Researchers led by Shigehiro Oishi at the University of Virginia found that people who move more often have more individualised self-concepts and are less likely to identify groups they belong to as central to their identity.[40]

Such patterns are not evenly realised throughout society – people who have more resources and education may be more mobile. But these broader trends coalesce in our social norms, our sense of possibility. Americans hold dear the Manifest Destiny dream of 'starting over' in more western regions of our own country.

So do greater shared resources and uniformity produce a more collectivist culture in Britain? Political systems reflect the individualistic or collectivist orientations of cultures. The structure of our settlements and spaces shows the crystallisation of these systems over time. Smaller and more homogenous nations often tend to have more generous and extensive welfare systems than large and ethnically diverse countries like the US.

In addition to being a small place, Britain also has one of the most centralised systems of government known to the modern developed world.[41] Think of those distant county councils still ruling upon what happens in the traffic ways of places like Yoredale. In America, local speed limits and parking regulations may change from one small city to another within a single urban area. Central government in London has a great amount of control over what happens in other cities and counties around the nation. British mayors have historically been relatively weak – both in the extent of their authority and control of their own budgets. Britain sometimes feels like it's still run as one little kingdom. But it is a kingdom in which providing housing and health care for all citizens has been assumed as a basic responsibility of the state – essential collectivist assumptions almost unknown in the US.

Despite these dramatic differences, both America and England rank among the most individualistic countries of the world, according to many metrics. In the twentieth century, both nations adopted collectivist programmes and policies such as social security and national insurance. Depression, war, and the austere conditions of recovery united societies against common enemies, paving the way for a more egalitarian approach. But the greater security and prosperity enabled by social support ironically strengthened individualism by making people less dependent on family and other traditional support networks.

New York University sociologist David Garland has argued that the American and British welfare systems (excluding Scotland's devolved services) are now more similar to each other than they are to their Nordic, continental, and antipodean counterparts in many ways. Not having to rebuild as extensively as her continental cousins, Britain experienced lower growth rates, leading to tighter constraints on social spending. The combination of universal benefits across a wide range of areas with a tight budget meant that the level and quality of benefits and services did not keep up with rising living standards.[42] State agencies became major forces in developing the post-war landscape, bringing us council housing, NHS facilities, and, of course, those lovely roundabouts. These common institutions – many whose counterparts vary widely between regions, states, and cities in the US – shape places, people, and experiences similarly across the country.

Daily activities ranging from listening to the BBC to drinking tea have a certain consistency across Britain. British social norms dictate another collective (but maddeningly inefficient) practice of fetching rounds of tea for the entire office in workspaces of a certain small size. Confounded by my inconsistent preferences for milk and/or sugar, my British colleagues will politely inquire if Americans drink coffee instead of tea – imagining we enjoy the same shared culture of beverage norms and practices with a darker brew. But having never been to Kansas, I can't say what form of caffeinated beverages may be most popular there.

America is known for its patchwork welfare systems and porous social safety net, but this was not always the case. In the nineteenth century, the US pioneered strong welfare provisions such as pensions for Civil War veterans, mothers, and children. But the US has relied heavily on the private sector to provide services like healthcare, and Britain has increasingly moved closer to the American model. Both countries have been reluctant to take actions supporting the collective good of their citizens that might endanger the freedom of the few to make enormous corporate profits. The 'American Dream' embodied in the frontier spirit of individualism is now indeed a dream. Today, intergenerational social mobility is lower in the US than in the UK, Germany, or Sweden.[43] Despite seemingly divergent attitudes, systems, and support structures, inequality has skyrocketed in both the US and UK.[44]

The link between personality, place, and political ideology is a linchpin in understanding macro-level environmental psychology. The individualistic character of America's harsh and violent frontier origins has been entrenched, normalised, and amplified through individualistic political systems, economic models, and land-use policies. But whether building through the private or public sectors, both countries have consolidated the behaviour settings of everyday life into increasingly bigger-scale operations.

In the decade between the years in which Yoredale and Midwest were studied, the researchers started to notice some significant changes in the two towns. In Yoredale, behaviour settings such as abattoirs disappeared as central meat processing was determined to be more economically viable than local plants. Bicycle runs gave way to more efficient highways teeming with more efficient motor vehicles, which rising affluence had enabled people to purchase. These changes took place in the context of bigger shifts in both countries, where male employment rates have declined since the 1960s as blue-collar industries like manufacturing, shipping, and steel were shut down and outsourced overseas. Employment rates peaked at ninety-two per cent in 1971 for men in Britain, although they have grown for women since then.[45]

At the same time, new types of settings evolved. Many of Yoredale's new settings, such as motor vehicles operator classes and typing classes, were connected to its schools. In Midwest one could also now find kindergarten classes and tractor-pulling contests. But in Midwest, habitat innovation was driven overwhelmingly by the private enterprise system. The American town also saw significant growth in behaviour settings associated with another pillar of the community: the church. Ecclesiastical settings grew from thirteen per cent of the town's settings in the '50s to twenty-two per cent in the '60s – a hint of the mega-churches to come. Meanwhile in Yoredale, church-related settings were shrinking.[46]

As the researchers continued studying the Midwest area into the '70s, similar forces reshaped both towns. In Yoredale, a new government policy consolidated smaller rural district councils into one larger district government. Small-town schools and churches, including Midwest's, were amalgamated into bigger entities with the promise of greater efficiency, better services, and specialisation. Settings like algebra classes and football games within these larger schools tended, in turn, to be larger than those at the now extinct smaller schools. The single pastor of the new nine-hundred-member church might be better qualified than the six pastors who had previously led congregations of 150. But those six pastors lost their meaningful roles and, presumably, their livelihoods. And along with them, around eighty per cent of church members who had held important roles and responsibilities in the small churches were now less valued in the new church.

Barker identified five great classes of authority systems – government, school, religious, business, and voluntary – and, in each of these, institutions grew increasingly larger in Midwest, Yoredale, and their wider countries. In larger institutions, more people slip through the cracks. Is a large school really more efficient when it produces a greater number of drop-out students, who then end up in counselling centres, courts, jails, and dole lines? As institutions in all these domains grew larger, they also lost the complexity and diversity we find in collections of many smaller settings.

Britain does function more like one collective Lego-set whole than America does – from the universal provision of NHS services to the common standards of potatoes and crisp packets. But both countries have prioritised the needs of corporations over the common good of their citizens, resulting in the inequality we now see.

Looking back on his career during a train trip through the Midwest, Roger Barker wrote: 'In 1940 I only asked, "What do people do in these towns?" In 1977 I ask in addition, "What do these towns do to people?"'[49] He looked at the towns differently because his decades of research analysing the larger patterns of human behaviour had led him to focus on the movements of the many above the few. But also because the ecosystems of the towns, the larger systems they were embedded in, had evolved. In Midwest and Yoredale, people were losing agency in the everyday spaces of their lives.

Midwest is actually a town called Oskaloosa, and Yoredale is called Leyburn. In 2016, the people of both these communities voted decisively for the walls and borders many believed would renew that autonomy and agency. This is not out of character with the political landscape of either place. But it is also not going to bring back the everyday spaces that supported this long-gone way of life.

'Small is indeed beautiful,' Barker concluded in 1978, 'to people who want to reduce the risk of being helpless and expendable.'[50]

CHAPTER 6

The Ruin Porn Phenomenon

Detroit, fractal aesthetics,
and *The Timeless Way of Building*

In 2009 a new kind of pornography hit the internet. It didn't involve any vulnerable groups of people, but the question of whether anyone was harmed in its production was still contentious.

Ruin porn is not really new. People have been travelling to see the ruins of Tintagel, Machu Picchu, and Angkor Wat for centuries. But recently, these degenerates have started seeking new extremes of crumbling civilisation to satiate their unseemly cravings for sagging and wrinkly buildings. And people in Detroit aren't very happy about it. As my Paper Tiger TV comrades and I called Detroit activists and urban farmers in the autumn of 2010, preparing to shoot *Rerooting the Motor City: Notes on a City in Transformation*, we encountered suspicions about our intentions to their city: 'OK, we'll talk to you, but this better not be another ruin porn.' The people we spoke to were tired of out-of-town camera crews and European tourists swooping in to 'capture' Detroit the way you would photograph Pompeii or Stonehenge. They were tired of seeing Detroit represented as a dead civilisation, an empty city.

We had set out on a long winter drive from New York to Detroit to counter mainstream media representations of a desolate ghost town with stories of a living, growing city. But it was easy to see why visiting and photographing these decaying relics of the industrial age was so enticing. The stately ghost of Michigan Central Station, Gothic caverns of a lace-like theatre, a single house in a sea of grass, slowly returning to the open prairie.

Why do we like old buildings? Can it be boiled down to a golden ratio of factors like ceiling height and room width? Is it because they use more natural materials like wood and stone? Is it because, as architect Christopher Alexander says, they were constructed in a time when our built environment grew slowly, piece by piece? Or is it because the wear and tear of time produces fractal patterns like those found in nature? Are older buildings more malleable and responsive, and does this impact how we act in them? Why do we find old trees and churches beautiful but not old people? Where do we draw the line between the captivation of ruin and the disgust of decay? And why do some buildings and building materials seem to age better than others?

In a world where we are increasingly surrounded by touch screens and digital toilets, why are people so drawn to these accidental monuments to the decline of twentieth-century capitalist civilisation? And why do so many people in nations like America and Britain still prefer to live in a 'traditional home'?[1] These are two different questions, each with many answers. But they also have some of the same answers, and these may be the ones that tell us the most about them.

■ ■ ■

People have searched for golden ratios and building variables to predict and explain our aesthetic preferences throughout history. The ancient Greeks believed that moderation held the key to both beauty and well-being. Since Euclid of Alexandria set down the geometric laws of lines and triangles, people have used his 'golden section' to structure buildings, compose landscapes, and explain our perception of beauty. If you can remember anything about the golden ratio from the ancient history of school geometry, you will probably recall an image of a rectangle with a fern-like curve inside it. This large rectangle is divided into two smaller rectangles, and the smaller one divided again, into ever-more miniature versions of the same shapes.

The golden ratio expressed in these shapes is found naturally in the curved patterns of nautilus and abalone shells, sunflower seeds, and rose petals, all of which express the same curvature found in the golden rectangle. These proportions are said to have been used consciously in ancient buildings, such as the great pyramids at Giza and the Parthenon in Athens, to instil a sense of beauty and calm. Euclidian geometry and the golden ratio went on to become keystones of western architecture, aided by a Roman architect and military engineer named Vitruvius. Vitruvius had a lot to say about Greek and Roman architecture, city-building, and construction – ten papyrus scrolls worth of observations, theories, and instructions – dedicated to his boss, Caesar Augustus, in the decades leading up to the common era. As the only major work on architecture to survive antiquity, his *Ten Books on Architecture* has played an important role in translating these ideas to the Renaissance and spreading them since then.

Vitruvius proposed a triad of virtues that architecture must possess to be successful, *firmitas, utilitas, and venustas*, translated

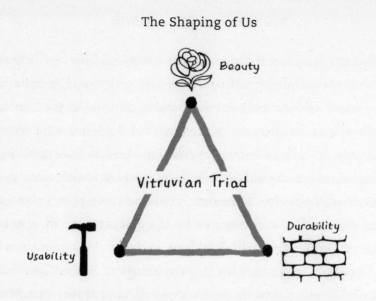

Beauty

Vitruvian Triad

Durability

Usability

The trio of virtues which architecture must embody.

as durability, usefulness, and beauty. Many architects today still believe this triad holds the key to distinguishing 'architecture' from mere building. But Vitruvius is probably most famous for an icon most people don't associate with him: Leonardo da Vinci's *Vitruvian Man*. Leonardo's nude, four-armed, four-legged man inside a circle and a square was drawn to demonstrate and update proportional theories proposed by Vitruvius. Vitruvius catalogued what he believed to be ideal human proportions (eight heads to a body, arm breadth equal to height), which he also cited as the starting point for proportion in classical architecture.

Leonardo's drawing is said to express the organic symmetry of the human body, which he saw as the '*cosmography del minor mondo*' (the cosmography of the microcosm). He saw the idealised geometry of the human body as a miniature metaphor for the universe itself. More recently, social scientists have approached these questions of building beauty and quality by conducting studies examining how specific features impact our preferences.

Research has shown that people tend to find high-ceilinged rooms more beautiful, and to prefer curvilinear spaces over rectilinear ones.[2] We like exteriors featuring decoration, curved lines, and articulated facades – like the Chrysler Building, where the complexity of the structure is revealed in the elaboration of the surface.[3] And we do indeed find faces and buildings embodying golden proportions appealing. Although our perception of human beauty is also influenced by the aesthetics of their surroundings, as Maslow famously found – we perceive people as more beautiful when they are in more beautiful rooms.[4]

Research on building features can provide interesting insights, particularly into the different preferences various types of people hold for building styles and elements. It is clear, for instance, that architects tend to have a higher opinion of minimalist modern buildings and poured concrete than the general public does.[5] But looking at the photos which are inevitably used in such studies, it seems that even combining long lists of variables like building age, ornamentation, and colour variation will somehow miss the true sense of coherence that makes the buildings we love work.

Our efforts to compile lists of the perfect building ingredients have failed to produce an over-arching theory – a compelling and comprehensive explanation for why contemporary buildings so often fail to appeal and inspire in the way we achieved for thousands of years. Creating new buildings that people will love and cherish may be harder than finding a new element. Can the frameworks that explained our survival and well-being in natural environments explain what works in our buildings and neighbourhoods as well? Could this include things like coherence and complexity, mystery and legibility, prospect and refuge, along with the geometry and elements of the natural world itself?

Building upon these ideas, architectural scholars such as Grant Hildebrand have argued that our biophilic bias holds the key to our built-environment preferences. Beloved environments require a degree of complexity, depth, and variety that takes time to grow. And over time, we begin to find patterns in this complexity, such as the gently varying height of bluebells, the tidal ornamentation of the shoreline, the land-shaped form of wind-sculpted trees. We find this type of ordered complexity in coveted buildings and places around the world. But in the age of office parks, high-rises, and ten-lane highways, we tend to see less and less of it.

Like refuge and prospect, order and complexity are twins that work together. Throughout history certain societies and regimes have put greater value on order and control, while others have grown in more complex, organic shapes. Like a messy room, too much complexity can be disorienting. But as we've seen with sterile institutional buildings, too much order is boring, depriving us of the sensory stimulation we thrive on. Maybe our networks of motorways and office parks do display some kind of ordered complexity when viewed from aeroplanes. Or when we whizz through steel and concrete conurbations at 70 miles an hour. But this isn't how we experience them most of the time. This isn't how we experience them on a human level. While ordered complexity may be difficult to reproduce, we know it when we see it. Or when we hear it.

As Grant Hildebrand has observed, all known cultures in history have made their own versions of ordered complexity for the ear, also known as music. While many may have their doubts about heavy metal and minimal techno, we can usually agree on the distinction between music and noise when we hear it. In our houses, cities, and holy places, we see ordered complexity in the layout and elevation of individual structures and the weaving together of materials. But we also see this sense of coherence in the way the buildings come together with each other, the streets and spaces connecting them, and the landscapes they are rooted in. It takes more than repetition to achieve ordered complexity. Ordered complexity requires patterns such as symmetry, rotation, scale, and nesting. The kind of patterns we find in fractals.

What exactly is a fractal? It seems to be a somewhat slippery concept to pin down, even for mathematicians. Well, not so much slippery as rough and inter-dimensional. The mathematical definition differs from the popular conception of a fractal, which is largely informed by 'fractal art' posters resembling tie-dyed worm-holes found on the dorm room walls of college students.

Fractal comes from the Latin *fractus*, which means fractured or broken. Fractals are multi-faceted by definition, and the pattern of their irregularity repeats itself on different scales. Imagine looking at the coastline of British Columbia from high up in a hot-air balloon. This area of the Canadian coast is run through with numberless rivulets, inlets, and islands. This variegation occurs in a similar pattern all across the coastline. And if you were now to descend closer to the ground in your balloon, you would see this pattern repeated similarly at lower levels. All the way down to stepping out of the balloon and looking at the shoreline from a mouse's point of view. Or an ant's. This self-similarity – replicating the patterns of the whole on infinitely smaller levels of magnification – is found in nature and can be expressed with fractal mathematics.

The pattern results in what is known as the 'coastline paradox'. Because fractal forms like coastlines have deep levels of wrinkled complexity, it is almost impossible to definitively say what the length of the British Columbian coast is. When it comes to the natural world, the distance between two points is less straightforward than drawing a straight line between them, as Euclidian geometry aspires to do.

Fractal geometry is a relatively recent discovery. It was conundrums such as the coastline paradox that led a Frenchman named Benoit Mandelbrot to develop a new mathematical approach to model the complex forms and dynamics of the natural world. The Euclidian models that had defined our understanding of geometry since 300 BCE were inadequate to describe lightning, clouds, and mountains, he argued in his 1982 publication, *The Fractal Geometry of Nature*. What Einstein did for physics, Mandelbrot did for geometry.

The truly mind-boggling fact about fractals is that they technically exist in between the first and second dimensions. If you draw a line on a piece of paper it has one dimension. If you then draw two more lines to create a triangle, you have a two-dimensional shape. If you could possibly figure out how to draw a fractal on your piece of paper, it would have a dimension somewhere between 1 and 2. Or ideally, between 1.3 and 1.5 – this is apparently the fractal sweet spot, the patterns we find most appealing.[6] But don't feel bad if you can't wrap your mind around the idea of fractional dimensions! These dimensions apply to fractals as they would appear on a flat piece of paper. But if we were to look at a fractal in space, it would fall in between the second and third dimensions. Take the Romanesco cauliflower: in many natural fractals like this chartreuse bud, the self-repeating pattern is only a few layers deep. But mathematical fractals extend to infinity. Because their surfaces are so multi-faceted, fractals cannot be contained between the integer dimensions of our standard shapes.

And mainstream mathematicians were not very happy about this, when the very first fractals were discovered. Long before Mandelbrot, a Swedish mathematician named Helge von Koch created a fractal called the Koch snowflake in 1904. These terrible shapes were considered 'mathematical pathologies' by his contemporaries – monsters, to be locked away in the dark dungeons reserved for non-Euclidian geometry.[7] Thanks to Mandelbrot, these persecuted forms have been freed from the repressive rule of squares and triangles, and are now appreciated as a measure of ordered complexity. Ethnomathematician Ron Eglash describes fractals as 'self-organising systems'.[8] We find self-organising systems all over nature, like the clusters of cells in our own bodies, which are organised in clusters of clusters. Not everything in nature is fractal, however. Water can take on a disorderly liquid form or the orderly crystals of ice. Mid-way between these two extremes we find the fascinating fractal structure of snowflakes.[9]

One might assume that random forms and arrangements – the way a handful of rice falls to the ground – would be highly complex. But mathematically, complexity is measured by how difficult it is to create a model to represent the phenomenon. Both highly ordered forms, like the structure of crystals, and highly disordered formations, like the random distribution of fallen rice, are easy to represent – they are not very complex. But fractals, which display a level of order mid-way between these two extremes, have the highest complexity. The ordered

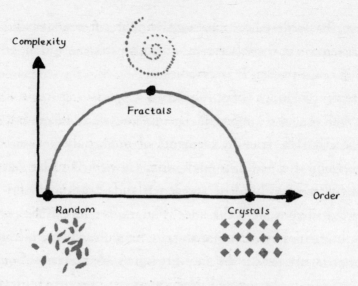

Fractals: ordered complexity found midway between randomness and order.
Source: Adapted from Eglash (2005)

complexity we see in fractals is a 'signature' of self-organisation.[10] We are quite fond of these fractal patterns, and they inspire us with the feeling of natural quality even when they are not naturally occurring.[11]

So can these types of patterns explain why we like old buildings as well?

The house is the primordial structure: the place we started building, the building from which all other building forms evolved. As our hunter-gatherer ancestors made their way hunting and gathering around the world, they began to build themselves different types of portable and temporary dwellings. The forms of our forebears' structures, as architectural theorist Nikos Salinagaros describes it, 'arose from within the material logic of their immediate surroundings and from the spatial ordering processes of their minds'.[12] Human neurological processes display fractal properties, as does the biology of our cells and lungs. The ordered complexity we find in vernacular building is an extension of these patterns – not only in trees and mountains but in our own minds and bodies.

Early dwellings were inherently close to nature in several ways. First, the materials themselves were recognisably of the earth. The friendly elements of mud, palm leaves, stone, and wood formed into new shapes with familiar patterns and surfaces. While the Aegean islands are known for their whitewashed stone walls and Thailand for its bamboo-stilted dwellings, New Mexico is known for its adobes. Natural building materials like wood display inherent self-similarity from the micro scale to the macro.[13] Spending time in rooms built with a good balance of wooden surfaces has been linked to a decrease in diastolic blood pressure and general sensation of comfort.[14] Vernacular dwellings were also of course particularly well-designed in relation to the climate and conditions – responsive to the threats, opportunities, and refuge needs specific to the people, place, and time.

Secondly, early buildings often echoed natural shapes and features in some way. Columns are said to mimic the form of trees, while arches may resemble shells or pine cones. Ornamental flora and fauna have decorated our buildings from the days of sphinxes and gargoyles to contemporary wallpaper.

Thirdly, traditional building forms consistently possess fractal qualities from their smallest details to the layout of floor-plans and the structure of cities.[15] The most obvious fractals in architecture are found in Gothic cathedrals like Notre Dame and in Hindu temples, with their cascading layers of ever smaller domes and gods and elephants. Like trees, whose branches and twigs repeat their overall form on smaller scales, iconic

Kandariya Mahadev Temple in Pradesh, India demonstrates fractal geometry, with larger domes composed of smaller, self-similar domes.
© Shutterstock

and religious structures like temples and palaces often repeat a particular form like an arch or triangle over a number of orders of magnitude.

Subtler fractal patterns can be found in simple bits of ornamentation, like the mouldings around our windows, door frames, and skirting boards. Mouldings may seem like boring features of stuffy buildings, which have little to do with nature. But the generous use of small-scale features creates a 'cascade of detail', which can display fractal characteristics in their relative scale without being identical in form. Like the Romanesco cauliflower, this cascade of detail does not extend to infinity, and is often approximately rather than exactly self-similar. We have inherited these detailed features from the lintel structures that sat atop the columns of Greek and Roman buildings, which seem to have been either consciously or subconsciously crafted in fractal forms.[16]

A cross-section of a Gothic column bears a striking resemblance to the 'monstrous' Koch snowflake (see overleaf). One of Mandelbrot's fractals, 'the devil's staircase', looks uncannily like a Doric cornice. In a less satanic light, segments of the Koch curve resemble the blooming silhouette of a tree. And if you stare at classical door and window frames long enough, you will start to see little tree silhouettes all around you, which may explain why people have taken such great trouble to ornament these building joints with such strange shapes. This fractal practice continued in western architecture through the use of simple features like mouldings, essentially until the rise of modernism.[17]

We also find fractal patterns in the layout of buildings, towns, and villages, as ethnomathematician Ron Eglash has demonstrated across a variety of vernacular African traditions. In Cameroon, he found palaces and entire urban areas laid out in rectangular fractal structures. The palace in the city of Logone-Birni was expanded over generations with larger, self-similar rectangular structures that housed greater numbers of family members and increased fortifications. In the traditional Ba-ila settlements of southern Zambia, circular village fortifications were formed from smaller circles for each family, centring on the chief's outer and inner family circles. Smaller still was the circle for the spirit people, the ancestors. And even the ancestors had a smaller circle for their own spirit people. A 'ring of rings', replicating its form on multiple scales.[18]

Fractals even seem to be woven into the fabric of vernacular African craftwork. We see them in the winding structure of

The 'monstrous' Koch Snowflake fractal © Andrew Crompton

Cross-section of a Gothic column © Andrew Crompton

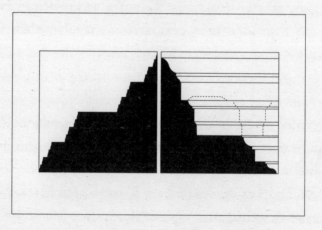

Mandelbrot's 'devil's staircase' fractal displays similar geometry to a
Doric cornice © Andrew Crompton

braided hair, concentric arrangements of increasingly smaller pots, and the weaving of fences. Speaking to a fence maker, Eglash discovered these fractals were in his fence for a very good reason. The higher parts of fences faced stronger winds. The reeds were woven tighter and tighter as needed for strength, resulting in a perfectly engineered fractal fence.

Eglash describes fractals as a common technology used for innovative and aesthetic advancements in a diverse array of cultures on the African continent. But he also suggests that the recurrence of fractal structures relates to a worldview – an understanding of the universe that seems more related to fractals than Euclidian squares. Fractal design expresses a conception of the infinite cycles of birth and rebirth, showing similarities with the Hindu notion of the universe as a microcosm on the tip of a pin, and Leonardo's cosmography of the microcosm.[19]

Is it possible to unravel the mystery of these miracles of ordered complexity? The sense of integration between the smaller elements of the greater whole? To parse the elements that make up these patterns? This is what architect Christopher Alexander and his colleagues set out to do in their canonical work, *A Pattern Language*.

When Max Jacobson first met Christopher Alexander, Alexander was in the process of deconstructing his own home. 'Chris at the time had a chisel and a sledgehammer and he was knocking all the plaster off the fireplace in his house,' Jacobson told me. 'He wanted to expose the true brick – get down to the meat of the building.' *A Pattern Language*, which Jacobson went on to co-author with Alexander and four others, is one of the top-selling architectural books of all time and among the most influential of the twentieth century. Its reach, as we shall see, has extended far beyond the scope of the built environment.

Like many famous theorists, Christopher Alexander is said to be brilliant, charming, dark, and brooding. Born in Vienna in 1938, he grew up in Chichester, England, after his family fled the Nazi invasion of Austria. Uniting the study of architecture, mathematics, and computer science in new and unique ways, he made his way from Oxford and Harvard to land at the University of California at Berkeley. He was a mysterious local celebrity in a big, pink house up in the hills in my childhood. Much bigger and pinker than the house The Band named their album after.

The College of Environmental Design at Berkeley wanted to make architecture a more scientific and rational discipline, and Alexander was to lead the charge. Max Jacobson was an architecture graduate student, not much younger than Alexander himself. Sometime after their initial encounter with the sledgehammer, Alexander and his right-hand woman, Sara Ishikawa, invited Jacobson to join them at their Center for Environmental Structure. This centre was funded by the National Institute for Mental Health – the same institute that had funded Calhoun's rats of NIMH research.

'They were convinced, as we were, that these patterns were important for mental health,' Jacobson explained. 'If you live in a room and it's only got light coming in from one side, you're not going to be happy with the glare. If you live above the sixth storey of a house or an apartment, you'll go crazy – there were some outrageous claims.'

A Pattern Language was also framed in reaction to what the authors saw as the decline of contemporary architecture. 'We had a bias at that time,' Jacobson said. 'We felt and said that modernism was producing terrible buildings. Here at Berkeley they would tear down a nice house and put up an apartment building that was just ugly as sin. So we were critics. We had a point of view. And the point of view was that bad architecture is cold, hard-surfaced. Too simple. Stark. Uninteresting.'

It took them ten years to complete their work. The result was a distinctly bible-like book: a thick, maroon-covered volume, embossed in gold. The 1171 pages of this treatise form only a third of the complete work – including several companion volumes such as *The Timeless Way of Building* and *The Oregon Experiment*.

If Roger Barker approached the study of human behaviour settings the way an ecologist would study frogs, then Alexander approached the study of environmental structure as a geneticist or a linguistic anthropologist would. The book was informed by the study of buildings, people, and places around the world. Some of this took the form of original 'research' which would probably not stand up to social science standards. Jacobson describes knocking on people's doors to ask them whether or not they used their backyards, from which they concluded that northern hemisphere dwellers did not use northern-facing backyards. But they also drew on the growing body of environmental psychology and behavioural evidence available at the time, including Barker's behaviour settings and Edward T. Hall's personal space bubbles.

'In order to define this quality in buildings and towns,' Alexander wrote in *The Timeless Way of Building*, 'we must begin by understanding that every place is given its character by certain patterns of events that keep on happening there.'[20] Like Hall,

Alexander believed that these patterns of behaviour constituted a language – a dance – differing from place to place. But while Hall and Barker focused on the human side of this inextricable dance, Alexander focused on the environmental side.

Like any language, the dialogue of our built environment has parts of speech. But this language has window panes instead of letters and garden paths for punctuation. Once we learn the language, we can use these letters to build the words of rooms, the paragraphs of buildings, and the books of towns and cities.[21] The book presents these patterns – 253 in total – which the authors suggest can be practically applied to design a house, a neighbourhood, or a town. We learn from Alexander and his colleagues that towns should have paved squares for dancing (63), rooms should have light from two sides (159), and windows should have window-seats (202). As with the recursive, self-similarity of fractals, we see echoes in these patterns from the micro scale to the macro.

For example, 'half-open wall' (193) suggests that our most beloved rooms tend to take the form of semi-enclosed spaces defined by features like breakfast bars, French doors, or trellised walls. This balance of enclosure and exposure – which we might also describe as refuge and prospect – enlivens these spaces with cosy nooks and active openings not found in floor layouts that are either cellular or completely open. At the neighbourhood level, they suggest similar patterns of semi-permeable space, partially enclosed so that 'smaller and more private pieces of land and pockets always open onto it' (67).[22] On the miniature scale of the children's bedroom, they suggest carving out crescent alcoves for each child's bed, centring around the common play space (143).

Alexander holds that all great architects and modest build-ers have used such patterns throughout history. Some, like the sixteenth-century Italian Andrea Palladio, recorded these pat-terns in books. Palladio, who entered the building trade as a stonemason, is often said to be the most influential architect in the western world. His *Four Books of Architecture* helped revive Vitruvius, spreading and building upon the architectural legacy of Rome and Greece. But others, like Frank Lloyd Wright, have tried to keep their patterns secret, like pharmaceutical compan-ies patenting medications.[23]

Christopher Alexander and Frank Lloyd Wright may differ in their attitudes to sharing, but have shared an interest in organic building forms and processes. Wright pioneered many of the bold moves that went on to define modern architecture. But he also believed that buildings should be fundamentally defined by and connected to nature. 'Nature builds a tree from the inside out,' Wright said, 'That's what organic architecture is. It's building the way nature builds.'[24] From the flowing horizontal form of his prairie homes to the spiralling elevation of the Guggenheim museum in New York City, Wright aspired to 'break out of the box' of Victorian architecture. He is credited with inventing the open-plan concept, breaking down the segmented layout of the house. He restructured the form of home to flow around a central fireplace, to grow out of the landscape, and connect the inside with the outside. Nearly sixty years after his death, Wright remains the most famous American architect. There are a number of potential explanations for why his designs have remained so popular and influential.

As with early vernacular architecture, Wright's style seems to respond to its surroundings, to grow inherently out of its geography. He wanted houses to be part of their environment instead of perched atop them. His prairie-style houses featured flat, low rooflines, stretching out like the infinite horizon of the landscape. Of his own house, built on the brow of a hill in Wisconsin, he explained, 'No house should ever be on any hill. It should be of the hill, belonging to it, so hill and house should live together, each the happier for the other.' And Wright's famous Fallingwater, the house he built over a waterfall in the 1930s, certainly embraces this principle to its utmost.

Grant Hildebrand has demonstrated that Wright's designs make cunning use of refuge and prospect, with shadowed, low-ceilinged refuges opening up to bright airy expanses. His structures often lead you up to the second floor, where living areas open onto cantilevered porches, allowing prospect of the street from a

Frank Lloyd Wright's Fallingwater in Mill Run, Pennsylvania
© Archive Photos/Stringer/Getty images

securely sheltered shelf. Wright sought to identify the geometric structure of the landscape and reflect these in his buildings.

But while Wright's buildings were deeply intertwined in a dance with the natural landscape, they didn't play quite as well with human organisms. He hated clutter, the mess of people and the things they brought with them. His solution? Design out storage space. Closets in his houses tend to be small, if included at all. Basements were worthy of extinction in his opinion. He even designed 'dun-coloured' clothing for his first wife Catherine to prevent her from upstaging his creations.[25]

His masterpiece – Fallingwater – has been plagued by structural problems and water damage, leading to expensive repairs and reinforcement. The ochre horizontal wings of this picture-perfect house have an unhealthy, waterlogged look up close. And the waterfall is not all to blame. The wide low roofs of his houses may fascinate us partly because they seem to defy gravity, but many cracked and leaked even soon after completion. And this should come as no great surprise, according to the logic of *A Pattern Language*. Wright pushed form and material to new extremes, including the quintessentially modern use of poured concrete as a sculptural building material. Many consider his Unity Temple in Chicago the first truly modern building, due to its ground-breaking construction out of a single building material: reinforced concrete. It would be foolish to think he could perfect these new patterns within the canon of his own work – or lifetime. Patterns are like genes. They must reproduce and evolve to survive. But other incarnations of modernism have adapted and advanced through the timeless way of building.

Reacting to the sterility and inflexibility of the International Style of modernism reigning in 1947, renowned *New Yorker* architectural critic Lewis Mumford wrote, 'I look for the continued spread, to every part of our country of that native and humane form of modernism which one might call the Bay Region style, a free yet unobtrusive expression of the terrain, the climate, and the way of life of the coast.'[26]

Along with Wright, leading California architects such as Bernard Maybeck, Julia Morgan, and Ernest Coxhead departed from the stiff structure and vertical orientation of the Victorian era they were born into to create more free, open, and horizontal arrangements. But they also adapted these ideas to the misty redwood forests and sunny hills of northern California, mixing in patterns from the California Mediterranean and bungalow styles to create the San Francisco Bay Region style.

Both Wright and the Bay Region architects were heavily influenced by the arts and crafts movement, which was essentially a reaction to industrialisation, the working conditions that accompanied it, and the perceived decline of traditional creation. Both were also deeply influenced by Japanese architecture. Maybeck is often portrayed as a counterpoint to Wright – the friendly, forest-dwelling architectural 'wizard of the west' versus the cool concrete 'wizard Wright', ruling over the plains and waterfalls of the east and Midwest. Maybeck's buildings share a freedom in the formation of horizontal and vertical space with Wright's, and an integrity with the natural environment. But Maybeck combined these advances with a grounding in earthy, natural materials and delight in historic detail. In fact, he and his contemporaries were so fond of their local redwood trees that they built their houses out of them.[27]

The Bay Region style also differed from some other branches of modernism in that it was deeply vernacular. It didn't even have a name, until Mumford gave it one. It evolved in the way vernacular buildings have grown throughout time: through repetition, sharing, and spreading simple patterns. 'The style is actually a product of the meeting of oriental and occidental architectural traditions,' Mumford said, 'and it is far more truly a universal style than the so-called international style of the 1930s, since it permits regional adaptations and modifications.'[28]

Consider the case of Berkeley brown shingle. These houses can be found all around Berkeley and other cities in the Bay Area. Like different trees of the same species, they share similar features: peaked roofs, wide overhanging eaves, dark wood mouldings and wainscoting, and, of course, their signature cedar or redwood shingles. Like a forest of redwood trees, each one expresses the patterns essential to the species in its own unique way. One tree may be taller or thicker while others have bifurcated trunks. The patterns formed by their branches are each unique, and yet the same. They come to be home to families of birds and caterpillars, who make their mark on each tree through their comings and goings.

We see the same sort of variation across a house type like the brown shingle. They range from simple bungalows to three-storey giants. Many feature a secondary peaked roof, popping out at right angles like a two-headed house. Others are adorned with enlarged dormers, bay windows, turrets, and smaller peaked roofs peeking out from underneath. Like the vernacular villas of Italian towns or the multi-coloured hillsides of Valparaíso, Chile, these dwellings create a complex symphony of variation, while maintaining order through the language of the patterns they share. And throughout this process, little kinks and issues are tested, smoothed over and corrected. The city grows like a forest.

Of course, we cannot meet the demands of today's housing crisis with spacious single-family homes made of old-growth redwood trees. But what is interesting about the little-known Bay Region incarnation of modernism is that it blended some of this movement's most beloved and innovative patterns with the vernacular process – the evolutionary growth of buildings and places.

Modern architecture is not inherently lacking in fractal qualities. Architect and mechanical engineer Carl Bovill has demonstrated that both Le Corbusier and Wright's buildings display fractal patterns in the relative dimensions of building surfaces and smaller components. But the rapid spread of mainstream modernism left Wright's organic emphasis in the dust, breaking with the vernacular and sometimes fractal traditions of building in a few key ways. Modernists put an end to ornamentation. Austrian-Czech architect and modernist pioneer Alfred Loos famously likened ornamentation to the moral corruption of tattoo art. His 1910 essay, *Ornament and Crime*, suggested that tattooed westerners who died outside of prison had simply not got around to committing their crimes yet. And this meant an end to mouldings and other detailed elements in which fractal dimensions were typically expressed in the west.

The dictum 'form follows function' has been attributed to Louis Sullivan, a mentor of Wright, who has been called the father of both modernism and skyscrapers. The functionalist fervour taken up by Le Corbusier and others prioritised utility over the other corners of the Vitruvian triangle. Modern buildings tend to lack a fractal quality because they favour plain surfaces and large, simple forms, like the big blocks of buildings filling most American downtowns. They refrain from variation and ornamentation in their silhouette down to their internal details. Following America's puritanical forefathers, they don't want any unnecessary frills getting between them and their all-holy function. Unnecessary ornamentation typically included the peaked and overhanging rooflines that have been found to symbolise home and shelter, even to those who grow up in flat-roofed high-rises.[29] Wright often flattened his rooflines, but he also extended them to maintain the feeling of shelter.

Features such as high ceilings also went by the board. Le Corbusier was very interested in the classical, Euclidian approach to beauty, meticulously designing his buildings in accord with the golden ratio. He carefully crafted his Unité d'Habitation around the dimensions of a six-foot man, but somehow got the odd idea that the ideal height was one allowing this man to reach the ceiling with his hand. Le Corbusier was equally fond of poured concrete, but less interested than Wright in pairing this component with local materials and colour palettes. Building materials became far removed from anything resembling the earth. Landscapes were forced to make way for buildings.

The built environment took on a hard, cold quality, making buildings unresponsive to their occupants. Design standards in institutional structures were specifically created to be resistant to human imprint, and this trickled down into other environments. People became less able to adapt and shape buildings to their needs. And when people feel alienated from their environment, they also feel alienated from each other. What began as breaking out of the box of Victorian architecture resulted in a distinctly boxier quality of life.

Malvina Reynolds's classic 1962 song satirising post-war American suburban conformism, made famous by Pete Seeger, pretty much sums it up:

> 'Little boxes on the hillside,
> Little boxes made of ticky tacky,
> Little boxes on the hillside,
> Little boxes all the same ...
> And the people in the houses
> All went to the university,
> Where they were put in boxes
> And they came out all the same'

It was inspired by a suburban tract home development on a hillside south of San Francisco. While Le Corbusier and his imitators were trying to house the masses of war-torn Europe in stacks of little boxes, the American middle class was sprawling out in little detached boxes of their own. Whether in the form of soaring high-rises or sprawling suburbs, these mass-produced dwellings deprived their occupants of agency and changed the relationship between people and their environments.

'The adaptation between people and buildings is profound,' as Alexander says. Or as he seems to mean, it should be: 'The patterns stay alive because the people who are using them are also testing them.'[30] This may be Alexander's most important point. The timeless way of building is a collaborative creation. It takes many people, working in their own ways, contributing their pieces to the greater whole over time.

■ ■ ■

So can you actually use *A Pattern Language* to build your own home? To create a structure in this timeless way of building? This was the little experiment I embarked on when I gave my partner a copy of the book for his birthday. Owain had been hard at work for six months transforming his derelict auctioned property into a home when I first came to visit him in Bristol. While this 150-year-old building had once housed a brewery, it was not exactly the spacious site you might imagine from this former industrial function. His future house was a deep, narrow, three-storey shell, though there weren't actually any storeys to speak of. There was little of the original structure he could make use of except the ancient stone walls – and even those he had to repoint.

The side walls were shared with the adjoining properties and the tangle of overlapping rights, responsibilities, wires, and drains with neighbouring parties didn't stop there, as I discovered when I began to help with some of the legal paperwork. In addition to his being obliged to give over half of the ground floor for emergency access to the pub behind and shop next door, the previous owner had retained ownership of a two-foot square hole in the ground floor!

Complexity was built into the site. Bringing order to this tall space between two buildings was a tall order. Have you ever found yourself walking down a city street and come across a building that seemed too narrow for people to possibly live in? That is this house. 'That tiny house!' everyone says. 'I've always wondered how anyone could fit in there.'

The secret is that it's not as narrow as it looks. While the front wall was about 8 feet (2.4 metres) wide, the back wall was 11.5 feet (3.5 metres). And compared to its width, the footprint is relatively long – almost 23 feet (7 metres). Luckily for us, tiny houses are all the rage these days. This American movement has been fuelled by enthusiasm for both mortgage- and clutter-free lifestyles. According to the Tiny House Town blog, most Lilliputians cap the tiny house quotient around 500 square feet (46 square metres). The combined 'usable' floor area of the first and second floors of Owain's tiny townhouse is around 441 square feet (41 square metres).

What is 'usable space', anyway? Are you using that lofted storage area above the bathroom? Are you using your staircase as a bench/phone booth/cocktail lounge? These are the kind of questions you ask yourself when you live in a tiny house. And living in one, you also find out just how usable these little nooks and crannies can be.

But one of the surprises about the house was how spacious it felt in the end. You can't do much on the ground floor other than unload your laundry, fix a bike, or fall down the hole that we don't own. But the sense of vertical volume gained climbing from the ground floor to the bedroom is significant. A friend of mine has a flat in London with almost identical floor area that feels smaller because it's all on one level. There might be less 'unusable space' in the horizontal version, but there is no sense of distance. We recognise vertical space in features such as high ceilings but we don't sell a house based on its cubic volume.

Within our small but tall building, there was the big question of how to divide the space between the different floors. Was there a golden rule or ratio that could help us here?

'A building in which the ceiling heights are all the same is virtually incapable of making people comfortable,' Alexander and his colleagues wrote. 'Vary the ceiling height continuously throughout the building.'[31]

I'm sure there have been some lovely buildings where the rooms all have the same height. But the authors make a compelling case for this pronouncement, drawing on various sources. One classic idea, proposed by Palladio and used traditionally in Japan, is that ceiling height should be proportional to room length. A sort of golden ratio approach, determining ceiling height by a measurement between width and length. Another theory posits that ceiling height should be determined by the geometry of our personal space bubbles in relation to the intimacy rating of the setting. In Anglophone architecture we traditionally find these common spaces on the lower floors, with ceiling height decreasing and intimacy increasing as one goes upstairs.

Variation, Alexander, et al. ultimately decided, is the key. And this seems to be at the root of many of their insights. Patterns such as 'structure follows social spaces' (205) encourage us to carve out a uniquely shaped space, formed to the specific needs of the inhabitants. On this subject we also have 'house for a couple' (77). That probably would have been a good pattern to consult before we began.[32]

'In the first years of a couple's life, as they learn more about each other and find out if indeed they have a future together, the evolution of the house plays a vital role,' Alexander wrote. Who would have thought that two people with seemingly similar tastes could hold such different views on bathroom tiles? I hadn't thought I had any views on bathroom tiles, for that matter. But I did have an idea of what a normal bathroom looked like, which turned out to be based on some different patterns than Owain's idea. And given childhoods shaped by the differing forms of the wee English cottage and the peak-roofed Berkeley brown shingle, we also had somewhat different ideas about the definition of a high ceiling. Owain followed his own instincts to turn the traditional ceiling height gradient upside down, transforming this awkward space into a ship-shape tiny house. The progressively higher ceiling heights give it a nautical feeling, as you wind your way from the dark depths in the hold to emerge up into the bright fresh air above, where the bedroom's double doors give onto a glossy wooden deck, and giant skylights open like sails in the wind.

Much of the genius of vernacular building comes down to this small-scale individual attention to detail – making decisions based on the specifics of the setting and occupants. When people make their own homes, they are much more likely to make the most of the opportunities at hand

'At the core of these books is the idea that people should design for themselves their own houses, streets, and communities,' Alexander explained. 'It comes simply from the observation that most of the wonderful places in the world were not made by architects but by the people.'[33]

The timeless way of building, it turned out, is a very time-consuming way of building. As all contemporary builders know, the complex dynamics of construction can be represented by a simple triangular diagram that functions as a practical update to the Vitruvian triad: fast, cheap, and good. But unlike the effect on an actual triangle, putting pressure on any two points of this system breaks the third point. You can build a house that is good and fast, but it won't be cheap. You can also build a good-quality house cheaply, but it will take a long time. You can build a house quickly and cheaply, but it won't be very good quality. And, since so much housing development in the post-war era has been in the form of speculative development, completely detached from those who will live there, this has been the dominant mode of building. We have weakened the 'good' point of the triangle, creating homes that don't perform well by any of the original Vitruvian virtues: durability, usability, and beauty. The decreasing quality of the built environment is partly due to how big everything has become. Even the finest bamboo flooring is pretty affordable when you only have 41 square metres to cover.

Our buildings hold up a mirror reflecting who we are. People did in fact become taller and larger over the course of the twentieth century. But our economic structures and their corporate incarnations nevertheless expanded disproportionately.

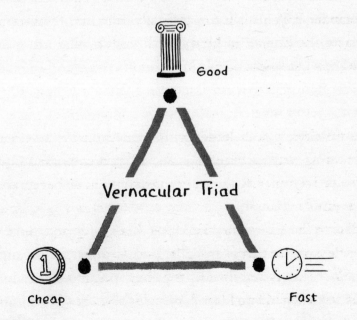

Building can embody only two of these three contemporary virtues.

'The great automobile factories and the highways surrounding them are never empty,' one 1950s' promotional film proclaimed of Detroit. 'Tens of thousands of men on one payroll. Money for new comforts and conveniences. Prosperity grows – prosperity greater than history has ever known.'[34]

Detroit was a city built for the machine age. With an area covering the size of San Francisco, Boston, and Manhattan combined, the Motor City was built by and for the automobile. And the unwieldy expansion of this city did not happen slowly, piece by piece. It was built quickly, in big chunks. Detroit was also destroyed by the automobile, as more than half of its residents got into those cars and drove out of the city to newly built suburbs. Peaking at a population of 1.86 million in 1950, the city had shrunk back to its 1910 size – 700,000 – by 2010. The vast majority of the white population fled to the suburbs, accompanied by an outward flow of wealth and resources. The car factories that had driven the city's growth collapsed, one after another, and manufacturing jobs plummeted from two hundred thousand in 1950 to fewer than twenty thousand by 2012.[35]

'Capitalism doesn't just destroy communities,' long-time Detroit labour union leader and former auto worker General Baker told our Paper Tiger team, 'It destroys itself. That's the lesson of Detroit. Let the rest of the world see what capitalism has in store for you.'

Henry Ford famously said that his customers could have a car any colour they wanted as long as it was black. But car manufacturers eventually realised that, using more colours, they could sell more cars to more people. If those cars didn't last very long, people would need to buy still more. American car-makers' strategy of planned obsolescence ultimately led many buyers to prefer Japanese and German cars, contributing to the decline of the American auto industry.

Yet standardised techniques of mass-production were soon applied to housing, with the development of cookie-cutter suburbs such as Levittown, Long Island – one of the first and largest of such planned communities, followed by clones in New Jersey, Pennsylvania, and even Puerto Rico. What we think of as mainstream modern architecture today says just as much about our economy, our values as a society, as it does about modernist aesthetics. Modernism was the clothing that capitalism put on for its global growth spurt.

Much of our built world is now created quickly and in large swathes. This violates a principle Alexander considers to be key to the beauty and success of many older environments: the process of 'piecemeal growth'.

'Any living system must repair itself constantly in order to maintain its balance . . . ' As he explained, 'All the good environments that we know have this in common. They are whole and alive because they have grown slowly over long periods of time, piece by piece.' Many studies have indeed suggested that people tend to prefer older buildings to newer ones when the buildings are equally well maintained.[36] But Alexander and others argue that the problem is the focus on the building as commodity – the perfect new building. Our culture – especially American – tends to prize the new flower in bloom.

While many find Frank Lloyd Wright's buildings beautiful, he does not seem to have taken much interest in their durability, in how they would perform and age over the long term. Wright believed that buildings should be designed around the personalities of their owners – part of his organic philosophy – the logical conclusion being that they had no need to outlast their owners. Many post-war buildings weren't even intended to make it that long. Ruin porn and other aesthetic schools of thought such as the ancient Japanese art of *wabi-sabi* appreciate the flower in its other stages of development – and decay. We like the natural world because it is alive. And with life comes death.

What clouds, lightning, coastlines, and trees have in common is that their form is never static. They are in motion – growing, changing, moving. But when we make a toaster or a modern home, we tend to think of it as a finished, static product. What does it do to our conception of ourselves, our communities, if we have no appreciation for the natural passage of time and of our place in a world that is alive and growing instead of a commodity? As with fake flowers, we don't like it when buildings lie to us – when they pretend to be something they are not. We feel disappointed, deceived.

Building at a human scale is not just about space and time – the distance at which we can make eye contact, the speed below which our skulls swiftly fracture on collision. Human nature is fractal in nature. The geometry of our own bodies, the functioning of our nervous systems, is characterised by fractal-like properties. The wrinkling of our skin and the branching of the tracheal bronchi in our lungs are fractal. 'The aesthetic appeal of fractal-like patterns is also explained by the fact that the nervous system is governed by fractal-like properties. . .' concludes biophilia researcher Yannick Joye, 'from the microscopic level of neural functioning to the macroscopic level of human behaviour.'[37]

Fractal patterns recur profoundly over time in physiological processes ranging from cellular function and neuron-firing patterns to breathing apparatus. The fractal functioning of our bodies defines the nervous system dynamics that structure our very consciousness.[38] As Nikos Salingaros explains, these patterns of ordered complexity appear to be progressing over time: 'Many scientists now believe that evolution has a direction: the increasing complexity from emergent life forms in a primordial soup to human beings is not random. . . while not speaking of "purpose", we may discern a flow of organisation toward a very specific type of organised complexity.'[39]

So how does Max Jacobson feel about *A Pattern Language* today?

'As time has gone on I've changed my attitudes about it,' Jacobson told me. 'And one of the things that has struck me is that so many of the patterns are designed to make people comfortable. After thirty-five years of practising architecture, I'm also interested in other kinds of environmental experience. I don't want to just be comfortable. I would like there to be some challenge. I want my interest sparked. I want to be thrilled.'

Throughout our environmental experiences, another pair of matched forces crucial to our aesthetic preferences seems to emerge: comfort versus awe. We like small, cosy spaces and climbable hills. But we are also drawn to the awe-inspiring scale of cliff faces, soaring skyscrapers, and magnificent monuments. Recent research from the University of Warwick has demonstrated that beautiful urban environments can provide restorative effects similar to those we gain from nature. A stroll beneath St Paul's cathedral or through the deliciously textured streets of New Orleans can have biophilic benefits. Urban areas rated as 'scenic' were found to correspond with higher rates of health and happiness. Cohesion – the quality of complex elements coming together to form a coherent whole – proved key to beauty. And as you may recall, cohesion was also a core component of the mystery novel model, along with complexity and legibility.[40]

In writing *A Pattern Language*, Jacobson and his colleagues believed beauty would arise from utility. 'We did not discuss beauty because we felt that if you put together things in ways that matched human needs, beauty emerged naturally,' he explained to me. Today, Jacobson thinks it's all right if the beauty and utility corners of the Vitruvian triad don't always align. Ideas grow and develop just as buildings, places, and languages do. The *Pattern Language* authors wanted their work to reflect the nature of its material: to be a collaborative, living process rather than a static, dead product.

Part of the reason *A Pattern Language* took so long to write was that there were debates about what form it should take. The authors considered a vehicle like a ring binder. They wanted a collectively editable format, enabling people to contribute and add to patterns. There was also the idea that the book could somehow be housed in the then-emerging medium of the computer. These vessels were ultimately rejected for aesthetic and practical reasons. A work about timelessness could not be communicated in the clunky form of a ring binder, they figured. And how would all these different ring binders get updated? Computers were in short supply, and were about as aesthetically pleasing as ring binders.

The ideal format for the work would be collectively editable and interconnected. But it would also function somewhat like an encyclopaedia. Each pattern in the book contains references to various other patterns, which would ideally be dynamically linked. The challenge of an appropriate format for *A Pattern*

Language had 'captured the imagination of the computer gangs,' as Jacobson called them.

Alexander's mathematically-informed work was closely followed by pioneers in the growing field of computer science. His 1964 work, *Notes on the Synthesis of Form*, was considered required reading by many computer-science researchers in the 1960s, and they kept up with his progress. With the publication of *A Pattern Language*, computer scientists saw a potential solution to a long-standing problem in software design. Instead of writing a new, bug-prone program to address every new challenge, software development could follow a pattern-language approach. Just like written languages, software programs could produce more reliable results if they were assembled from predefined patterns of code. The design patterns or software patterns approach was a game-changing revolution, and Alexander was its cult figure. His work is credited with influencing the Agile and Scrum approaches to software development (iterative models driven by 'self-organising' teams), object-oriented programming, and even *SimCity*, the virtual city-building game which reigned for years as the most popular computer game in America.[41]

In taking on Alexander's design patterns approach, developers found themselves facing the same problem the *Pattern Language* authors had faced. If only they had some kind of digital, inter-linked network of collectively editable documents to share their developing patterns... And, with that, the 'wiki' was born.

Ward Cunningham, who created the original wiki technology running Wikipedia, credits Alexander directly for its inspiration.[42] But while Alexander's disciples were busy building SimCities and writing Wikipedia articles, his principles proved more complicated to apply to actual buildings and cities. The timeless way of building was lost in the explosion of neoliberal globalisation over the past century. Our built environment has grown so big and so quickly that it has lost connection with the vernacular tradition. New technologies have allowed us to pop out new buildings and towns quickly and efficiently. In doing so we lost the quality that made them whole and liveable.

Yet, as our cities became further removed from the collaborative grammar of the pattern languages we had always used, technological development was creating new opportunities for collaborative development online. Many years on, we are seeing the seeds sown by *A Pattern Language* blossom, putting the power of distributed, vernacular building back into the hands of everyday people through initiatives like WikiHouse, as we will soon explore further. New models for harnessing the collective potential of ordered complexity range from high-tech to back-to-basics.

Of course, our love of old buildings is partly due to the collective sense of memory they hold, the stories they tell us about our history. The structure of our cities is a language – a language that speaks to us about our past, our present, and our future. It tells us about who we are and where we have come from.

The usability of the casement window, the beauty of Venice, and the durability of ancient stone walls were achieved thanks to the small and repeated contributions of many people over many years. We love old buildings because they envelop us in patterns we understand intuitively. And if our everyday environments possessed more ordered complexity, perhaps we might not be so starved for ruin porn.

Detroit ruin porn, in particular, seems to represent an extreme surrender to the reality of nature. Does the breakdown of rational factory land symbolise an acceptance that America is growing old? Will Americans as people – as a nation – take on the characteristics we associate with the elderly? Are we becoming resigned to our fates as we see in older nations? Like Mayan temples and Babylonian walls, the ruins of Detroit appear to tell the story of a lost civilisation. But these images overshadow the living reality of Detroit – the long, hard labour of Detroiters to construct new communities in new ways. And this style of community-driven development is intrinsically intertwined with ordered complexity.

To fix our built environment, we must also change the behaviour, culture, and community that we see reflected in it.

CHAPTER 7

The Big Fix

From lab rats and rational choice
to resilient cities

In 2010 the brand new Bank of America building opened for business in midtown Manhattan – a gleaming entity towering over Bryant Park like a giant narwhal, thrusting its single tusk up into the sky. As the first skyscraper to achieve the premium LEED (Leadership in Energy and Environmental Design) platinum certification, the crystalline structure was hailed as 'the world's most environmentally responsible high-rise office building'.[1]

A feat of environmental engineering, the fifty-five-storey building featured a rainwater collection system, waterless urinals, and green roofs. Daylight dimming and LED lights promised to reduce electricity usage, while carbon dioxide monitors automatically introduced fresh air when needed, and an innovative thermal storage system produced ice at night to cool the building by day. Approximately sixty-five per cent of energy used in the building was co-generated on site. Despite all these efforts, a different picture began to emerge over the first few years of the building's use.

In 2013 Sam Roudman made headlines with a *New Republic* article claiming the tower produced 'more greenhouse gases and uses more energy per square foot than any comparably sized office building in Manhattan'.[2] The 'toxic tower' used over twice as much energy per square foot as its aged neighbour, the Empire State Building, according to the exposé. Roudman's analysis has also faced criticism. Appropriate grounds for comparison of skyscrapers encompassing different uses, users, and technologies are hard to agree upon – a major point being that energy use per person may be more meaningful than energy use per square foot. But one point seems to remain clear: the designers and certifiers failed to consider how workers' behaviour in the building would affect the use of resources.

The building's primary tenant is, unsurprisingly, Bank of America itself, whose energy-intensive trading activities take up nearly a third of the tower. With five computer screens per desk, just one workstation in these brightly-lit, money-crunching floors can consume nearly as much yearly energy as it takes an average car to drive more than 4,500 miles. Mitigating energy use by workers was not part of the design brief, and was not considered in the LEED certification, which assessed energy use with computer models before the occupants arrived.[3]

'We did not attack the demand side, meaning the user side,' Roudman cites architectural project leader Serge Appel explaining. 'We attacked "How do you produce the energy and how do you bring that energy to the building?"'

We often explain urban problems ranging from sustainable design to the housing crisis through the rational economic logic of supply and demand. But what does it really mean for a building to be sustainable? Can buildings and cities be structured to change behaviour – to encourage people to use less energy or drive less – through their very design?

The construction industry is a little like a dinosaur: outmoded, slow to change, and very hungry. The sheer quantity of resources required to construct new buildings has long meant this industry has been considered to be one of the least sustainable in the world.

For the average British family, heating and powering the home is the largest source of greenhouse gas emissions, followed by transportation.[4] We see the reverse for American families, where transportation accounts for the majority of carbon emissions, largely due to the enormous output of motor vehicle fuel.[5] The buildings we live and work in and the journeys we make between them account for the majority of our environmental impact, in terms of carbon emissions.[6]

So how exactly can such resource-gobbling creations be called sustainable? There is nothing truly sustainable about constructing new buildings unless the way we interact with them is more environmentally efficient and resilient than what they replace. Green building certification schemes such as LEED and BREEAM (Building Research Establishment Environmental Assessment Method) are now the leading mechanisms for measuring and demonstrating environmental impact in the built environment.[7] Points are awarded for solar panels, LED lighting, smart meters, cycle-parking, reused or renewable building materials, etc. But seemingly sustainable buildings and technologies often impact our behaviour and well-being in ways that are counterintuitive. Smart meters may go unheeded, LED lighting can interfere with circadian rhythms, and technologically efficient housing developments may fail to foster community.[8]

Sustainable buildings have often failed to account for human interaction – both in terms of how we impact buildings, and how they impact us. A study from the Center for the Built Environment (CBE) at the University of California, Berkeley found that LEED accreditation of office buildings did not bring about any significant improvement in satisfaction with workspaces or buildings as a whole. LEED and other 'green' building standards did not appear to have improved working conditions in terms of lighting, acoustics, or office layout, and have even been linked to declining acoustic conditions.[9] These shortcomings may be related to the fact that these efficient new workspaces are also more likely to be open-plan.

If we are going to use all these resources to build these new 'sustainable' structures, wouldn't it also be worthwhile to make them work better for people from a well-being perspective?

Environmental psychology has grown from looking at how the built environment affects humans to encompass how to proactively minimise our impact on the natural environment.

'In the early years, environmental psychology was very much concerned with architecture and the built environment – people-environment fit at an architectural level,' my former professor, David Uzzell, recalled on a recent visit I made back to University of Surrey. 'Now, fast-forward forty years, the emphasis is much more on sustainability and environmental behaviour, things like environmental values.' What began as the study of how design influences behaviour has evolved to discover how we can intentionally redesign our own behaviour.

Two years after visiting the slick new development in Berkeley, California, that raised so many questions for me, I came back to my hometown to try to answer them. I talked to young burger-flippers and old Jewish comedians, life-long residents and transplants, city council members and radio journalists. I interviewed them to try to understand whether these big new buildings really had the power to enable people to drive less – to change their behaviour. While people typically expressed a desire to drive less, there were many barriers to changing their behaviour. I found that actions didn't always align with intentions. The messy complexities of life could not so easily be reconfigured with simple economic incentives and environmental ideals.

Psychologists originally assumed that people's behaviour was rationally determined by their attitudes. If people only had access to the right facts – if they knew that smoking was dangerous and leaving lights on was wasteful – they would change these destructive habits. These 'information deficit' models, as they were called, could be addressed through a simple, linear approach. If people could be nudged to adopt a desired attitude, such as 'I should drive less', this would lead them to change their wicked driving ways. Sort of like a societal machine where you put facts in one end and get actions out the other end. But as we've seen in various settings, people don't typically check a list of stated attitudes before they hop in the car to take the kids to school. Their actions are constrained by the realities of daily life and embedded in the structures of the city. We are swayed by the suggestions of the scenery.

Around the same time that Lee Robins was studying heroin addiction in Vietnam vets returning to the US, experimental psychologists were busy researching drug addiction in their favourite animal subject, the lab rat. But instead of being crammed together in overpopulated rodent high-rises, these rats were isolated in cold metal cages, sometimes starved, and even zapped with electric shocks in torture chambers known, after their creator, B. F. Skinner, as Skinner boxes.

Given the opportunity to consume drugs like heroin, morphine, cocaine, and amphetamines, the rats became serious drug addicts, often to the point of fatal overdose. These results were extrapolated to humans, cementing the notion that the irresistibly addictive nature of such substances is the cause of addiction. But Bruce Alexander at Simon Fraser University noticed something a bit odd about this experimental setup. Rats are naturally quite social, active, and sexual creatures. Deprived of playmates, mating mates, and productive activities, might not the rats act as strangely as most humans would under such conditions?

To test the hypothesis, Alexander and his colleagues set up a sort of rat paradise: a plywood enclosure filled with woodchips, climbing platforms, exercise wheels, wholesome food, and lots of rats for socialising. They even included tin cans (a rat's favourite refuge) and painted the walls with a pleasant prospect of widely spaced pine trees. Instead of Rat City, they called it Rat Park. The rats loved their Rat Park, and they also loved each other, quickly producing lots of rat babies – though not too many!

But Rat Park had a dark side of its own. On certain days, the rats in Rat Park were given a choice between simple tap water and a morphine-laced alternative, as were their less fortunate counterparts, who were housed in isolation. The isolated rats consumed significantly more morphine than the Rat Park rats – more than four times as much in one experiment.[10] Rats, of course, don't have access to information about the negative consequences of morphine addiction. They're not bombarded with public service announcements likening your brain on drugs to a fried egg (as American audiences were throughout the '80s). And even if they were, it might not make much difference.

The rats whose environment allowed them to be happy, healthy, and connected to other rats were far less prone to addiction than those whose environment did not. As we saw with the American servicemen in Vietnam, an estranged and stressful environment made the rats more likely to engage in destructive behaviour. In other words, our environment contributes to the shaping of our well-being. But well-being isn't just about how well we're doing as individuals. It's about how well we're doing as a community. The Skinner box researchers' great mistake was not just in overlooking the influence of the environment, but also the ways in which the environment facilitates community.

Running for president at the height of the Vietnam war in 1968, Robert Kennedy made a speech at the University of Kansas that would help transform our understanding of well-being. The irony of measuring national success in terms of gross domestic product (GDP), he explained, was that this economic measure counts profits resulting from air pollution, ambulances, nuclear warheads, and prison construction.

'It counts the destruction of the redwood and the loss of our natural wonder in chaotic sprawl . . . Yet the gross national product does not allow for the health of our children, the quality of their education or the joy of their play . . . it measures everything in short, except that which makes life worthwhile.'[11]

GDP has long been used as an indicator of how well a country is doing. Today, the US is one of the wealthiest countries in the world as measured by GDP per capita and percentage of global personal wealth. As of 2015, almost forty-five per cent of worldwide financial assets were concentrated in North America.[12] But this addiction to ever-increasing prosperity is not linked to ever-increasing well-being. Up to a certain level, greater wealth brings people greater happiness and security, allowing them to feed and clothe their family, get a good education and have some free time to go to the beach. But once certain core needs have been met, well-being levels plateau.[13]

Despite wealth roughly doubling since the 1970s in the UK, life satisfaction has increased little.[14] And with great wealth, we also often find great inequality. The US has the highest degrees of income inequality in the world, with the UK following not far behind in third place, and Sweden, surprisingly, second.[15]

In the rat universe, a park-like environment fitted out with luxuries like woodchips and tin cans may lay the groundwork for well-being. But in the human universe, the uneven distribution of resources has a negative impact on everyone's well-being.

When wealth is distributed unevenly, we all suffer – not just the poor. In *The Spirit Level*, Richard Wilkinson and Kate Pickett have demonstrated that nations with greater levels of inequality experience devastating social and health outcomes. The destructive effects of inequality are seen in both poor and wealthy nations in the highly developed group of OECD (Organisation for Economic Co-operation and Development) countries. But rich countries with high inequality have the worst outcomes in matters that range from mental health to obesity and include drug abuse, violence, teen pregnancies, trust, and community life.[16]

In the face of this gaping disconnect, bodies like the UK government and the UN are increasingly investing in understanding and enhancing well-being as an alternative to GDP. Well-being is a measure of how well we are doing as a society. And your personal well-being has more to do with the well-being of your broader community than how many mindfulness apps and Lululemon leggings you have.

Thirty years ago, a UN commission headed by Norway's first female prime minister, Gro Harlem Brundtland, famously defined sustainable development as that which 'meets the needs of the present without compromising the ability of future generations to meet their own needs.'[17] According to the so-called Brundtland Report, well-being is a key component of sustainability as well. Sustainable development has been likened to a three-legged stool, requiring a balance between environmental, economic, and social sustainability. And, like all three-legged stools, it needs three equal legs to stand up: a structure or system is environmentally sustainable to the extent that it allows biological life to flourish and remain diverse; it is economically sustainable if societal wealth and welfare can prevail; and it is socially sustainable if it supports continued psychological and social well-being on both an individual and societal level.

More recently, we have seen the rise of the resilient cities movement – shifting from an emphasis on maintaining the status quo to building societies that can repair and rework themselves in the face of chaotic change. Well-being is an integral part of resilient structures and societies, but too often this leg of the stool is missing. We talk about sustainable cities from an environmental and economic perspective, forgetting the human factors that make these urban ecosystems function.

■ ■ ■

From time to time, I find myself talking to a man at a bar about the housing crisis. He works in tech or finance or architecture, and he has all the answers. The solution to the housing crisis, he explains to me between swigs of Heineken, is to build as much high-rise housing as quickly as we can.

'It's a simple problem of supply-and-demand – increase the supply and the price will drop.'

'But what if they're uncomfortable, nondescript, and badly built?' I say. 'What if living there makes people feel like soulless clones?'

'Well,' he tells me, 'that's not very rational.'

Rational city planning has long been aligned with advancing the course of progress – a vehicle for behaviour change on a cultural scale. Many would argue that city planning has also been used as a method of social control. The ancient Romans have been called 'urban choreographers' for their cunning use of urban design to manage their subjects. They were so fond of boundaries that they even had a special god to rule over and protect them – his name was Terminus.

Paris, the 'city of light', is said to have gained this name from the city's central role in the Enlightenment – the intellectual movement asserting the importance of reason and rationality – and also because of Georges-Eugène Haussmann's pioneering use of gas lamps, lighting the way for new cafés and department stores, shooing away the vermin, rats, and other 'undesirables'.

Paris before Haussmann was, by all accounts, better known for the stench of its streets and high infant mortality rate than for the taste of its macarons and beauty of its courtesans. The Emperor Napoleon III commissioned Haussmann to

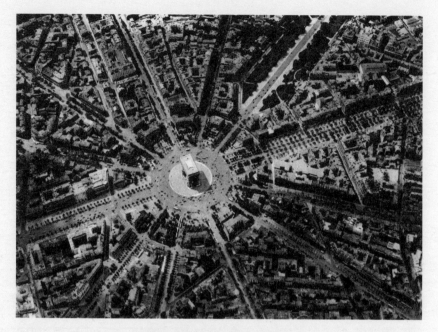

Haussmann's boulevards, Paris
© Print Collector/Getty Images

modernise the city in 1853, entrusting him with enormous powers that combined the functions of mayor, city planner, and director of public works. He used his great, centralised authority to construct sewers, railroad stations, parklands, and civic buildings,[18] but he is perhaps best known for carving wide boulevards through the city's old residential districts. Haussmann's boulevards made way for modern advances in sanitation and traffic engineering. They also facilitated the rapid deployment of troops at a time of great urban strife and disturbance: Napoleon III had risen to power as a result of major civil unrest and public revolt by unemployed workers. These fresh channels of commerce and circulation were also useful in clearing out some of the sources of this disturbance, and suppressing further difficulties.[19]

This urban makeover has often been compared with Robert Moses's remodelling of New York City and its broader watershed in the mid-twentieth century. Like Haussmann in France, Moses took on the task of modernising New York for a new era. And, also like Haussmann, he was granted enormous unilateral powers, which he wielded in what is often called a top-down approach to city planning. A great fan of Haussmann's, Moses similarly used transportation arteries as a tool for remaking the city in a new image – for moving some people out, inviting others in, and controlling who went where. He intentionally made the underpasses leading to a new state park beach too low for public buses to fit under, thus excluding low-income, bus-riding African Americans from the sandy havens of Long Island.[20]

Fortunately for everyone who likes the way Paris looks today, Le Corbusier didn't get the chance to 'refresh' the French capital as he had drawn up plans to do, replacing old neighbourhoods with his 'towers in a park' model. But Moses reshaped large portions of New York into forms Le Corbusier would have been proud of. Under his direction, the city agency in charge of urban renewal 'cleared' three hundred acres of city land for housing alone, on which towers containing 28,400 new apartments were erected. [21]

The urban renewal projects of American cities in the 1950s and 1960s were not only costly and socially destructive, but ultimately ended with more housing dismantled than constructed.[22] Federal policy and regulations mandated racial segregation, leading to further inequality, crime, and alienation.[23] Many white Americans left New York City for the new suburbs of Long Island with the help of a post-World War II programme providing low-interest mortgages (the 'GI

Bill') – a game-changing step up in the American dream that ethnic minorities, like African-Americans, were systematically excluded from.[24]

Today, we are faced with new visions of the urban future for America and beyond – visions aspiring to reverse the damage of car-oriented planning. Unfortunately, these models of sustainable development also have the potential for unexpected consequences. The utopian visions of suburban cul-de-sacs and functionalist mega-structures both promised access to light, air, and open space. But such well-meaning projects failed to foresee how the scale and density of development would impact human perception and interaction, and how they would fail to enliven public space.

So can we plan cities and design buildings rationally? Is our behaviour really any more rational than our preference for the fractal silhouette of a magnolia tree over the rectilinear form of a 'big box' store?

Economic theory has traditionally been grounded in what is called 'rational choice theory', which proposes that the macro-scale movements we see socially and economically are the result of many individual actors making rational individual decisions. In order to understand what we see happening on a societal level, we need to understand the dynamics of these individual decision-making entities, which in the worldview of economics are either consumers or firms – buyers and sellers.

Imagine we are at a medieval marketplace where there are a variety of merchants peddling their wares. And among these many merchants there are a great number of shoemakers offering footwear of the pointy-toed, curly-toed, and knee-high boot varieties. How might we understand the dynamics that determine how much these shoemakers charge, and how much medieval customers will pay for them? The rational choice worldview is based in the fundamental premise that buyers and sellers of any era make logical choices between the available options, ultimately selecting the shoes that will help them best achieve their shoe-related goals – whatever those may be. This assumes that shoe-buyers assess the various options and form preferences based on information such as costs and benefits (will the pricier curly-toed shoes attract more beautiful maidens?), the probable course of events when wearing such shoes (will they one day become entangled in one's stirrups?), and take these details into account in deciding which ones to buy and what is reasonable to pay for them. The rational choice model essentially assumes we conduct cost benefit analyses in all our daily decisions, and act logically in accordance with these mental Excel spreadsheets.

Psychologist Daniel Kahneman, along with his collaborator Amos Tversky, was a key force in challenging modern economists' core assumption of human rationality. These two men, who by all accounts had wildly opposite characters, made an interesting team for the study of human character. Tversky, who grew up in Israel, was unabashedly confident. Kahneman, who spent his formative years hiding from the Nazis in French barns and chicken coops, was deeply self-doubting – constantly questioning himself and his ideas.[25] Together, they spent decades studying how people act when they are faced with decisions about economic dilemmas and risks. Tversky sadly passed away before the Nobel committee got around to recognising their work. Kahneman is the only psychologist to have been awarded the Nobel Prize in economic sciences, but he considers it a joint award.

In his 'intellectual memoir', *Thinking, Fast and Slow*, Kahneman recalls how he first became aware that the economists working in the building next to his own department were studying an alien species. One seemingly unremarkable day in the 1970s, Tversky handed Kahneman an essay on the psychological presumptions of economic logic. Opening the document, Kahneman read; 'The agent of economic theory is rational, selfish, and his tastes do not change.'[26]

He was struck by this strange combination of traits which did not seem to be describing the species his discipline studied – namely, humans. The good news, according to Kahneman, is that we are not entirely selfish. The bad news is that we are quite often irrational. And beyond this, our tastes and preferences seem to change quite a lot. The only logical conclusion was that these economists were studying an entirely different species – a species which Kahneman's behavioural economist colleague Richard Thaler has identified as 'Econs'. These Econs – which I imagine to be boxy robotic creatures – have only one way of thinking and making decisions. Econs employ only the 'slow thinking' from Kahneman's title, which is more commonly known in psychology circles by the unstimulating name of 'System 2'. This slow-thinking system is the part of our consciousness we often identify with. It is careful, considerate, and logical. It can solve complex maths problems, analyse memories, and rationally compare the costs and benefits of two houses you might buy – just like our medieval man compares prospective shoe choices at the marketplace.

Humans use this slow-thinking system all the time. But we also use fast-thinking, known as 'System 1'. Kahneman describes this system as labouring under the general impression that 'what you see is all there is'. The fast-thinking system is very good at drawing quick connections about things that 'go together' in simple categories like apples and oranges, and associations, like monkeys and bananas. The fast-thinking system functions swiftly and automatically, requiring no sense of effort or control. It can recognise facial expressions, navigate a simple landscape, and form a rough stereotype of a person based on what their house looks like. Like an excitable dog whose interest is piqued by every passing squirrel, this part of our consciousness reacts strongly to changes and is not very picky about the quality or quantity of the information it takes in.

Kahneman and others have found that these fast and slow systems work together and impact each other in interesting ways. The slow system can direct the fast system to be on the lookout for particular things – as you might train a dog to be on alert for the scent of explosives rather than squirrels. The fast system offers feelings, impressions, and intuition to the slow system. And if the slow system accepts these messages, they can form the basis of attitudes, beliefs, and intentions.

Economists traditionally used rational choice models to describe both how they thought Econs *should* make choices, and how they actually behaved. Kahneman and Tversky set out to understand how humans behave in reality. More specifically, they set up studies using gambling scenario word-problems to understand and model the irrational and yet predictable ways that humans systematically make 'illogical' decisions.

One of their earliest and most influential revelations was the finding that people tend to place greater value on losses than gains. We assign greater value to things we already possess – be it a bicycle, a parking space, or an apartment – than to those we might be able to obtain. This flies in the face of 'expected utility theory', the basic foundation of the rational choice model. Utility theory proposes that we value wealth in terms of its usefulness or 'utility'.

According to this theory, if you and I both have £1,000 today, we should both be equally happy because this amount of money has the same utility for both of us. But let's say you had £500 yesterday and I had £1,500. If we were both Econs, we would be equally happy because we would both be able to purchase the same amount of robot fuel or whatever it is that Econs do with their Econ money. But since we are humans, you would probably be very happy and I would probably be very unhappy because I have lost a lot of money while you have gained the same amount. Utility theory does not account for this reality of lived human experience.[27] Our perception of the brightness of a lamp or loudness of a car's engine is not objective or constant. It is impacted by the brightness or loudness of our surroundings, or the context we have just come from. And our perception of the value of money, shoes, and houses is similarly not consistent. It is based in relation to our background, which forms a sort of baseline.

Essentially, traditional economic theory assumed we use only the slow-thinking system of our minds, ignoring the big picture of human cognition and decision-making. Even the concept of 'making a decision' falls in the deliberate, slow-thinking camp. The cognitive sciences now estimate that approximately ninety-eight per cent of human cognition falls outside the realm of 'conscious' thought.[28]

Using his fast-thinking system, our medieval man may swiftly reach a resolution to buy the pricier curly-toed shoes because they remind him of snails, which he is so fond of eating (he is a medieval Frenchman, it turns out). And upon purchasing his snail-inspired shoes, he irrationally values them even more than before he bought them. Perhaps one reason we attach greater value to things within our ownership is that they have become tied up with our identity. Insight such as this, introduced in Kahneman and Tversky's ground-breaking 1979 essay 'Prospect Theory: An Analysis of Decision Under Risk', turned the basic presumptions of economic theory on their head, and led to the development of behavioural economics. (Despite similar hypothetical grounding in our dislike of risky scenarios like the possibility of losing a limb to a lion, this line of thought is unrelated to the theory of prospect and refuge.)

But psychologists have not been immune to the pervasive influence of this seductively logical vision of human behaviour. When psychological researchers first started thinking about how to motivate pro-environmental behaviour in the early 1970s, they imagined that people simply needed more information – information about the nature and scale of environmental problems, and information about how they could change their behaviour to address these problems. They developed their thinking further to produce a particularly popular model known by the unfortunately dull name of the 'theory of planned behaviour'. As you might imagine, this approach assumes that we respond logically to available information, make plans, and behave in accordance with these plans. Returning to our medieval man's shoe choices, this framework accounts for social norms (are your friends wearing curly-toed shoes?), and potential 'barriers' (do the shoes fit your feet?). But it still imagines that we think and behave much like Econs – albeit Econs who have a potentially more altruistic orientation than those traditionally studied by economists.

Econs with the potential to be motivated by goals other than self-interest.

The theory of planned behaviour has been plagued by a pesky problem known in psychology circles as the 'value-action gap', which boils down to the fact that people often don't behave in line with their stated values, plans, and intentions. As with the petrified woodchip experiment in Arizona, convincing people to drive less, live more densely, or buy curly-toed shoes turned out to be much harder than putting up a sign delivering rational facts and directions. And like the Petrified Forest rangers who kept on using counterproductive signs about the large number of people stealing woodchips, many governmental and non-governmental organisations have persisted in trying to change behaviour with information.

'How can we change behaviours?' David Uzzell, a leader in the psychology of behaviour change, questioned. 'We can't change a behaviour without changing the culture, and products, and buildings that are part of it. We have to address the conditions which encourage and constrain action, as much as the actions themselves.' And even when we do revamp our buildings and products, people are often not as easily re-engineered.

Take smart meters, for instance – a seemingly straightforward way to deliver useful and pertinent information. Studying the introduction of smart meter energy-use feedback in a university office, Niamh Murtagh and her colleagues found that approximately £60,000 could be saved annually by switching off all computers every evening – the equivalent of two researchers' salaries.[29] Surely a rational Econ would plan accordingly and turn off its computer if only it had access to the proper information? Perhaps an Econ would. But humans do not, according to Murtagh's findings. Forty-one per cent of participants failed to take even a single look at the individual energy feedback provided through the study. While some significant reductions in energy use were found, engagement diminished over time. And, falling prey to the dreaded value-action gap, participants' self-reporting of their pro-environmental behaviour had no relation to how much energy they used, or how much attention they paid to their smart meter. Although individual energy feedback may be a good starting point, Murtagh concludes, stronger motivational forces must be marshalled to engage the masses in changing their behaviour.

'No one ever made a decision because of a number,' Daniel Kahneman has written. 'They need a story.'[30]

Despite his demonstration that utility theory fails to accurately model human behaviour at the most basic level, the rational choice model remains 'to this day the most important theory in the social sciences,' according to Kahneman.[31] Unrealistic economic models are still employed in planning our cities and social policies. Yet, beyond the full picture of costs and benefits, many of our reactions and actions are simply not 'logical'. We have an emotional relationship with the environments in our lives, just as we do with people.

Climate change and its related gang of global environmental ghouls presents what may be the gravest survival threat the human species has ever faced. But paradoxically, understanding the enormity of this threat may make people less likely to take action to combat it. The spectre of climate chaos is terrifying. But it is also difficult to identify. When we want to mobilise people to action, we try to unify them against a common enemy.

In the UK, I was surprised to find how large 'the War' still looms in the collective consciousness. Red paper poppies bloom every year to commemorate fallen soldiers – a tradition that began just after the end of World War I. There is a common, righteous sense of unity in the country gained from the collective effort of triumphing against extreme evil in World War II – a unified moral high ground that was lost for many Americans in my parents' generation with the falsely premised atrocities of Vietnam. But combating climate change is more like fighting cancer than fighting Hitler. And this is not something we are psychologically well-equipped to do. The scale of the crisis and chaos can leave people feeling that it is too late to do anything about it, or that their individual actions won't make an impact.

Many people simply ignore the mounting evidence of this problem. Others cope by developing a belief that the negative outcomes will be more strongly felt elsewhere. Alternatively, those who accept climate change may become more authoritarian and less accepting of others.[32] The rational choice approach fails because it focuses on the individual rather than groups as agents of change. When we focus on change at the individual level, it is nearly impossible to achieve the greater collective shifts needed to confront these enormous challenges. While it may be fairly easy to change people's attitudes to specific issues like recycling or forest-fire prevention, changing individual attitudes to individual issues doesn't achieve very much. Like experimenting on rats in Skinner boxes, attempts to manipulate people in isolation don't tell us much about how to motivate the greater societal changes critical to resilience.

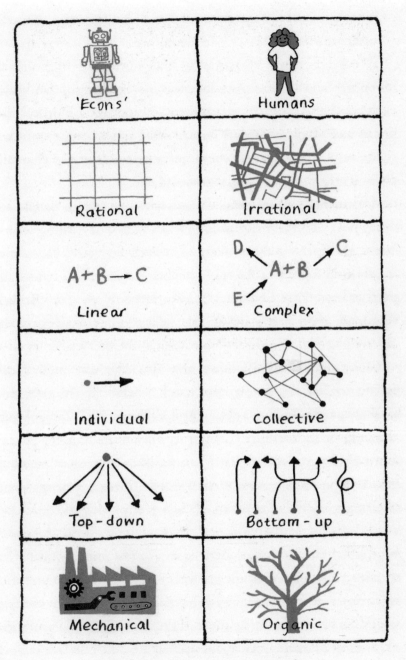

'Rational' planning versus organic growth

From petrified woodchips to natural gas reserves, rationally quantifying how swiftly our fellow humans are sucking up precious resources may lead to an 'every man for himself' mentality. In Murtagh's study for instance, focus groups expressed a strong and indignant belief that 'the government' should not call on individuals to save small amounts of energy when others used even more!

So how can we encourage pro-environmental behaviour without triggering the 'petrified wood effect'?

A growing body of research indicates that when people see themselves and their communities as capable of dealing with a threat, they are far more likely to actively engage.[33] This sense of common agency is known as collective efficacy – the same phenomenon that provided a counterpoint to the 'Broken Windows' theory explaining the relationship between crime and evidence of disorder in New York and Chicago. At its core, collective efficacy is really not a new idea. We hear much about the survival of the fittest, and much less about the collective basis of success, known as biological altruism. The Vervet breed of monkeys, for instance, cry out to warn their monkey pals of approaching predators, putting themselves at greater personal risk. Vampire bats have a lovely practice of regurgitating blood to nourish underfed members of their group. And, of course, we have the sterile worker bees and termites, who devote their lives to building the cities and skyscrapers of the insect world with no hope of reproducing themselves. Darwin himself noted the importance of such altruistic behaviour in *The Descent of Man*, coming to believe human's 'sympathetic' or collective orientation was critical to our species' great success.[34]

Collective efficacy requires social cohesion, combined with a readiness to take action for the common good.[35] We particularly tend to look to community for support and agency when individual control is limited, meaning collective efficacy is especially relevant for the scale of our current conundrum. It seems to go hand-in-hand with a strong sense of group identity. [36]

A few years after their famous petrified wood findings, Robert Cialdini and his colleagues in Arizona conducted another study to see if they could use social norms to encourage pro-environmental behaviours rather than stealing woodchips. If you have stayed in a hotel room any time recently, you may have found a small placard in the bathroom inviting you to hang your towels up if you don't need them to be washed. You may have also found yourself wondering whether this small action would make much impact among the enormous number of towels that must be washed in hotels and houses every day. Cialdini and his colleagues set out to test whether the sometimes counter-intuitive tool of social norms could be leveraged to convince more guests to adopt this energy-saving behaviour. Once again they scurried around hotel rooms placing different signs in different bathrooms, with the important caveat that they didn't hide in people's showers to watch what they did. They compared one sign with a simple appeal to 'Help save the environment' with another saying, 'Join your fellow guests in helping to save the environment'. As they expected, 'fellow guests' were significantly more persuasive.

But which fellow people are most influential in motivating our pro-environmental behaviour? In a second experiment, the researchers tested what kind of peers we are most strongly influenced by. They planted more little signs in different hotel rooms. Some emphasised the social norms of 'fellow citizens', while others gave specific statistics for men and women, and all expressed that these peer groups were 'helping to save the environment'. Finally, they threw in one last sign claiming that 'Seventy-five per cent of guests who stayed in this room' had reused their towels. They expected that this last option would be the least successful, assuming that guests' identities as citizens, men or women, and environmentally concerned people would be more important than their identities as guests of room no. 303, and that these more important identities would influence their actions more strongly.

To their surprise, the social norms of fellow room-lodgers had the strongest apparent impact. Nearly fifty per cent of guests reused their towels in this condition, as opposed to only forty-one per cent using the gender identity appeal, and thirty-seven per cent for the standard 'save the environment' messaging.[37] Whether in Rome or in room no. 303, it seems we are impelled to do as our fellow Romans or roomers do. And perhaps this is also because we strangely feel some kind of connection or common identity with those who have occupied the same places as us, even in the transitory space of a hotel room. The hotel towel signs worked not just because people have a sheep-like desire to conform, but because their small actions become more meaningful and powerful when joined by many others.

Drawing on research such as that carried out by Cialdini, Canadian environmental psychologist Doug McKenzie-Mohr has created an evidence-based framework called 'community-based social marketing', which has been successfully used by organisations and policymakers around the world to tackle environmental issues – often working at the neighbourhood or workplace level.[38] This practical approach offers simple steps to identify barriers to change and combine the power of social norms with other tools, like feedback. If the individual smart-meter feedback in Murtagh's study had been delivered in a creative, interlinked way designed to play into the power of collective efficacy, for instance, perhaps it would have been more effective.[39]

Collective efficacy inspires people to believe in the power of their actions – individually and communally – to make an impact. And this makes people much more likely to take those actions.

How do we foster collective efficacy in the everyday spaces of our lives – from the small scale to the large?

The very first project my consultancy ever took on was a new co-working space in Clerkenwell called Huckletree, which aimed to be London's first 'fully sustainable' co-working venue. Grigoriou Interiors, a firm specialising in sustainable design, brought us on board to help craft a workspace that would encourage people to waste less and share more. New to the co-working business, the founders also had concerns about how to create a communal and cooperative workspace: a village centre and innovation hub where freelancers and start-ups would benefit from interacting, and respect each other's working needs and space.

Our first task was to help create a space 'etiquette' that would encourage equitable management of shared resources within the workspace and motivate specific sustainable behaviours, like saving paper and turning out the lights. Like many others before them, the powers that be had assumed that rational signs, rules, and regulations would be the best way to get people to behave as they wanted them to. The Huckletree etiquette, we suggested, could be communicated by employing both more subtle and more interactive channels of communication – appealing to a collective sensibility, and invoking social norms. The encouragement of behaviour that is sustainable on a global level and respectful of one's office-mates on a local level essentially draws on the same psychological principles at different scales.

To create a respectful working community, we advised, the interaction design should foster a culture of trust and responsibility rather than borders and penalties. As we've seen before, when people's personal space is cramped they tend to be less amicable. Instead of delineating exact desk territories with unsightly markings, we suggested indicating separate spaces with task lighting to subtly rein in those expanding tendencies we tend to find in co-workers, while also giving people control over lighting. And rather than didactic signage directing people not to linger with laptops at the kitchen table, why not use a high table with stools to suggest a place for perching rather than nesting? Crafting a space with semi-enclosed nooks and enclaves helps people feel secure and able to focus, which may in turn make them more communally spirited. We worked with the designers to suggest partial screens and permeable curtains to define a space where people have room to retreat and to meet.

The Huckletree office made use of recycled materials, sourced cradle-to-cradle products, and considered environmental impacts such as reduced chemical content to achieve Ska rating – an environmental assessment credential for interior design. But crucially, with our help, they also considered how people would interact with the space. Drawing on Cialdini's research, we suggested a playful visual communication strategy, emphasising collective efficacy. Little owls and songbirds decorated the office walls, beckoning members to 'join the flock' in key energy-saving behaviours (the office operated a complete energy shutdown policy every night). Passing by the light switch, a cartoon smokestack billowing CO_2 reminded you that energy has an environmental cost. Wondering where to chuck an empty container? Recycling and landfill bins were adorned with graphic tips from a friendly seagull, reminding you what goes where – and that the things you throw 'away' might end up in some other animal's home.

In accounting for human factors, Grigoriou Interiors were able to create a space that fostered community and engaged occupants in doing their part to reduce their waste and energy use, instead of a sterile automated office box.

But what does this all mean for shaping resilient cities? Can we harness the power of collective efficacy to build sustainable and equitable urban areas? Like language, cities are great collective creations. Some see them as centres of exchange and creation, intellect and enlightenment, art and intrigue. Others see them as the messy cesspools resulting from the societal shifts towards agriculture and industrialisation – living piggy-banks constructed as containers for surplus capital. But most agree that the future of our cities is deeply entwined with the future of our societies.

As geographer David Harvey has written, 'The question of what kind of city we want cannot be divorced from that of what kind of social ties, relationship to nature, lifestyles, technologies, and aesthetic values we desire. The right to the city is far more than the individual liberty to access urban resources: it is a right to change ourselves by changing the city.'[40]

Haussmann's transformation of Paris redefined what it meant to be Parisian – the elegant and fashionable identity we associate with Paris today. This cultural change was not a magical transformation whereby sooty scullery maids were transformed into Cinderellas by the magic of fairy godfather Haussmann's wand. As we often see, the modernisation and beautification of the city involved moving the scullery maids out and the ballgown-clad princesses in. And rather than turning pumpkins into carriages, this magic trick is most effectively performed by demolishing the scullery maids' decrepit old housing, and replacing it with gleaming new dwellings for the leisurely ladies.

While Haussmann cut the cloth for the new urban persona of the nineteenth century, Moses helped create the new suburban identity of the post-World War II era. As Harvey has examined, the suburbanisation of the US did not merely create new transportation and residential infrastructures, it transformed the American lifestyle in ways that restructured the economic landscape and massively increased oil consumption. This suburban transformation created a different kind of American. A home-owning, debt-burdened, geographically isolated American, who Harvey argues was less likely to strike and more likely to vote conservatively.

We are now experiencing what many see as an urban renaissance. While resources, and those with them, fled British and American cities in the second half of the twentieth century, they have now returned with a vengeance. Building densely in our cities holds the potential to craft a more resilient society – a future in which people spend more time communing in human parks and less time commuting in isolated cars.

But there is no doubt that big buildings also mean big business. When so-called sustainable development takes the form of luxury housing and corporate banking headquarters, we must ask who this 'sustainable lifestyle' will be available to? If you build it, they may indeed come. But it is unclear who 'they' will be, or what you will have accomplished. Are we changing people's behaviour with urban design, or simply swapping one set of city residents for another once again? The 'green-washing' of luxury residential and commercial developments – sometimes benefiting from generous tax cuts by virtue of their 'sustainability' credentials – may have detrimental consequences for the future of the planet.

When we encourage people to focus on financial success, they tend to become more manipulative, hierarchical, and prejudiced against difference. They become less empathetic, and less concerned about environmental issues.[41] When we narrowly focus our understanding of the world through an economic lens – seeing people as buyers and sellers, seeing cities as development opportunities – we become more selfish and individualistic. We become like Econs. This is the compelling argument Tom Crompton makes in *Common Cause: The Case for Working with our Cultural Values*. While simple financial incentives may be effective for individual issues, Crompton argues, the vast scope of the problems we are facing and the level of societal change needed requires a greater shift in cultural values. But financial incentives sound like great tools for changing behaviour. What's wrong with encouraging people to buy a hybrid car because Cameron Diaz has one?

'Hybrid cars are taking celebrities by storm, with the Toyota Prius, as driven by Hollywood A-listers such as the likes of Will Ferrell, Cameron Diaz and Leonardo DiCaprio . . .' boasts a hybrid-boosting British website. 'It helps send out the message that the owner cares about the environment they live in, that they are trying to make the world a better place. It is becoming a status symbol, and that can only help sales and the environment.'[42]

Psychological research has demonstrated that motivating pro-environmental behaviour with this sort of messaging subtly strengthens selfish values, ultimately detracting from the very aims it claims to promote. Motivation depends on the interplay between what are known as *intrinsic* and *extrinsic* drivers.[43] A watermelon, for instance, is intrinsically valuable for humans as a source of nourishment and amusement, whereas the currency we might use to pay for it has value only in the extrinsic worth we assign to it. Well-being is an intrinsic measure of personal or national achievement, while GDP or personal wealth are extrinsic measures.

Similarly, intrinsic motivation involves taking an action for its inherent value, whereas extrinsic motivation is oriented towards a goal distinguishable from the action itself. Having the desire to garden because you enjoy being active in the sun and eating delicious watermelons with your children are examples of intrinsic motivation. But a desire to garden based in the belief that herbaceous borders will impress your neighbours and raise your property values is extrinsic motivation in action. Intrinsic values are those of personal growth, community cohesion, and well-being. Extrinsic values are the trappings and image of material 'success', such as the celebrity-style social status of hybrid vehicles.[44]

Research has shown that extrinsic rewards – especially money itself – can have a negative effect on intrinsic motivation.[45] If you reward a child with pocket money for good grades, will they continue to work hard when you're short on cash? The reward tactic may work for specific issues that happen to serve a person's self-interest at the moment – especially those that are local or visible. But if we encourage people to buy electric vehicles because they're cheaper, what happens when the price of oil goes down? As we see in the US, gas-guzzling SUVs once again become hot-sellers.

Crompton's plea for the importance of intrinsic motivation is supported by the work of Shalom Schwartz, who taught at the Hebrew University of Jerusalem, where Kahneman and Tversky collaborated. Conducting studies in almost seventy countries, Schwartz consistently found similar expressions of the same essential values around the world. But as we have seen, some cultures tend to value individualism, self-enhancement, and extrinsic goals, while others prioritise collectivism, self-transcendence, and intrinsic goals. This large body of research has shown that bigger-than-self values (such as universalism and benevolence) are difficult to pursue or even contemplate simultaneously with self-enhancing values (such as power and hedonism).[46]

By refocusing our cultural values on collective causes, we may be able to heal our societies physically and psychologically. Valuing the simple and communal things in life not only makes us better citizens but can make us happier and healthier. People who are oriented towards intrinsic values – the watermelon lovers – tend to have a better sense of well-being, engage in more pro-environmental behaviour, and have smaller carbon footprints.[47] Surrounding ourselves with nature increases our perception of the value of nature in and of itself. And natural settings can also enhance our interpersonal relationships. Time spent in beautiful natural environments encourages us to be more generous, empathetic, and helpful. The nature of our everyday spaces has great power to foster pro-social interaction and positive emotions.[48]

But the fact that we find we now spend our days and lives surrounded by toasters and digital billboards instead of butterflies and oak trees may be fundamentally reframing the way we perceive and think of the world. Spending less time among living things changes our outlook to thinking more functionally than perceptually – to value things extrinsically, including nature itself.

Semantic memory research has shown that we rely on perceptual information to process ideas about things that are alive. The idea of a leopard, for instance, will bring up the concept of spots. But thinking about a non-living thing like a toaster tends to activate functional information – probably toasting, unless you have found some other handy use for your toaster.[49] As we become more and more surrounded by things designed to do something for us – for us to use – we are strengthening these thought patterns. This functional framework may be making us see the world as something to use and consume rather than to take joy in or be part of.[50]

Our buildings and cities represent and reinforce the values of our societies. So do sterile skyscrapers and automated HVAC systems encourage us to value wealth and personal success over community and resilience?

The problem we keep encountering in applying rational choice models to sustainable development and behaviour is that the real dynamics are played out with humans rather than Econs. If we build cities for Econs rather than humans, we may end up being more like Econs ourselves. Do we want to be a society of self-centred, robotic beings who prioritise the wealth of the few over the well-being of the many? We can keep working within the traditional economic models, building the world to work out as they tell us it should. Or we can take a step back from what we are doing with our precious shared resources, and ask if it makes sense.

'Too much of this creates this', urban innovator Andrew Campbell explained to me, pointing to a photograph of sparkling high-rises looming over a sprawling sea of informal shacks and huts. His organisation, Massive Small, envisions alternative forms of ordered complexity for the shape of things to come, as we will soon examine further.

We do need to invest in dense, collective systems of housing and transportation. But we must do so in a way that is socially sustainable – from the micro-scale of well-being in a living space to the macro-scale of equality in housing affordability. Fixing the housing crisis will take more than big new buildings. It will take big policy changes to protect vulnerable renters from excessive rent hikes and unwarranted evictions. It will require new and creative ways of thinking about what housing means, how it fits into society, and how we distribute and cultivate land. We need a more diverse ecosystem of development. We need to build housing with the intrinsic goal of creating homes rather than the extrinsic goal of producing real estate. Of course, sustainable cities must be economically viable as well. But as we shall soon see, enabling people to house themselves can also help create more economically and environmentally resilient communities.

Cities are testaments to the collective efficacy of humankind – at least they have been historically. And the future of our cities is more critical and complex than a simple supply-and-demand formula might suggest. Just as sustainable buildings require more than smart meters and LED lighting to foster sustainable behaviour, a sustainable city is made of more than high-performance buildings. It is made of the people who live and move around the city; the natural world that surrounds it and runs through it

A truly sustainable building is a socially sustainable building; a place where people want to make a home, raise healthy children, and commune with their neighbours – just like the happy rats in Rat Park; an office so well-suited to its people and purpose that it doesn't need to be retrofitted every five years; an office that speaks to people about how to conserve resources and share ideas.

Sustainable structures provide the best return on investment through their durability, usability, and beauty. A resilient building is built to last, but is also flexible enough to adapt to change. Resilient cities are those that enable collective efficacy. And cities do this best when they are built with collective efficacy.

CHAPTER 8

The Shape of
Things to Come

Half a house, WikiHouse, and the IKEA Effect

As senseless police shootings ricocheted across American cities from Baton Rouge and Tulsa to Charlotte and Milwaukee in 2016, the Avon and Somerset Constabulary in the south-west of England opted for a radically different approach to policing. What if police forces invested in making cities safer by engaging communities in recreating their streets as better public places?

Inspired by the success of *woonerfs* and pocket parks from old to Nieuw Amsterdam, communities around the world have taken up liveable streets tools to make their public realm safer for walking, cycling, breathing, or simply being a child. But according to Georgie Burr of Sustrans, the St Pauls district of Bristol is the first place the sustainable transportation charity has taken on a project with the primary goal of making streets safer in terms of criminal activity.

In 2015, Rosa Parks Lane was a hotspot for what the British call anti-social activities (in the divergence of American and British English, 'anti-social' Americans somehow became people who don't like going to parties while anti-social Brits became drug-dealing vandals). Like her namesake, Rosa Parks Lane was quiet and unassuming – a little walkway, cutting through a neglected scrap of green space on the edge of St Pauls. Wedged between landowners, the lane had become overgrown with a thick curtain of vines, obscuring sight lines from the back windows of adjacent terraced houses and around the bend of the path itself (providing too much mystery, in this context). The lane became known in the neighbourhood as a place where people were selling crack under the cloak of the overgrowth. It suffered from what urbanist Jane Jacobs called not enough 'eyes on the street', a self-perpetuating problem that quickly escalates as people avoid a shrouded space, making it feel even less safe. People were afraid to walk and cycle through the lane, so it was also a broken link in Bristol's pedestrian and cycling network. The poor state of the path felt disrespectful towards its namesake.

And this is where Sustrans came in. The Bristol-based, UK-wide organisation works first and foremost to improve cycling networks and make it easier for people to get around without cars. Of course, this sort of change can take more than telling people statistics about car pollution and painting a few new bike lanes. 'We're invested in helping create communities where you don't just want to get in your car and zoom off', Georgie Burr, who was then a community engagement officer, explained to me in 2016. Working with communities to redesign their public streets and spaces, Sustrans discovered a secondary outcome: people felt safer. Human-centred street improvements work like a medication developed to treat one ailment that has an off-label benefit for another condition.

Word got around to Avon and Somerset police, who approached Sustrans with a proposal. They would fund the charity to trial a community engagement project in St Pauls, a 'high demand' area for policing time and resources. Burr worked with the St Pauls community to identify five key trouble spots, reimagine the design of these spaces, and test interventions.

Rosa Parks Lane was where Burr saw the greatest change. The physical adjustments themselves were quite simple. But simple changes can help build stronger communities, transforming how people interact in a space. Engagement activities helped connect local residents with an adjacent school and housing association – all of whom were suffering from the fear arising from the lane. People got together to cut down the vines, remove tagging, and organise monthly community clean-up days. They planted a wildflower meadow, hung bird boxes, and painted a rosy mural of Rosa Parks on a utility box. Further plans in collaboration with the city include removing the prison-bar style barriers at both entrances and calming traffic on bordering roads with coloured surfacing designed by local schoolchildren.

By late 2016, before permanent works were installed, the efforts had already paid off, according to Burr. 'Cutting the greenery in this lane has literally reduced crime,' she said. Neighbours – especially women – felt safer walking, cycling, and smelling the wildflowers in this newly colourful corridor.

Ironically, Sustrans can often see official crime data rise in transitioning spaces like Rosa Parks Lane because people feel empowered to tackle anti-social activity. Stronger communities are more likely to report crime and more likely to deal with crime themselves. 'By connecting people through disrupting their street, you enable them to come together, and maybe they realise they have a shared issue around concern with drug-dealing or housing conditions, and form a group to deal with it that has nothing to do with you,' says Burr. Temporary 'disruptions' like occupying a parking spot with a pop-up park can sow the seeds for community cohesion and pro-active growth. The transformation of Rosa Parks Lane was achieved, it seems, by bolstering the collective efficacy of the community.

So if collective efficacy is key to motivating both pro-environmental and pro-social behaviour, how can we strengthen or inspire more of it?

Collective efficacy and ordered complexity are two sides of the same coin. These twin forces are simple principles we can use to guide the creation and restoration of streets, buildings, and communities. They are tools to shape ourselves, our landscapes, and our future.

Setting out to study environmental psychology, I imagined I would discover perfect design solutions – that research would reveal the recipe for the ideal office and the healthy house. A legion of futuristic design and construction technologies now promise to bring biophilia back into our built environment. Some designers hope that 3D printers will enable us to ornament our window frames and building facades once again at little additional expense. Others are experimenting with 3D printing compounds combining concrete with resilient organic materials like algae. Meanwhile, well-being building certification programmes like the WELL building standard are helping to raise awareness about the importance of health and happiness in the built environment. Assembling this evidence base in an accessible framework is a great step forward. But similarly to LEED, the WELL standard may fall prey to technical, add-on solutions. It's easy to focus on superficial fixes like supplementing oversized corporate offices with water features.

Time and again, we find that fixating primarily on the details of physical design fails to produce successful spaces. Even the most exquisitely executed museum will encounter unforeseen usage patterns and challenges beyond the fantasy of the building as a perfect finished product. A shared-space street design that works wonderfully in the Netherlands may not play out the same way in the UK or the US.

'You can't rewrite the built environment by just changing the built environment,' architect and WikiHouse co-founder Alistair Parvin explained to me. 'You've got to lift up the bonnet and look at the economics that are the real forces that shape it.'

Whatever name we may choose to analyse and label these forces – economics, psychology, behaviour – we must rework them as well to reshape our world. Around the globe and from the micro scale to the macro, where we see collective efficacy and the ordered complexity it creates, we see wonderful cities, workplaces, and public spaces.

In December 2016, Tomiquia Moss, chief of staff to the mayor of Oakland, California, spoke about the housing crisis at a forum in San Francisco. 'It's not just about the intersection of housing and transportation, but access to educational outcomes, food, and health. What we're talking about is a problem where our communities are not whole, evidenced by the housing crisis.' She made these statements days after the devastating Ghost Ship fire left thirty-six dead in an informally settled artists' warehouse. 'There is no silver bullet,' Moss said. 'We need to be as creative, innovative, and nimble as possible.'

In what are supposedly the most successful cities and countries in the world, we ironically find ourselves locked in to trying to solve our current crises with the same tools that helped cause them. With great wealth, we often find poverty of creativity and innovation. The large structures, budgets, and regulations of big development are anything but nimble. The complex rules, regulations, and financial systems we have set up to keep our buildings risk-free may inadvertently push us into riskier places.

Massive animals once reigned as the mightiest creatures in the land. Those T-Rexes and mastodons must have thought they had really nailed the survival of the fittest game. Where are they now? Scientists generally believe that a giant asteroid hit the Gulf of Mexico sixty-five million years ago, setting off a series of catastrophic environmental changes visible in fossil records. Many now theorise that dinosaurs' great stature may have put them at a fatal disadvantage in this chaotic time. When the going gets tough, smaller species can adapt more nimbly to get by on less.[1]

One reason government agencies like the Avon and Somerset police are so fond of public-realm interventions like bike lanes and traffic-calming planters is that these human-scale tweaks can achieve much with a light touch. It's easy to try things out and learn before committing to a final decision. Our housing and public transportation infrastructures are more cumbersome beasts. Reworking them is complicated, costly, and difficult to undo. But surely there must be pioneering examples of projects recapturing the collective efficacy of ordered complexity in the domain of housing and urban development?

Like the people of Midwest, American thinking sometimes seems constrained by the rigid frameworks of professional, spatial, and legal structures. And like the Yoredalers who had more time for 'esthetic and muscular activities', British housing innovators are dreaming up a wonderfully complex and plucky array of solutions to the housing crisis. The US often looks longingly to European public housing models. Just like gun control and the disarmament of police officers it enables, there is no doubt that a good supply of affordable housing prevents senseless deaths and hardship. But British social housing has not been without its difficulties, and these are important lessons for all to learn from.

Housing provision in the UK is often framed as a problem of market versus state, painting as villains either the council housing of the post-war years or the market-rate development dominating since the Thatcher era. But the two models share an over-reliance on a single mode of housing production – a monoculture. And both have deprived their occupants of agency and efficacy.

'With housing estates, the state treated poor people as dependent consumers. But equally, the private sector version doesn't do that much differently. The difference is with poor people we build housing like filing cabinets for humans, whereas for rich people it's like a permanent hotel,' Alastair Parvin of WikiHouse told me. 'What they're doing is creating an incredibly fragile society and fragile humans.'

What if we could collectively create our cities and share resources as easily as we can edit Wikipedia pages? This is what Parvin and his colleagues at WikiHouse have set out to facilitate.

A Pattern Language may have had more substantial impact on *SimCity* than on real cities in the twentieth century, but the open-source technologies and frameworks it inspired are now finally enabling Alexander's vision to become a reality. WikiHouse is fostered under an organisation called 00 (pronounced 'Zero Zero'), whose strange name is 'a mystery to all and subject to personal interpretation', mine being that nihilistic robots from the future founded the collaborative studio in an effort to save humanity from destroying ourselves in the impending corporate robot takeover.[2]

I met Parvin at 00's Hackney studios, where he drew wonderful little pictures on tracing paper demonstrating how the horizon of the sky and sea may have been the only straight line known to humankind in ancient times.

'What most people call bad design isn't bad design,' said Parvin, 'It's really good design for a totally different set of economic outcomes, which is producing real estate.' Until we start driving housing production with the goal of housing people rather than producing real estate, it will continue to be badly designed for the social, environmental, and economic needs of everyday families. 'The housing crisis is mis-framed as a numbers game when it's not,' Parvin explained.

Highly developed nations ranging from the US and UK to China and Australia are not experiencing housing crises because it's technologically or financially impossible to build the required housing – these are some of the world's largest economies. It's because we are approaching the problem the wrong way around. For decades, we have relied on speculative, debt-dependent development. And the speculative development housing machine works by making a profit on land values. It's a system rigged to prioritise packaging housing units into smaller portions with higher price tags, planned obsolescence rather than good quality, and profit above well-being. The product of this system is somewhat like an anecdote Woody Allen tells in *Annie Hall*.

'Boy, the food at this place is really terrible,' one old woman says to another at a Borscht Belt resort.

'Yeah, I know,' the other replies, 'and such small portions.'

To which my inner Jewish grandmother adds, 'and so pricey!'

The housing crisis is not just a crisis of supply. It is a crisis of unaffordability, inequality, and poor quality – resulting in environmentally, economically, and socially unsustainable buildings. The housing crisis is the failure of a complex system. A perfect storm.

In the UK almost half of all new homes are built by just ten companies. So it's not very surprising that this lack of diversity in the ecology of our built environment generates a lack of ordered complexity. Imagine if a savannah once teeming with a variety of mammals, insects, and plant species came to be dominated solely by hyenas, cockroaches, and Bermuda grass. It would look odd. And moreover, it wouldn't be a sustainable ecosystem. According to a report by Parvin and Andy Reeve, *Scaling the Citizen Sector*, speculative development is often not feasible on small sites (defined as fewer than thirty units in the UK) – exactly the kinds of end bits in our urban fabric we most need to make use of. The nooks and crannies that can enliven a city when we plant tiny homes or businesses in them. The little pieces that bring complexity to the greater whole.

Parvin realised early on in his career that the best way to address the multiple problems of the housing crisis was to scale up what some call the 'citizen sector' – also known in Britain as self-build and custom-build. 'The moment you put the end user in charge of procuring their home, they are still procuring a financial asset in most cases, but they're primarily procuring the place they're going to live and bring up their kids,' said Parvin.

'Every country has an imperative to tackle climate change right now, but the only people with an economic incentive to put more insulation in the walls are the people who are going to pay the heating bills. Yet they're the only group we have yet to take seriously as a scalable force.'

And in a manner any good environmental psychology researcher would be proud of, Parvin and his colleagues set about addressing this problem by identifying the barriers to change. What issues were getting in the way of people taking a more active role in their own housing?

'It's too damn difficult' – too difficult for people to sell and procure land, figure out what they want to build, how to build it, and manage the whole timelessly time-consuming building process. Meanwhile, in a different part of their brains, 00 were always interested in the success of open source software like the wiki technology behind Wikipedia and the Linux operating system – technologies influenced by the *Pattern Language* model of an open source book created through many small contributions.

'We'd seen the way [open source] had transformed the software industry – what would that mean for architecture? And that loop didn't really close for us at 00 until we saw digital fabrication. We realised for the first time that you could share design solutions as code and replicate them as code. . . We realised these digital tools could solve the "too damn difficult" problem – going from experiment to a scalable digital supply chain, which companies and citizens can use to find each other and build better homes.'

Parvin hopes to do for housing development what Wikipedia and Airbnb have done for knowledge-sharing and hotel accommodation. Critically, WikiHouse combines the distributive potential of the open-source framework with the burgeoning possibilities of digital fabrication. We're at the dawn of what many are calling the fourth industrial revolution – a shift which people like Parvin believe will reshape society even more profoundly than steam trains and factories, hopefully for the better. Instead of organising our lives and towns around centralised factories and retail outlets, digital fabrication technologies like 3D printers and CNC machines hold the potential to redistribute where and how we make things ranging from houses to toothbrushes.

CNC machines (computer numerical controlled lathes) are the less sexy sister of the digital fabrication family. Everyone gushes about 3D printers – which have been used to 'print' multiple-storey buildings. But many architects are actually more excited about the potential of CNC machines. One of the key tools in the WikiHouse stack is a technology called WREN, which they describe as the first building system designed for open, digital manufacturing: a kind of digital Lego.

The desks in 00's studio – a little urban laboratory nestled in a barn-like industrial space – are strewn with miniature wooden models of the big Lego pieces that can be put together to build a WikiHouse. Though before all the Lego enthusiasts jump out of their seats it is important to note that they are not actually Lego or even block-shaped. They look a bit more like a cross between giant ice lolly sticks and Lincoln Logs (miniature, notched logs American children use to build model log cabins, which were invented by one of Frank Lloyd Wright's sons).

I will not pretend to understand the inner workings of this complex web of interconnected technologies. But WikiHouse's central platform is a community library of 3D models, which

A WikiHouse barn raising/WikiHouse CC BY

The completed WikiHouse barn/WikiHouse CC BY

share common design principles, and can also be freely shared. Anyone can use these tools to cut their very own Lego/Lincoln Log set using a material like structural plywood. And these can be easily put together without standard construction skills or power tools, using pegs and wedges hammered together with a wooden mallet, which you can also print.

The basic frame on the smallest WikiHouse can be put up like a barn by a few people in a single day. The larger, three- and four-storey creations they envision will require a bit more machine-power to assemble. Windows, shingles, toilets, and other trimmings can be added using local materials or additional printable pieces. Prototypes have been built in places like Haiti, Washington State, and Korea. But WikiHouse means much more than a nifty, high-performance plywood house.

Like Wikipedia, WikiHouse is meant to function as an open community library, which people can borrow from, add to, and build upon: 'a full, open, urban development model'.

'Housing is not a noun, housing is a verb,' says Parvin, quoting architect and self-building advocate, John Turner. 'We flip from seeing houses as objects, assets, to seeing them as a continuous process of supporting peoples' lives.'

WikiHouse and a growing number of other projects like it actively engage citizens in the process of housing. In other words, WikiHouse is a platform for collective and self-efficacy. It puts the power of vernacular building and piecemeal growth back into the hands of everyday people.

When instant cake mixes made their supermarket debut in the 1950s, American housewives were initially suspicious. These boxes of floury powder promised to make cake-baking as easy as pie – well, much easier than pie, actually. Cake mixes were too easy. The manufacturers discovered that requiring the addition of an egg instilled the process with just enough effort to make the housewives happy with their work. To feel they had indeed 'baked the cake'. The cake also looked and tasted better. And handling the egg was an enjoyable biophilic act – what other food has such an iconic and primal form? Various factors may have played a role, but the greater sense of effort gained from a little extra labour is believed to have been essential to the subsequent success of the cake mix.[3]

While we might imagine that taking on greater labour, costs, and time would lessen the value of a chair or cake, the reverse seems to be the case. We place greater value on things we have worked to create. The IKEA effect, as this phenomenon has been called by business psychologist Michael I. Norton and his colleagues, may not be as counterintuitive as it first appears. People typically say their jobs are less enjoyable than other activities they engage in, like spending time with friends or going out for a meal. But they also tend to rank their work as one of the most rewarding activities.[4] A wide range of research into this seemingly contradictory attitude has consistently confirmed that as we expend more effort on a particular activity or piece of work, we also value it more highly. Even rats, our favourite old animal stand-ins for human nature, prefer food sources that they have to work harder to acquire.[5]

Norton and his colleagues conducted four studies in which they asked participants to fold origami cranes and frogs, assemble IKEA boxes, and even build 'sets of Legos' (as the American researchers refer to them). They then asked the builders to bid for their creations, and compared the prices with bids and other evaluative measures from people who hadn't built them. The builders consistently out-bid the non-builders. 'Labour leads to love,' as the researchers wrote, but only when tasks are successfully completed. When people had failed in their attempts to fold paper cranes and construct Lego sets, the IKEA effect weakened – as it also did when they were forced to dismantle their creations. Intriguingly, the IKEA effect works even when people have no opportunity to personalise their creations – as with the IKEA boxes and Lego sets. While most participants' origami skills left much to be desired, they loved their imperfectly personalised products all the more. Builders valued their crumpled crane-like creations nearly five times as much as non-builders. Beauty is in the eye of the builder.

'The moment people are involved with their built environment they have a totally different relationship to it,' said Parvin. When the roof starts leaking or a door starts creaking, they have the power to fix it themselves. And this self-efficacy may start to spill over into other areas of their lives. 'They don't have to grow the trees. But with IKEA people feel more attached. Strangely, people think things like WikiHouse are about choice. Actually, people don't want as much choice. They want the freedom to customise, but don't necessarily want the burden of choice over it.'

Having lived through (and in) a self-build process first-hand, I can agree that the IKEA effect may plateau at a certain point. After the third readjustment of unruly floorboards, one starts to develop some less than positive feelings towards these creations.

Looking back at the success of co-working spaces, Hogeweyk, and Monderman's shared-space streets, we could say these spaces are successful because they are flexible. They are responsive to their users. They allow people to interact with each other, to find their way, and potentially even shape the space. They enable choice, within limits.

But have you have ever actually tried to edit a Wikipedia page? If you are not so comfortable with lifting up the HTML bonnet of your webpages, you may have discovered that it's not as easy to edit as you thought. Wikipedia does not employ what is called a WYSIWIG (What You See Is What You Get) editing tool. What you see is not what you get. In the same way, most people don't want too many choices and options. They need a framework to be flexible within.

In the early 2000s, Chilean architect Alejandro Aravena found himself faced with a seemingly impossible task: build housing for a hundred families on a 464-square-foot (5,000-square-metre) inner-city plot with a budget of only £5,764 ($7,500) per dwelling. That standard government subsidy had to cover not only the costs of construction and infrastructure, but the land itself. And since this land, on which the families had been squatting for thirty years, was in the city centre, it was nearly three times as expensive as the suburban land usually used for social housing. Completed in 2004, the Quinta Monroy development in the northern port city of Iquique was the first project fully realised for Aravena's firm, Elemental.

Parvin calls himself a strategic designer while Aravena calls himself a participatory designer, by which they seem to mean much the same thing. Elemental defines itself as a 'do tank' rather than an architecture firm.[6] "'No one should be interested in the design of bridges",' says Parvin, citing architectural insurgent, Cedric Price. '"They should be concerned with how to get to the other side." We should be less interested in hospitals and more interested in health.'[7]

By carrying out in-depth community consultation and analysing the economic, political, and zoning landscape, both Parvin and Aravena believe their profession can better understand the questions they are trying to answer, rather than merely supplying new versions of answers to the wrong questions. In Aravena's case, the answer was to build half a house. But not just any half: 'half a good house,' as they called the project.

Operating within the constraints of such a tight budget, something had to give. Working with the families, Aravena's team realised that squatting came along with great self-building skills and experience. Most families had the resources within their networks to take on minor construction and decorating work themselves. The true skeleton and organs of a house – the structural walls, kitchen, and bathroom – must be robust. With this sturdy framework in place, each family filled in the remaining portion. Leaving room for growth was critical to truly solving the social problem presented by Quinta Monroy rather than just the architectural answer to the question of how to build X houses with Y budget.

Quinta Monroy's residents were able to personalise their homes according to the needs of their family structures, aesthetic preferences, and budgets. They also had room to evolve from being economically struggling families into comfortable, middle-class families. Not having ample room to accommodate a multiplying, extended family, the designers discovered, had been a critical barrier to the economic growth of poor families.

Instead of being limited by the confines of tiny kitchens and bathrooms associated with housing for the poor, Quinta Monroy families could redefine their space as they redefined their lifestyles. The result was a housing form that is not so far from the classic British terraced house. But like Goldilocks, they had to try out the more extreme options before arriving at this happy medium. The detached home model – common in subsidised housing relegated to cheaper, sprawling, suburban land in Chile – would only accommodate thirty families on the site.[8]

High-rise housing would have efficiently accommodated all hundred families on the land. But in addition to the negative impact on well-being, mental health, and social consequences known to accompany high-rise housing for low-income families, Aravena and his team foresaw another problem. The high-rise is a stubborn, inflexible form of building. It does not enable its inhabitants to extend and adjust their living space as easily as smaller, less structurally intensive buildings. The high-rise is not a nimble creature. So they finally settled on a simple form – three-storey rows of houses, gathered in groups of twenty families and arranged around central collective courtyards. And they weren't joking about the half-a-house thing. Beyond a continuous, first-floor structure connecting the row, there was literally a gap half the width of the house between each unit when the families received them. The initial look was somewhat stark: a set of concrete teeth rising up from the Chilean desert.

Materials were chosen carefully to allow for the right balance of grounding structure and growth potential. Building the exoskeleton with concrete blocks rather than frames was an important decision, for example, complemented by wood for flexible elements such as non-structural walls. Families quickly took the shaping of their homes into their own hands. One group built out a balcony on the first floor, while another had theirs on the second floor. Some put in ornate bay windows and wood-frame siding, while others opted for bright turquoise and pink paints. Inside, they gradually laid tiles of their choosing, arranged the space to meet their needs, and populated their new home with the trappings of their lives. Gradually, they brought complexity to the orderly frames they began with.

Crucially, Elemental wanted social housing to be valued as an investment rather than an expense. And their hard work seems to have paid off. According to Aravena, all of Elemental's projects have tripled in value.[9] By contrast, conventional subsidised Chilean housing declines in value over time, due to poor quality and location.

'Quality is a property that gains value with time,' Aravena said in an interview with *Dezeen*. 'Housing designed that way is not just a shelter against the environment, it's a tool to overcome poverty.'[10]

With houses like those in Quinta Monroy, the Chilean government has invested in these families as well as enabling them to invest in the creation of their own future – an asset that Aravena suggests can enable these families to get a loan for something like starting a small business. The incremental model has now evolved far past its humble beginnings in Iquique. Elemental have built 2,500 units in places ranging from Monterey, Mexico, to a prototype for the Make it Right Foundation's project providing housing in New Orleans in the wake of Hurricane Katrina. In the process they have adjusted the form to range from cheerful rows of red peaked roofs to an elegant white-washed version.

Elemental's Villa Verde half-houses in Constitución, Chile
© Image courtesy of Felipe Diaz Contardo

Critically, Elemental have made the plans for four incarnations of incremental housing available for download from their website, so that others can make use of them in the open sharing model that WikiHouse hopes to spread.[11]

While architects like Aravena and Parvin design to empower the collective creation of ordered complexity, others are revolutionising urban development and government policy. One London-based social enterprise is assembling a network of innovators, organisers, and governments from around the world who are working to bring about this kind of change on what they call a 'massive small scale'. Massive Small's mission is essentially to reignite Christopher Alexander's timeless way of building for the twenty-first century.

'It's how we developed cities for millennia,' executive director Andrew Campbell explained. 'It's only in the last hundred years or so that we've lost the art.'

In 1965, Alexander wrote an essay, confusingly titled 'A City is Not a Tree'. Alexander – and related urban thinkers like Jane Jacobs and complexity theorist Michael Batty – generally seem to be telling us that cities are naturally similar to fractal patterns of ordered complexity like those we see in trees. But Alexander was referring to the mathematical idea of a tree *diagram*, where you take two categories of things – say people and cars – and devise separate pathways for each of them. This was the approach to city planning that modernists like Le Corbusier and Louis Kahn advocated. The great visions they drew – of rational, linear cities – segregated living areas from leisure and working functions and placed them each in their own neat box.

Our innate, fast-thinking instinct to divide information into simple categories helped our survival in the environments in which we evolved, but has not served us well as we became increasingly powerful crafters of our own environs. Modern urban development has often been less than successful. The model of handing big parcels of land over to large developers to create masterplans and build in one fell swoop has rarely been able to produce whole and healthy places. The core problem is that we have constricted the organic growth of cities by trying to plan and control them too precisely. The master-planning process is expensive, slow, and leaves much-needed land vacant for long periods. Their outcomes – such as the British new towns – have tended to have a static quality which renders them unable to respond to social and economic life. This monolithic model doesn't work in terms of the scale and pace of creation.

From luxurious gated communities to council estates, giant projects have a self-destructive habit of trying to control every outcome.

Many of the South African government's well-meaning attempts to bring order and infrastructure to informal settlements have backfired because 'in a sense they've tried to prescribe where all the leaves are on the tree, rather than focusing on understanding the branches – the conditions that lead to the emergence of the leaves,' Campbell explained to me. They tried to impose too much order. And, as we've seen with the fractal nature of trees and other organisms, this isn't an ideal order of things for us – or most other living things.

One of the concepts underlying the Massive Small revolution is complexity theory, which boils down to understanding that 'a few simple conditions give rise to highly complex conditions in the future'. Twentieth-century planners tried to approach this complex and intertwined system as if it were a simple equation, say, $X + Y = Z$, assuming that the proper ingredients will consistently deliver the desired outcome of Z. Planners tried to model the living, growing organism of the city with the rational calculations of a machine.

'But actually what we find in complex systems is that all of these different, interacting factors affect each other over time, creating outcomes that can't be predicted,' said Campbell. 'You can't necessarily tell what's going to come out of the end of a complex system. And if you try and apply a linear, conveyor belt methodology to a complex system, you get weird outcomes that weren't anticipated.' Like the growth patterns of mycelia and flights of starlings, cities, at their best, are self-organising systems of collective behaviour.

'Cities, as part of societies and economies, not only hold together without any top-down control but actually evolve their own coordination from the bottom up, their order emerging from these millions of relatively uncoordinated decisions,' Michael Batty wrote, in his 2008 essay on the fractal structure of cities.[12] Even Haussmann didn't fill in all the lines at once in his modernisation of Paris. He planned out grand streets and avenues, but left space for these to be developed piece by piece with smaller buildings originating from various sources.[13]

'When you create too little order in a space, you don't create innovation or bottom-up activity from the people. Then when you try and create too much order you get these weird outcomes and the space doesn't work,' explained Campbell. 'It's just the right amount of order the government needs to put in place to get the maximum amount of output from people. It's like the Goldilocks story.'

What does the right amount of order look like? As we are often reminded, fifty-four per cent of the world's 7.3 billion people now live in urban areas. The majority of the next billion people on the planet will live in cities, and many estimate that the bulk of urban growth in the next decade will happen in 'informal' settlements like those we find around Mumbai and Lima.[14] And with increasing numbers of homeless people and refugees in European and North American cities, the secrets to successful incremental urban development may be needed in unsuspected places. A total lack of order in these areas runs the risk of devastating disaster. When fires start, as they often do with improvised electrical wiring, they quickly spiral out of control in the absence of water systems and clear pathways, wiping out entire areas.

The solution? Governments can lay the groundwork for growth by establishing American-style grid systems, delineating different plots of land while keeping clear access ways. As people develop the area and it grows to become a more formal settlement, the grid will provide a framework to add infrastructure – such as proper electrical systems to stop fires starting, water to put fires out, and other great wonders of the modern world like electric lighting. This creates breathing room and enables a safe exit strategy. The incremental approach has had great results in places like Peru, Burkina Faso, and Mauritania, as covered in Massive Small's manifesto, 'The Radical Incrementalist'.

But aren't street grids a bit square and inorganic? Didn't we find that American four-way intersections bring us head-to-head in traffic accidents? That long-stretching straight roads drive us to speed and bore us to death? It's the general structure of the grid that's critical, Campbell explains, but 'the grid can get modified by context and that's good; that makes it more exciting'. A grid doesn't have to take the chequerboard form of square blocks lacking a natural hierarchy of street traffic volume, as we find in some US cities. In fact, it probably shouldn't.

Based on the historical success of adaptive grid patterns – used from the times of Roman military camps to Savannah, Georgia in the US and Belhar, South Africa – Massive Small suggest long rectangular blocks in a 2:1 ratio of length to width. These may be flexibly adapted to create an array of varied street structures, including a wonderful pinwheel formation with a central public square, and T-junctions – bringing a bit more of that mystery we are so fond of in our environments. Going a step further, governments and other top-down actors can seed a site with resource- or engineering-intensive elements like toilets or structural walls running part of the width between two lots in these blocks. These structural walls could provide a bone structure for people to start building their dwellings. They would become a stabilising framework to support the first stages of growth, expanding with many little structures over time.

'At the end of the day it's the people who are going to make those decisions and it's OK if one guy wants to stick his window the other way,' said Campbell. 'It's part of the fine-grained natural quality, and that's a good thing – individuality.' As we saw with the half-houses, the optimum level of order requires planting a tree in the right place, giving it water, and maybe even a trellis to climb on. The tree then has the freedom to grow in its own magnificent, unpredictable complexity.

Ordered complexity on the streets of Manhattan © author.

So what is the way forward? The Massive Small Collective is uniting people around the world to share lessons, build collective efficacy, and join together to achieve the big changes we need through many small, distributed projects. And the product of these collective processes is ordered complexity.

Cycling through the eerily quiet Mitte district of Berlin in the summer of 2016, I came across a street of row houses that stopped me in my tracks. Each house in the long stretch of five- and six-storey townhouses had the fresh look of recent construction. And their newness was striking in contrast to the fact that each house was completely unique: a rainbow variety show of giant, green-glass windows and little portholes, modern minimalism and simple yellow brick, French balconies and rooftop gardens. At least one or two were, frankly, quite ugly. But it didn't matter, because the fine-grained variation upon a theme was so delightful as a whole.

The Berlin Mitte townhouses, it turns out, are an example of what Campbell considers one of the best success stories of top-down intervention combined with bottom-up development to create massive small change. The Mitte model is quite similar to the grid and subdivision framework for informal settlements, scaled to a different social and economic context. Instead of selling off a whole block of land to a private developer, Berlin's government sub-divides it into smaller lots, which they invite people to submit Kickstarter-style proposals for, and sell off as cheaply as possible.[15] Approximately sixty per cent of German housing is self-built, including co-housing models like the *baugruppen*, which enable groups of families to pool their resources for larger developments.[16]

'The Radical Incrementalist' suggests that citizen-driven approaches can save the families who live in them as much as forty per cent of what they would pay for a market-rate developer to do the dirty work.[17] 'The mayor of Berlin finds that he actually balances his budget more effectively with this model because he has the space developed quickly, he's got families on the land paying their council tax, and he's also got socially stable families, which provides a variety of benefits in the long run or even medium term,' Campbell explained.

There's no need to reinvent the wheel. Or the townhouse. The Berlin approach is just a twenty-first-century hack to get back to how great cities like London, New York, and Paris were built in the first place – through the collective action of many small builders. Looking at a row of similar terraced houses in London or Lower East Side tenements in New York, you'll notice that the brickwork and ornamentation varies from house to house and block to block: ordered complexity, the product of collective efficacy.

'We don't like to walk down a street where everything is completely standardised,' said Campbell. 'It's eerie, it makes us feel like we're not wonderful special little snowflakes, which in fact we are'.

Berlin has also been a leader in pioneering projects where communities of artists, 'green punks', and other innovators have been able to transition from temporary uses of valuable urban land to the collective development of larger urban areas. On the same visit to Berlin I had the opportunity to see one of these success stories, the Holzmarkt 'village', under construction. City officials had planned to develop this prime part of the river Spree waterfront as a media centre – using standard, top-down development methods to create what would have likely been a string of glass office towers, as like each other as they are like those found in New York or Hong Kong.

When Juval Dieziger and his friends first came upon the space, it was a forgotten piece of urban land which neither the city government nor private investors had any interest in. 'It was like between the concrete the trees were growing again and the trees were growing in squares,' he told me. Like many Berliners, they were looking for a place to party. But they wanted to dance outside. 'We had one rule in the Bar 25 [venue] that no trees were cut. On the dance floor we had a tree in the beginning.'

Using excess wood from nearby sites of construction and destruction, they built a club and restaurant, sleeping huts, and community spaces. Transitioning from this 'temporary use' to the long-term right to develop the site was more complicated. But Juval and his merry band were a crafty bunch. They narrowly secured the winning auction bid on the site through a classic poker bluff. After consistently claiming they could afford no more than a certain amount, they showed their winning hand at the last minute, outbidding the other hopeful buyers. Then came the trickier process of collectively managing the design, development, and financing of the space.

Juval and his group were inspired by the Tower of David, a forty-five-storey office complex in Caracas whose story is a parable to rival its namesake in Jerusalem. Construction on the tower, which was intended as a banking headquarters, was abruptly halted by the death of its main financial backer, David himself, in the midst of the mid-'90s Venezuelan banking industry collapse. Left as a concrete skeleton, the tower was stormed by settlers from Caracas's informal-dwelling population, who took it over as a vertical city believed to have reached a population of five thousand.

Researchers like Jean Caldieron have chided the architecture community for glamourising the Tower of David, which he says did not enjoy the community spirit and collective efficacy found in many of Caracas's more horizontal informal settlements. The tower was represented rosily at the Venice Biennale, but *Homeland*'s portrayal of it as the empire of a powerful drug cartel may have some basis in truth – minus the kidnapping-of-Damian-Lewis bit.[18]

Like the Venice Biennale judges, Juval and his friends were inspired by the idea of a skeletal form that could be populated over time. Holzmarkt's financial backers, however, were not so enthusiastic about this vision of incremental development. If the Holzmarkt group went bankrupt and the bank had to sell the building, what would they have to sell?

'You have to understand the laws of capitalism,' Juval told me. 'That's why everything looks the same now – because it's all built by banks.'

They found ways to compromise their desires with the bank's requirements. The tree-loving clubbers realised that building all their structures as little wooden huts wasn't practical. Their kindergarten building is a blocky, concrete structure, playfully splashed with bright colours and the wide open jaws of a tiger face chomping on a window. In the process of managing a multi-million-euro-project, they have also faced some of the same difficult dilemmas and realities as those big developers.

'It's also changed my mind,' says Juval. 'Before we would always say, "Oh, these bad developers!" But it's true – it costs what it costs.' Holzmarkt, along with an adjacent project called Eckwerk, is an impressive demonstration that a citizen group can successfully lead urban development, contributing to the growth of the city in a way that invests and builds upon its own special strengths rather than a one-size-fits-all solution. 'Most people who come here say, "Ah, this is only possible in Berlin," but it's not true. You need definitely to fight,' says Juval.

So can projects like this provide a role model for other cities?

The post-industrial powerhouses of Berlin and Detroit have shared much with each other, from electronic music to DIY city regeneration strategies. In Detroit, the realisation that there would be no one big solution to these big problems came early. The decline of the city was already well under way in the 1980s when General Motors announced plans to build the first new car-manufacturing plant in the city for more than fifty years. The GM plant promised to revitalise the depressed inner city with thousands of jobs by replacing an out-dated Cadillac facility slated to shut down on the other side of town. To avoid the prospect of losing yet another major employer from the city, Mayor Coleman A. Young signed on, using eminent domain (the US equivalent of a compulsory purchase order) to buy and raze 1,500 homes, churches, and business in an area called Poletown, relocating the 3,400 former residents.[19]

Poletown had once been a thriving Polish-American neighbourhood, known as one of the last working-class, white strongholds in the inner city. Like other parts of the city, it was past its prime. But many said the neighbourhood shone with a special inter-ethnic harmony between Polish, Albanian, Latino, and African-Americans in tired and tense Detroit.

'In many ways I think Poletown was a turning point because all of the promises that were made never came through,' Sharon 'Shea' Howell, co-founder of Detroit Summer and the Boggs

Center to Nurture Community Leadership, told our Paper Tiger team in 2010. 'People really thought that it was all right to flatten an entire community because they actually believed that the Cadillac plant would hire enough people to justify destroying all those lives and all that property and all that memory.' But the plant didn't ultimately create as many jobs as promised – robots were already taking over manual labour in the '80s – a now familiar story. With all those employees gone, the plant didn't generate the additional economic activity anticipated. And it certainly didn't save the city. Yet top-down leaders and investors still clung to the hope that centralised, monolithic projects like monorails and sports stadiums could breathe life into Detroit.

Labour activists started to realise they could no longer look to big companies and factories to generate the resources needed to feed and heal their communities. Legendary labour leader Grace Lee Boggs attributed this to the early failures of the corporate industrial system, 'In Detroit, because of the demonstration of deindustrialisation, we recognise that we have to re-imagine work. We have to re-imagine how we relate to one another, that the jobs that paid us income also turned us into consumers and robbed us of some of our creativity . . . of our relationship to community.'[20]

As Detroit descended into bankruptcy, shutting down services and buildings, communities took matters into their own hands. Detroit has become a front-runner in 're-routing' the dysfunctional structures of the old city. The distributed, citizen-driven economy that Parvin envisions is already in full swing – using organic fabrication technologies like apple trees and bee hives as much as their digital equivalents. Beneath the post-industrial surface of the city lies a thriving network of food and labour activism, DIY maker-spaces, and creative reuse of the urban fabric.

One of the most basic ways to build collective efficacy and ordered complexity is by enabling people to grow and cook their own food again: 'The initiation of this urban gardening movement was started about twenty years ago, primarily by older African-American women who had roots in the south, who called themselves the gardening angels,' Shea Howell explained. 'It was about community memory, about beauty, and about how do you make a place have meaning? But it was also about food because Detroit is officially a food desert.'

These urban gardening projects have been so successful that corporate investors like the Hantz Farms group started to take interest in large-scale urban farming projects in Detroit. And with urban farming, how could you go wrong? Bringing the nourishing, biophilic properties of fruit trees and green beans back into the ailing city sounds like a win-win solution. But the problem with large-scale industrial farming is that, like the Poletown plant, it now relies on robots and other automated processes to do much of the work. Many of Detroit's small-scale farmers carried the familial memory of share-cropping servitude. Their families had broken free from working on former plantations in the south when they came to Detroit in the Great Migration of African-Americans to urban industrial centres during World War II. The last thing they wanted now was to go back to working on a big, top-down farm.

Does it matter whether ordered complexity and collective efficacy are motivated from the top down or bottom up? The best projects, according to Andrew Campbell, are those that come from the bottom but also receive support from the top. Projects such as Sustrans's work at Rosa Parks Lane are not without their issues. Georgie Burr worries that work like this may simply move 'undesirable' activities to other areas rather than dealing with the root of the problem.

'It's hard to talk about innovation when people just want more money for their youth centres and don't want their housing to be damp.' The police-funded effort is to some extent a top-down initiative. But it also reflects the rich history of street art, sustainable urban innovation, and creative interaction with the city landscape that very much originated from the bottom up in Bristol. And community members are taking their own steps to regenerate the public realm alongside the Sustrans project.

Tired of avoiding a different troubled alleyway in St Pauls, Michele Curtis took matters into her own hands with a paintbrush and a vision of jungle animals. Lions, giraffes, and a little elephant family filed in to brighten the dark brickwork, all set in an open savannah scene dotted with acacia trees. Michele is a small woman, fond of bright colours, who sparkles with as much energy as her creations. She grew up in the Afro-Caribbean community of Bristol's Easton and St Pauls neighbourhoods and rediscovered her artistic talents recently after a career change led her to enrol in a graphic design course. When a friend suggested she draw something for Black History Month, she was inspired to create portraits honouring the overlooked heroes of Bristol's black community.

'Why look to America for black icons, when we have so many on our doorstep that I wanted to recognise and celebrate?' she recalled.[21]

Bristol is known worldwide today as the birthplace of Banksy, or at least his signature street-art style. But in its heyday as England's second largest city, Bristol was called 'the city that made America' because of its major role in sending British ships to the New World, many of which were involved in the notorious triangle trade. The wealth and growth of the city were inextricably tied up with the slave trade and many of Bristol's landmark streets, buildings, and statues still bear the names of slave merchants and owners. Curtis wanted to revise the environment of her city to tell a different story about black history, rather than the negative mainstream images associating St Pauls with crime and drug-dealing. Stories about people like Roy Hackett, a Bristolian counterpart to Rosa Parks. Hackett helped organise the 1963 Bristol bus boycott which successfully overturned the Bristol Omnibus Company's discriminatory practices against hiring people of colour.

Curtis is working to bring these stories to the walls of St Pauls through a visionary public mural project she calls 'The Seven Saints of St Pauls'. People walking through St Pauls can learn about Roy Hackett and other iconic black Bristolians through seven murals of Michele's portraits spread around the neighbourhood. The Seven Saints of St Pauls celebrates the unique impact that iconic black Bristolians have had on the city – the positive distinctiveness of St Pauls. Bringing together memory, history, and creation, projects like this inspire young people and strengthen collective efficacy.

The Sustrans project worked like a prescription for liveable streets with off-label relief for anti-social activities. And this is a good tool to have in our environmental medicine chests. But bottom-up projects like Michele's hold the potential to enhance the well-being of our communities so we don't need to be medicated in the first place.

When it comes to health itself, more of this kind of innovation is needed as well. One cloudy day in August 2016, Tim Ahrensbach took me on a tour of 00's latest experiment at the intersection of co-working spaces and well-being. The Health Foundry is an incubator for digital health start-ups created in collaboration with Guys and St Thomas' Charity in London. At some point after their mysterious genesis, 00 became co-working tenants at Impact HUB Islington. Their journey as a practice has blossomed through the evolution of the British Impact HUBs and the broader co-working model as they became architects of the King's Cross branch as well as operators and co-owners at the Westminster, Brixton, and Islington locations.

The Health Foundry represents a new phase, in which 00 were commissioned to deliver the whole package, not just as workspace designers and operators, but to apply their wider design thinking and urban regeneration philosophy, and combine that into a space. When it comes to workspaces, 00 are experts in achieving the right balance between order and complexity, collective and self-efficacy.

'We have an informal, what we call the 60:40 design rule. The sixty per cent is basically the outline, the perimeters of what you're designing, and then the first specs of colour to guide what you do. And the forty per cent is what you design with the community over time', Ahrensbach explained. 'So people come in and it feels almost unfinished, but there is an openness to allow people, with you, to come up with what that then is.'

The Health Foundry space in Lambeth, London, certainly felt unfinished on the day of my visit. The workmen were hard at work hammering and drilling, but Ahrensbach assured me the first team would be moving in within a few days. Bringing users into the space would allow them to get feedback on issues like sound quality and layout. To test out the space in real time – or, shall we say, space.

But certain issues – the colour scheme, for instance – fall squarely in the sixty per cent that the designers established at the outset. In this case, a minimal, white palette with mild blue and orange accents, including a flock of crane-necked architect's lamps.

'You don't want people to say, "I want X colour," because that's not relevant.'

Soliciting open input on issues like colour scheme is a well-known faux pas, leading into a quagmire of squabbling over personal preferences. 'But how do we make this yours? How do we make it the community's?'

The Health Foundry represents the next generation of co-working spaces as entities that can help us fundamentally redefine things like the way work and health fit into our lives. It scales up from shared workspace for freelancers to a model that helps big institutions like Guy's and St. Thomas' Charity foster a 'massive small' model for health innovation, and repurpose underused spaces in big hospital facilities. Bringing more diverse activity into this part of Lambeth – monopolised by giant institutional buildings and mammoth roundabouts – should also support urban regeneration.

Beyond serving as a collaborative work and incubation space, the Health Foundry aims to function as a crossroads, drawing in different stakeholders from Guy's and St Thomas' hospital and beyond. Health start-ups, especially digital ones, rely on involving all sorts of people in the design and development process. That means doctors and nurses, but also patients. Ideally, the Health

Foundry would like to improve and support people's well-being before they get to the point of being patients. One initiative they envision to help facilitate this is transforming an abandoned play space in front of the Foundry into a garden, where local GPs can prescribe gardening activities for their patients.

'What's really exciting is that the client, the charity is really seeing this as a massive learning opportunity,' said Ahrensbach. 'This has a dual impact for them – on the start-ups and supporting them – but it's also learning that they would never gain if they had commissioned research for the same amount of money.'

Can this help transform how we design and manage health-care spaces? Ahrensbach sees bringing people who are traditionally thought of as being on different sides of the health equation together – redefining their roles – as a big part of this. 'The vision is to break down this idea of who is a health provider and who is a person that needs health support,' he said. The bigger step of course is to bring health out of hospitals and into our everyday lives – something that both gardening prescriptions and digital health initiatives may be able to support.

How can we rebuild the world we want to be defined by? Was Winston Churchill right when he said, 'We shape our buildings, and afterwards our buildings shape us'?

We are shaped by our homes, cities, and workspaces. But we have lost the agency we once had in shaping these spaces. Collectively, however, we hold the power to reshape our lives, society, and well-being through the ordered complexity of our small, collected actions. What motorways, high-rises, huge hospitals, and immense open-plan offices all have in common is that they don't tend to enable collective efficacy. Speeding down a ten-lane super-highway, we don't want people to spontaneously negotiate their paths as they do in a shared-space intersection. This isn't to say that we shouldn't have any highways. But as these fast-paced and super-scaled structures take over more of our world, we have less collective efficacy as a society. And, as we saw in Midwest and Yoredale, when our everyday spaces don't support autonomy, we become expendable people, a disengaged society.

Do we want to build bigger hospitals and more prisons? Or do we want to create homes, streets, and public spaces supporting a society that won't need as many hospitals and prisons? What are the big and small ways we can shape our own paths and destinies? How can we rewrite the secret scripts of our lives?

We can't all have half a house. And not everyone is cut out to take on the timeless (time-consuming) way of building for themselves. But we all have half-finished spaces in our lives. The empty lots and blank walls of our homes, streets, offices, and gardens are waiting to be enlivened. And in rewriting these spaces, we also redefine ourselves – not as helpless consumers or angry NIMBYs, but as builders of a resilient world.

How can you bring ordered complexity into your own home, workspace, or street? What little actions can we take to contribute to the greater transformation of our communities exemplified by the work of WikiHouse, Massive Small, and Detroit's urban farmers? The simple act of making a space your own elevates daily life – functionally and psychologically. Bring order to your desk and bedroom, but don't be afraid to embroider these places with the beautiful complexity of life. Paint walls in colours you love, build your own bookshelves, and populate your space with personal touches and glowing lamps.

Question whether the layout of your workplace works for the people and purpose of that space, whether your street functions as a public space or a parking lot, and how unequally land may be divided in your community and country.

Create little ecosystems. Consider how you arrange a room in terms of refuge and prospect, craft semi-sheltered nooks, and make the most of natural elements like light and views. Carve human-sized spaces out of oversized offices and intersections.

Bring biophilia and creativity into the built environment – from fostering wildflowers and birdhouses in neglected pockets of the urban fabric to sharing a simple bowl of seasonal fruit with your office-mates. Invite people into underused spaces with enticing seats, nourishing food, and inspiring murals. Connect the inside with the outside. Manipulate lighting to reflect the changing intensity, direction, and colour of the sun.

In all these realms, you can balance order and complexity, mystery and legibility, comfort and awe, individual and collective space. We need quiet corners to retreat to and replenish energy, as well as commons for the creative work ahead. Make space to meet your neighbours, share your garden with friends, and consider the needs of those who have less space.

Shifting to a collective way of cultivating our everyday spaces gives communities the power to re-orient their values. And like fractal patterns of self-organising systems, these small changes reverberate at the macro-scale of how we interact with the planet as a species.

To build a resilient future, we must take an active role in the shaping of our own environments – the shaping of us.

Acknowledgements

This book owes a great deal to many people, beginning with my parents for their loving support and encouragement in the journey of writing it, and the many other journeys that led to it. Thank you to my mother, Melissa Riley, for never tiring of tracking down obscure library books and hashing ideas out late into the night. And to my father, Alan Bernheimer, for his invaluable editorial insights, and for inspiring me to write.

Thanks to my agent Kirsty McLachlan and my editor Andrew McAleer, who helped me craft the many ideas and experiences of this book into a coherent story, and to the other talented people at Little, Brown who helped produce it, especially Lucian Randall and Amanda Keats. And I am grateful to have had the pleasure of collaborating with illustrator Grace Exley.

Many thanks to my 'peer reviewers', Paul Duguid, Max Jacobson, Fin McNab, Alice Shay, and Lindsay Taylor Graham, who lent their valuable time and insights to reading and commenting on various chapters. I am incredibly grateful to the many others I spoke with in the process of writing and researching, whose work and insights were deeply influential, including Alistair Parvin, Andrew Campbell, Georgie Burr, Tim Ahrensbach, Juval Dieziger, Rachel

Acknowledgements

Fisher, Laura Hartman, Gemma Drake, Hugh Petter, Andreas Kruger, George Lakoff, Bill Kutik, Katrina Johnston-Zimmerman, and the inspiring people our Paper Tiger Television team spoke to in Detroit in 2010. Thanks are also due to those who generously shared images of their work, including Andrew Crompton, Pieter de Haan, Elemental, Felipe Diaz Contardo, Impact HUB Berkeley, WikiHouse, Michael Waltuch, and Deane Kensok.

This book owes a huge debt to the hundreds of researchers whose work it discusses and synthesises, as well as the invaluable review articles and volumes compiled by environmental psychologists such as Robert Gifford, Paul A. Bell and his colleagues, Stephen R. Kellert and his colleagues, and Dan Stokols. And to the many great innovators, activists, designers, urbanists, writers, builders, and everyday people whose work it has built upon.

Thanks to my mentors at the University of Surrey, Professor David Uzzell and Birgitta Gatersleben, and the many other great teachers I have had the privilege of learning from. I would also like to thank Sarah Hewitt, who co-founded Space Works Consulting with me, as well as our colleague Clara Weber, who was a close collaborator in the beginning of this venture, and her partner Hannes Pahl, who generously built and maintained our first website. Many thanks as well to the partners who were part of projects, such as those at Impact HUB Kings Cross, Huckletree, Happy City, and the *Tomorrow's Home* report, as well as my colleagues at Paper Tiger Television, OpenPlans, Streetfilms, and the Urbanistas network.

And finally, I would like to thank the many other friends and family who have offered their wisdom, support, and spare beds to sleep in along the way, especially Alexa Clay, Joanna Milczarek, and Owain Exley.

Notes

Epigraph p. vii

1   Hall, E. T. (1959), *The Silent Language*, Garden City, NY: Doubleday, 163.

Introduction

1   Hansard HC Deb, vol. 393, col 403–73 (28 October 1953) [Electronic version]

2   Health Research Funding. (2014). '14 Shocking Heroin Relapse Statistics' http://healthresearchfunding.org/shocking-heroin-relapse-statistics/

3   Note: the study did find that servicemen with previous histories of 'anti-social behaviour' were more likely to be actively involved in combat and to use drugs. But once personal history was accounted for, exposure to combat could not be singled out as a cause of heroin use.

4   *The Debate Continues*, BBC, 28 October 1950. Accessed 14 March 2016, http://www.bbc.co.uk/iplayer/episode/p00s7dfd/the-debate-continues

5   New Yorkers and Cars [blog post], StatsBee blog, NYCEDC, 5 April 2012, https://www.nycedc.com/blog-entry/new-yorkers-and-cars

Chapter 1

1   Noordelijke Hogeschool Leeuwarden (2007), *The Laweiplein: Evaluation of the Reconstruction into a Square with a Roundabout*. Leeuwarden, Netherlands: Noordelijke Hogeschool.

2   Satran, J. (26 June 2015), The Secret History of the War on Public Drinking [blog post], The Huffington Post, http://www.huffingtonpost.com/2013/12/14/public-drinking-laws_n_4312523.html

3   Burn-Murdoch, J. (30 November 2012), Where are the world's deadliest major cities? The Guardian DataBlog [blog post], http://www.theguardian.com/news/datablog/2012/nov/30/new-york-crime-free-day-deadliest-cities-worldwide

4   Sampson, R. J., & Raudenbush, S. W. (2001), *Disorder in Urban Neighborhoods – Does It Lead to Crime?* National Institute of Justice Research in Brief. NCJ 186049, Washington, DC: United States Department of Justice, National Institute of Justice.

5   Appleyard, D. and Cox, L. (2006), 'At Home in the Zone: Creating Liveable Streets in the US', *Planning*, 72 (9), 30–35.

6   Biddulph, M. (2010), 'Evaluating the English Home Zone Initiatives', *Journal of the American Planning Association*, 76 (2), 199–218.

7   New York City DOT. (2015), 'New York City Cycling Risk: Changes in Cyclist Safety Relative to Bicycle Use in New York City 2000–2015', New York: NYC DOT. http://www.nyc.gov/html/dot/downloads/pdf/nyc-cycling-risk.pdf

8   Martin, Leslie (2007), 'The grid as generator', in Carmona, M. & Tiesdell, S. (eds.), *Urban Design Reader*, Oxford: Architectural Press/ Elsevier 63–69; Reps, J. W. (1965), *The Making of Urban America*. Princeton, N.J.: Princeton University Press.

9   Appleyard, D. (1981), *Livable Streets*, Berkeley: University of California Press.

10   Waddel, Edmund (1997), 'Evolution of Roundabout Technology: A History-Based Literature Review', *Compendium of Technical Papers*, 67th Annual Meeting, Institute of Transportation Engineers, Boston.

11   Waddell, (1997).

12   Tranick, R. (2007), 'What is lost space?', in Carmona M. & Tiesdell S. (eds.), *Urban Design Reader*, Oxford: Architectural Press/Elsevier 59–63.

13   Waddell, (1997).

14   Grana, A. (2011), 'An Overview of Safety Effects on Pedestrians at Modern Roundabouts', *Sustainable Development and Planning V*, 150, 261–272.

15   Halvorsen, S. (2017), 'Losing Space in Occupy London: Fetishising the Protest Camp', in Brown G., Feigenbaum A., Frenzel F., and McCurdy P. (eds.), *Protest Camps in International Context: Spaces, Infrastructure and Media of Resistance*, Bristol, UK: Policy Press 163–178.

16   Wargo, B., and Garrick, N. (2015), 'Shared Space: Could Less Formal Streets be Better for Both Pedestrians and Vehicles?', *Transportation Research Board Annual Meeting 2016*, Washington, DC.

17   Gould, J. (3 May 2017), 'The Street Where Eric Garner Died Struggles to Recover', *WNYC News*, http://www.wnyc.org/story/street-where-garner-died-struggles-to-recover/

Chapter 2

1   Grahn, P. & Stigsdotter, U. K. (2010), 'The Relation Between Perceived Sensory Dimensions of Urban Green Space and Stress Restoration', *Landscape and Urban Planning*, 94, 264–275.

2   Bell, P. A., Greene, T. C., Fisher, J. D., & Baum, A. (2001), *Environmental Psychology*, 5th ed., Fort Worth, TX: Harcourt College Publishers.

3   Felstead, Alan, (2012), 'Rapid Change or Slow Evolution? Changing Places of Work and Their Consequences in the UK', *Journal of Transport Geography*, 21 (March), 31–38.

4   Kim, J., and de Dear, R. (2013), 'Workplace Satisfaction: The Privacy–Communication Trade-Off in Open-Plan offices', *Journal of Environmental Psychology*, 36, 18–26.

5   Hall, E. T. (1968), 'Proxemics [and comments and replies]', *Current Anthropology*, 9 (2/3 April–June), 83–10, 84.

6   While some of Hall's methodologies and assumptions in cross-cultural comparison have not held up to the test of time, his principle of personal space as a form of communication has persisted as an important concept.

7   Hall, E. T. (1968), 84.

8   Hayduck, L. A. (1981), 'The Shape of Personal Space: An Experimental Investigation', *Canadian Journal of Behavioural Science*, 13(1), 87–93.

9   White, M. (1977), 'Interpersonal Distance as Affected by Room Size, Status, and Sex', *Journal of Social Psychology*, 95, 241–249.

10   Savinar, J. (1975), 'The Effect of Ceiling Height on Personal Space', *Man-Environment Systems*, 5, 321–324.

11   Bell et al., (2001).

12   Bell et al., (2001).

13   Wells, M., Thelen, L., and Ruark, J. (2007), 'Workspace Personalisation and Organisational Culture: Does Your Work Space Reflect You or Your Company?' *Environment and Behavior*, 39, 616–634.

14   Brennan, A., Chugh, J. S., and Kline, T. (2002), 'Traditional Versus Open Office Design', *Environment and Behavior*, 34 (3), 279–299.

15   Sommer, R. (2007), *Personal Space, Updated: The Behavioral Basis of Design*, Bristol: Bosko Books.

16   Sundstrom, E., and Sundstrom, M. G. (1986), *Work Places: The Psychology of the Physical Environment in Offices and Factories*, New York, NY: Cambridge University Press.

17   Duffy, F. (1992), *The Changing Workplace*, London: Phaidon.

18 Becker, F., and Steele, F. (1995), *Workplace by Design: Mapping the High-Performance Workspace*, San Francisco: Jossey-Bass.

19 Galinsky, E., and Tahmincioglu, E. (2014), 'Why Citi Got Rid of Assigned Desks', *Harvard Business Review* (12 November 2014) https://hbr.org/2014/11/why-citi-got-rid-of-assigned-desks

20 Veitch, J. A., Charles, K. E., Farley, K. M., and Newsham, G. R. (2007), 'A Model of Satisfaction with Open-Plan Office Conditions: COPE field findings', *Journal of Environmental Psychology*, 27 (3), 177–180.

21 Danielsson, C. B., and Bodin, L. (2009), 'Difference in Satisfaction with office Environment Among Employees in Different Office Types', *Journal of Architectural and Planning Research*, 26 (3), 241–257; De Croon, E. M., Sluiter, J. K., Kuijer, P. P. F. M., and Frings-Dresen, M. H. W. (2005), 'The Effect of Office Concepts on Worker Health and Performance: A Systematic Review of the Literature, *Ergonomics*, 48 (2), 119–134.

22 Haapakangas A., Helenius R., Keskinen E., and Hongisto V. (2008), 'Perceived Acoustic Environment, Work Performance and Wellbeing Survey Results from Finnish Offices', in 9th International Congress on Noise as a Public Health Problem (ICBEN) 21–25 July 2008, Mashantucket, Connecticut, USA

23 Haapakangas A., et al. (2008).

24 Zweigenhaft, R. L. (1976), 'Personal Space in the Faculty Office: Desk Placement and the Student–Faculty Interaction', *Journal of Applied Psychology*, 61 (4), 529–532.

25 Hedge, A. (1982), 'The Open-Plan Office: A Systematic Investigation of Employee Reactions to Their Work Environment', *Environment and Behavior*, 14, 519–542.

26 Dazkir, S. S., and Read, M. A., 'Furniture Forms and Their Influence on Our Emotional Responses Toward Interior Environments', *Environment and Behavior*, 44(5), 725; Papanek, Victor (1995), *The Green Imperative: Natural Design for the Real World*, New York: Thames and Hudson.

27 Lohr, V. I., Pearson-Mims C. H., and Goodwin, G. K. (1996), 'Interior Plants May Improve Worker Productivity and Reduce Stress in a Windowless Environment', *Journal of Environmental Horticulture*, 14 (2), 97–100.

28 Vischer, J. (2008), 'Towards a User-Centred Theory of the Built Environment', *Building Research & Information*, 36 (3), 231–240.

29 Cook, M. (1970), 'Experiments on Orientation and Proxemics', *Human Relations*, 23, 61–76.

30 Clearwater, Y. A., and R. G. Coss (1991), 'Functional Esthetics to Enhance Well-being', in Harrison, Clearwater & McKay (eds.), *From Antarctica to Outer Space*, New York: Springer-Verlag, 410.

31 Bjerstedt, A. (1960). 'Warm-Cool Colour Preferences as Potential Personality Indicators: Preliminary Note', *Perceptual and Motor Skills*, 10, 31–34.

32 Gosling, S. (2008), *Snoop: What Your Stuff Says About You*, London: Profile Books.

33 Wells-Lepley, M. (2012), 'Personalisation: Clutter or Meaningful Personal Displays?' *Business Lexington*.

34 Haber, Gilda Moss, (1 March 1980), 'Territorial Invasion in the Classroom', *Environment and Behavior*, 12 (1), http://eab.sagepub.com/content/12/1/17.

35 Williamson, J. M., Lounsbury, J. W., and Han, L. D. (2013), 'Key Personality Traits of Engineers for Innovation and Technology Development', *Journal of Engineering and Technology Management*, 30, 157–168.

36 Glass, D. C., and Singer, J. E. (1972), *Urban Stress*, New York: Academic Press.

Chapter 3

1 Eccles, L. (25 June 2015), 'Housing Experts Declare War on the "Selfish NIMBYs" Who Block Home Building and "Deny Their Children a Place on the Property Ladder"', the *Daily Mail*, http://www.dailymail.co.uk/news/article-3138107/Housing-experts-declare-war-selfish-nimbys-block-home-building-deny-children-place-property-ladder.html

2 Devine-Wright, P. (2009), 'Rethinking NIMBYism: The role of place attachment and place identity in explaining place-protective action', *Journal of Community & Applied Social Psychology*, 19(6), 426–441.

3 Silver, A. and Grek-Martin, J. (2015), 'Now We Understand What Community Really Means: Reconceptualising the Role of Sense of Place in the Disaster Recovery Process', *Journal of Environmental Psychology*, 42, 32–41.

4 Bernheimer, L. (2014), *Tomorrow's Home: Emerging Social Trends and Their Impact on the Built Environment*, Winchester, UK: Adam Architecture.

5 Theodori, G. L. (2001), 'Examining the Effects of Community Satisfaction and Attachment on Individual Well-being', *Rural Sociology*, 66, 618–828.

6 Gifford, R. (2007), 'The Consequences of Living in High-Rise Buildings', *Architectural Science Review*, 50 (1), 1–16.

7 Gehl, J. (2006), *Life Between Buildings* (2nd ed.), (Koch, J., trans.), Copenhagen: The Danish Architectural Press.

8 Le Corbusier (1923), *Urbanisme*, translated as *The City of Tomorrow and Its Planning*, Etchells, F., London: Architectural Press, 1.

9 Gifford, (2007).

Notes

10   Ramsden, E., and Adams, J. (2008), 'Escaping the Laboratory: The Rodent Experiments of John B. Calhoun and Their Cultural Influence', *The Journal of Social History*, spring 2009.

11   Ramsden and Adams, (2008).

12   Baum, A. and Paulus, P. B. (1987), 'Crowding', in Stokols D. and Altman I. (eds.), *Handbook of Environmental Psychology*, 1, New York: Academic Press 533–570.

13   Worchel, S., and Teddlie, C. (1976), 'The Experience of Crowding: a Two-Factor Theory', *Journal of Social Psychology*, July 34 (1): 30–40.

14   Bell et al., (2001).

15   Warerkar, T. (13 June 13 2016), 'Would You Pay to Live in NYC's Micro First Micro-Unit Building?' Curbed NYC, https://ny.curbed.com/2016/6/13/11924900/carmel-place-micro-living-kips-bay-cost
Note: currency conversions made as of 7 July 2017.

16   Gould, J. K. (12 June 2016), 'The Costly Fallacy of NYC's First Micro-Apartments', *New York Post*, http://nypost.com/2016/06/12/the-costly-fallacy-of-nycs-first-micro-apartments

17   Gifford, (2007).

18   Oda, M., Taniguchi, K., Wen, M. L., and Higurashi, M. (1989), 'Effects of High-Rise Living on Physical and Mental Development of Children', *Journal of Human Ergology*, 18, 231–235.

19   Cohen, S., Glass, D. C., and Singer, J. E. (1973), 'Apartment Noise, Auditory Discrimination, and Reading Ability in Children', *Journal of Experimental Social Psychology*, 9, 407–422.

20   Gillis, A. R. (1977), 'High-Rise housing and Psychological Strain', *Journal of Health and Social Behavior*, 18, 418–431.

21   Edwards, J. N., Booth, A., and Edwards, P. K. (1982), 'Housing Type, Stress, and Family Relations', *Social Forces*, 61, 241–267.

22   Saegert, S. (1979), 'A Systematic Approach to High Density Settings: Social and Physical Environmental Factors', in Gurkaynak, M. R. and LeCompte, W. A. (1979), *Human Consequences of Crowding*, New York: Plenum Press, 67–82.

23   Marshall, C. (22 April 2015), 'Pruitt-Igoe: the Troubled High-Rise That Came to Define Urban America – a History of Cities in Fifty Buildings, Day 21', the *Guardian*, https://www.theguardian.com/cities/2015/apr/22/pruitt-igoe-high-rise-urban-america-history-cities

24   Newman, O. (1966), *Creating Defensible Space*, Darby, PA: Diane Publishing.

25   Lewicka, M. (2015), 'Place Attachment: How Far Have We Come in The Last Forty Years?', *Journal of Environmental Psychology*, 31, 207–230.

26   Gifford, (2007).

27   Gifford, (2007).

28   Clapson, Mark (2003), *Suburban Century: Social Change and Urban Growth in England and the USA*, Oxford: Berg.

29   Hobbs, F., and Stoops, N. (2002), *Demographic Trends in the Twentieth Century: Census 2000 Special Reports*, US Census Bureau, https://www.census.gov/prod/2002pubs/censr-4.pdf

30   RICS, CABE (2007), *Sustaining Our Suburbs: Suburbia All Grown Up'*, London: Royal Institution of Chartered Surveyors; DEFRA (2013) *Rural-Urban Classification for England*, Government Statistical Service.

31   Williams, Raymond (1973), *The Country and the City*, Sheffield: Spokesman Books, 2.

32   Department for Communities and Local Government (2011), *English Housing Survey: HOMES 2011*. London: DCLG.

33   ONS (2012), *2011 Census, Population and Household Estimates for England and Wales*, March 2011, Office for National Statistics.

34   Williams, Katie (2009), 'Space Per Person in the UK: A Review of Densities, Trends, Experiences, and Optimum Levels', *Land Use Policy* 26 (2009), S83–S92.

35   Gordon, Ian (2008), 'Density and the Built Environment', *Energy Policy*, 36 (2008), 4652–4656.

36   Department for Communities and Local Government (2016), *English Housing Survey 2015–2016: Headline Report*, https://www.gov.uk/government/statistics/english-housing-survey-2015-to-2016-headline-report

37   Boys Smith, N., and Morton, A. (2013), *Create Streets: Not Just Multi-Storey Estates*, London: Policy Exchange and Create Streets.

38   Dempsey, N., Brown, C., and Bramley, G. (2012), 'The Key to Sustainable Urban Development in UK Cities? The Influence of Density on Social Sustainability', *Progress in Planning*, 77, 89–141.

39   Taylor, M. (2015), *Garden villages: Empowering Localism to Solve the Housing Crisis*, London: Policy Exchange.

40   Devine-Wright, P. (2011). 'Enhancing local distinctiveness fosters public acceptance of tidal energy UK case study', *Energy Policy*, 39, 83–93.

Chapter 4

1   CNN (29 December 2013), 'Dementia Village: A New Experiment Out of the Netherlands', Sanjay Gupta MD, http://www.cnn.com/TRANSCRIPTS/1312/29/hcsg.01.html

Notes

2   Passini, R., Rainville, C., Marchand, N., & Joanette, Y. (1995), 'Wayfinding in Dementia of the Alzheimer Type: Planning Abilities', *Journal of Clinical and Experimental Neuropsychology*, 6, 820–832.

3   McHenry, H. M (2009), 'Human Evolution', in Ruse, Michael and Travis, Joseph, *Evolution: The First Four Billion Years*, Cambridge, Massachusetts: the Belknap Press of Harvard University Press, 263.

4   Wayman, E. (16 April 2012), 'A New Aquatic Ape Theory', Smithsonian.com, http://www.smithsonianmag.com/science-nature/a-new-aquatic-ape-theory-67868308/

5   Leakey, M. G., Feibel, C. S., McDougall, E., and Walker, A. (1995), 'New Four-Million-Year-Old Hominid Species from Kanapoi and Allia Bay, Kenya', *Nature*, 376, 565–571.

6   Zimmer, C. (29 August 2016), A 3.2-Million-Year-Old Mystery: Did Lucy Fall from a Tree?', the *New York Times*, https://www.nytimes.com/2016/08/30/science/lucy-hominid-fossils-fall.html

7   Falk, J. H., and Balling, J. D. (2010), 'Evolutionary Influence on Human Landscape Preference', *Environment and Behavior*, 42(4), 479–493.

8   Davies, K. (2001), *Cracking the Genome: Inside the Race to Unlock Human DNA*, New York: Free Press.

9   Lieberman, D. E. (2013), *The Story of the Human Body: Evolution, Health, and Disease*, New York: Pantheon Books.

10 'Natural' (2015). *New Oxford American English Dictionary*, 10.1093/acref/9780195392883.001.0001

11 Wilson, E. O., and Kellert, S. (1993), *The Biophilia Hypothesis*, Washington, DC: Island Press.

12 Many humans can, however, hold their breaths for much longer under water. The so-called 'mammalian diving reflex', found in aquatic mammals and humans but not in other primates, is one of the strong arguments for the waterside ape theory.

13 Kellert, S. R. (2008), 'Dimensions, Elements, and Attributes of Biophilic Design', in Kellert, S. R., Heerwagen, J. H. and Mador, M. L., 3–19 *Biophilic Design: the Theory, Science, and Practice of Bringing Buildings to Life*.

14 Kaplan, R. and Kaplan S. (1989), *The Experience of Nature: A Psychological Perspective*. Cambridge: Cambridge University Press.

15 Hinrichsen, D. (1999), 'The Coastal Population Explosion', *The Next 25 Years: Global Issues*, National Oceanographic and Atmospheric Association, http://oceanservice.noaa.gov/websites/retiredsites/supp_natl_dialogueretired.html

16 Barton, J. & J. Pretty (2010), 'What is the Best Dose of Nature and Green Exercise for Improving Mental Health?', *Environmental Science & Technology*, 44, 3947–3955.

17 Adler, J. (June 2013), 'Why Fire Makes Us Human', *Smithsonian Magazine*, http://www.smithsonianmag.com/science-nature/why-fire-makes-us -human-72989884/?no-ist

18 Holick, M. F. (2005), 'The Vitamin D Deficiency Epidemic and its Health Consequences', *Journal of Nutrition*, 135 (11), 2739–2748.

19 Ulrich, R. (1986), 'Effects of Healthcare Environmental Design on Medical Outcomes', Canadian Association for Person-Centred Health.

20 Joye, Y. (2007), 'Architectural Lessons from Environmental Psychology: The case for Biophilic Architecture, *Review of General Psychology*, 11 (4), 305–328.

21 Joye, Y., and van den Berg, Agnes (2011), 'Is Love for Green in Our Genes? A Critical Analysis of Evolutionary Assumptions in Restorative Environments Research', *Urban Forestry & Urban Greening*, (2011), doi:10.1016/j. ufug.2011.07.004, 3.

22 Joye and van den Berg (2011).

23 Summit, J., and Sommer, R. (1999), 'Further Studies of Preferred Tree Shapes', *Environment and Behavior*, 31 (4), 550–576.

24 Orians G. H., Heerwagen, J. H. (1992), 'Evolved Responses to Landscapes', in Barkow, J. H., Cosmides L., and Tooby J. (eds.), *The Adapted Mind: Evolutionary Psychology and the Generation of Culture*, Oxford University Press; New York: 1992, 555–579.

25 Lohr, V. I. and Pearson-Mims, C. H. (2006), 'Responses to Scenes with Spreading, Rounded, and Conical Tree Forms', *Environment & Behavior*, 38 (5), 667–688.

26 Falk and Balling (2010).

27 Lieberman, D. E. (2013), *The Story of the Human Body: Evolution, Health, and Disease*, New York: Pantheon Books, 165.

28 Appleton, J. (1975), *The Experience of Landscape*, London: Wiley, 32.

29 Hildebrand, G. (2008), 'Biophilic Architectural Space', in Kellert, S. R., Heerwagen, J. H., and Mador, M. L. (eds.), *Biophilic Design: The Theory, Science, and Practice of Bringing Buildings to Life*, Hoboken: Wiley, 263–276.

30 Melville, H. (1994), *The Piazza Tales*, Albany, NY: NCUP, Inc., 5.

31 Kaplan, S. (1987). Aesthetics, Affect, and Cognition: Environmental Preference from an Evolutionary Perspective. *Environment and Behavior*, 19 (1), 3–32.

32 Han, K. T. (2007), 'Responses to Six Major Terrestrial Biomes in Terms of Scenic Beauty, Preference, and Restorativeness', *Environment and Behavior*, 39, 529–556.

33 Kaplan, R., Kaplan, S., and Ryan, R. L. (1998), *With People in Mind: Design and Management of Everyday Nature*, Washington, DC: Island Press.

34 Woollett, Katherine, and Maguire, Eleanor A. (2011), 'Acquiring "The Knowledge" of London's Layout Drives Structural Brain Changes', *Current Biology*, 21 (24), 20 December 2011, 2109–2114 http://www.sciencedirect.com/science/article/pii/S096098221101267X

35 Squire, L. R., and Kandel, E. R. (1999), *Memory: From Mind to Molecules*, New York: Scientific American Library.

36 *The Edge* (17 October 2012), BBC, 'Brains Plus Brawn: A Conversation with Daniel Lieberman', http://www.bbc.co.uk/programmes/b07v0hhm#play

37 Lieberman, (2013).

38 'The Waterside Ape', (14 September 2016), *BBC Radio 4*, http://www.bbc.co.uk/programmes/b07v0hhm#play

39 Lieberman, (2013).

40 Lieberman, (2013).

41 Salingaros, N. A., and Madsen, K. G. (2008), 'Neuroscience, The Natural Environment and Building Design', in Kellert, S. R., Heerwagen, J. H. and Mador, M. L. (eds.) *Biophilic Design: The Theory, Science, and Practice of Bringing Buildings to Life*, Hoboken: Wiley 59–83.

42 Wener, R. (2012), *The Environmental Psychology of Prisons and Jails: Creating Humane Spaces in Secure Settings*, Cambridge: Cambridge University Press.

43 Browning, W., Ryan, C., and Clancy, J. (2014), *14 Patterns of Biophilic Design*, New York: Terrapin Bright Green.

44 Heerwagen, J. H., and Wise, J. A. (1997), *The EcoLogic of Color, Pattern, and Texture: A Synthesis of Research for the Design of Office Environments*, Herman Miller Inc.

45 Ulrich, R. (2008), 'Biophilic Theory and Research for Healthcare Design', in Kellert, S. R., Heerwagen, J. H., and Mador, M. L., *Biophilic Design: The Theory, Science, and Practice of Bringing Buildings to Life*, Hoboken: Wiley 87–104.

46 Fredrickson, B. L., and Levenson, R. W. (1998), 'Positive Emotions Speed Recovery from the Cardiovascular Sequalae of Emotions', *Cognition and Emotion*, 12 (2), 191–220.

47 Ulrich, (2008).

48 Melzack R., and Wall P. D. (1965), 'Pain Mechanisms: A New Theory', *Science*, 150(3699), 971–9.

49 Ulrich, R. S. (1993), 'Biophilia and the Conservation Ethic', in Kellert, S. R., and Wilson, E. O. (eds.), *The Biophilia Hypothesis*, Washington, DC: Island Press 73–137.

50   Ulrich, R. S. (1999), 'Effects of Gardens on Health Outcomes: Theory and Research', in Cooper-Marcus, C., and Barnes, M. (eds.), *Healing Gardens: Therapeutic Benefits and Design Recommendations*, New York: John Wiley 27–86.

51   Wei et al. (2014), 'Field Study of Office Worker Responses to Fluorescent Lighting of Different Cct and Lumen Output', *Journal of Environmental Psychology*, 39, 62–76.

52   Harvard Health Letter (May 2012), 'Blue Light has a Dark Side: Exposure to Blue Light at Night, Emitted by Electronics and Energy-Efficient Lightbulbs, Harmful to Your Health', (updated 2 September 2015) http://www.health.harvard.edu/staying-healthy/blue-light-has-a-dark-side

53   Ilic, Ognjen, Bermel, Peter, Chen, Gang, Joannopoulos, John D., Celanovic, Ivan, and Soljačić, Marin (2016), 'Tailoring High-Temperature Radiation and the Resurrection of the Incandescent Source', *Nature Nanotechnology*, 11, 320–324.

54   Heerwagen, J. H. (2005), 'Psychosocial Value of Space', *Whole Building Design Guide*, https://www.wbdg.org/resources/psychspace_value.php

Chapter 5

1   Bell et al., (2001).

2   Barker, R. G., & Barker, L. S. (1978), 'Social Actions of American and English Children and Adults', in Barker, R. G., and Associates (eds.), *Habitats, Environments, and Human Behavior*, San Francisco; London: Jossey-Bass, 99–120, 197.

3   Wicker, A. W. (1984), *An Introduction to Ecological Psychology*, Monterey, CA: Brooks/Cole Publishing, 36.

4   Bell et al., (2001).

5   Conway III, L. G., Houk, S. C., and Gornick, L. J. (2014), 'Regional Differences in Individualism and Why They Matter', in Rentfrow, P. J. (ed.), *Geographical Psychology: Exploring the Interaction of Environment and Behavior*, Washington, DC: American Psychological Association 31–50.

6   Varnum, M. E. W., and Kitayama, S. (2010), 'What's In A Name: Popular Names are Less Common on Frontiers', *Psychological Science*, 22(2), 176–183.

7   Kitayama, S., Ishii, K., Imada, T., Takemura, K., and Ramaswamy, J. (2006), 'Voluntary Settlement and the Spirit of Independence: Evidence From Japan's "Northern Frontier"', *Journal of Personality and Social Psychology*, 91 (3), 369–384.

8   Krulwich, R. (10 October 2012), *Obama's Secret Weapon in the South: Small, Dead, But Still Kickin'*, National Public Radio, KQED Public Media, http://www.npr.org/sections/krulwich/2012/10/02/162163801/obama -s-secret-weapon-in-the-south-small-dead-but-still-kickin

Notes

9   John, O. P., Naumann, L. P., and Soto, C. J. (2008), 'Paradigm Shift to the Integrative Big-Five Trait Taxonomy: History, Measurement, and Conceptual Issues', in John, O. P., Robins, R. W., and Pervin, L. A. (eds.), *Handbook of Personality: Theory and Research*, New York, NY: Guilford Press 114–158.

10   Murray, D. R., and Schaller, M. (2014), 'Pathogen Prevalence and Geographical Variation in Traits and Behaviour', in Rentfrow, P. J. (ed.), *Geographical Psychology: Exploring the Interaction of Environment and Behaviour*, Washington, DC: American Psychological Association 51–70.

11   Alik, J., and Mcrae, R. (2005), 'Toward a Geography of Personality Traits: Patterns of Profiles Across 36 Cultures', *Journal of Cross-Cultural Psychology*, 13 (28), 13–20.

12   It is an acknowledged issue in cross-cultural psychology that people may asses their own personality with reference to the norms of their culture, which may make these comparisons less than ideally objective.

13   John et al., (2008).

14   Gosling, S. D., and John, O. P. (1999), 'Personality Dimensions in Non-Human Animals: A Cross-Species Review', *Current Directions in Psychological Science*, 8, 69–75.

15   Oishi, S., Talhelm, T., and Lee, M. (2015), 'Personality and Geography: Introverts Prefer Mountains', *Journal of Research in Personality*, 58 (2015), 55–68.

16   Rentfrow, P. J., Jokela, M., and Lamb, M. E. (2015), 'Regional Personality Differences in Great Britain', PLoS ONE 10 (3).

17   Jokela, M. (2009), 'Personality Predicts Migration Within and Between US States', *Journal of Research in Personality*, 43, 79–83.

18   Rentfrow, P. J. (2010), 'Statewide Differences in Personality: Toward a Psychological Geography of the United States', *American Psychology*, 65 (6), 548–58.

19   Davis, A., and Mishel, L. (12 June 2014), 'CEO Pay Continues to Rise as Typical Workers Are Paid Less', issue brief no. 380, *Economic Policy Institute* http://www.epi.org/publication/ceo-pay-continues-to-rise/

20   Barker & Associates (1978), *Habitats, Environments, and Human Behavior*.

21   Schoggen, P. (1989), *Behaviour Settings: A Revision and Extension of Roger G. Barker's Ecological Psychology*, Stanford, CA: Stanford University Press, viii.

22   Scott, M. M. (2005), 'A Powerful Theory and a Paradox: Ecological Psychologists After Barker', *Environment and Behavior*, 37 (3), 295–329, 301.

23   Schoggen, (1989).

24   Schoggen, (1989), 249.

25 Schoggen, (1989).

26 Barker, R. G., and Schoggen, P. (1978), 'Behaviour-Generating Machines: Models Midwest and Yoredale', in Barker & Associates (eds.), *Habitats, Environments, and Human Behavior*, San Francisco: Jossey-Bass, 265–284.

27 Barker, R. G. & Associates (1978), *Habitats, Environments, and Human Behavior*, San Francisco: Jossey-Bass.

28 Barker & Associates (1978), 120.

29 Wicker, Allen W. (November 1969), *Journal of Personality and Social Psychology*, 13 (3), 278–288, http://dx.doi.org/10.1037/h0028272

30 Hall, E. T. (1969), *The Hidden Dimension*, Garden City, NY: Anchor Books, 129.

31 Hall, (1969), 139.

32 The rats referred to here are not from Calhoun's experiments: see chapter 4 page 132.

33 Schoggen, (1989).

34 Barker & Associates, (1978).

35 Lynn, R., and Martin, T. (1995), 'National Differences for Thirty-Seven Nations in Extraversion, Neuroticism, Psychotics, and Economic, Demographic and Other Correlates', *Personality and Individual Differences*, 19 (3), 403–406.

36 Seligman, M. E. P. (1975), *Helplessness*, San Francisco: Freeman.

37 Barker & Associates, (1978), 283.

38 Barker & Associates, (1978), 290.

39 Belden Russonello Strategists LLC (2013), *Americans' Views on their Communities, Housing, and Transportation*, Washington DC: Urban Land Institute DI https://uli.org/wp-content/uploads/ULI-Documents/America-in-2013-Final-Report.pdf

40 Oishi, Lun and Sherman (2007), in Rentfrow P. J. (ed.), *Geographical Psychology: Exploring the Interaction of Environment and Behavior*, Washington DC, American Psychological Association, 31–50.

41 Booth, P. (2015), *Federal Britain: The Case for Decentralization.* London: Institute for Economic Affairs.

42 Garland, D. (2016), *The Welfare State: A Very Short Introduction*, Oxford: Oxford University Press.

43 Garland, (2016).

44 Sherman, E. (30 September 2015), 'America is the Richest, and

Most Unequal, Country', *Fortune*, http://fortune.com/2015/09/30/america-wealth-inequality/

45 Spence, A. (2011), *Labour Market*, Social Trends 41, London: Office for National Statistics.

46 Schoggen, (1989).

47 Schoggen, (1989), 315.

48 Steger, M. B. (2013), *Globalization: A Very Short Introduction*, Oxford: Oxford University Press.

49 Barker & Associates, (1978), 285.

50 Barker & Associates, (1978), 296.

Chapter 6

1 The Future Homes Commission (2012), *Building the Homes and Communities Britain Needs*, London: RIBA.

2 Vartanian, O., Navarrete, G., Chatterjee, A., Fich, L. B., Gonzalez-Mora, J. L., Leder, H., Modrono, C., Nadal, M., Rostrup, N., and Skov, M. (2015), 'Architectural Design and the Brain: Effects of Ceiling Height and Perceived Enclosure on Beauty Judgements and Approach-Avoidance Decisions', *Journal of Environmental Psychology*, 41, 10–18.

3 Frewald, D. B. (1990), 'Preferences for Older Buildings: A Psychological Approach to Architectural Design', *Dissertation Abstracts International*, 51 (1-B), 414–415.

4 Maslow, A. H., and Mintz, N. L. (1956), 'Effects of Esthetic Surroundings: I. Initial Short-Term Effects of Three Esthetic Conditions Upon Perceiving "Energy" and "Wellbeing" in Faces', *Journal of Psychology*, 41, 247–254.

5 Gifford, R., Hine, D. W., Muller-Clemm, W., Reynolds, D. J., Shaw, J., and Shaw, K. T. (2000), 'Decoding Modern Architecture: A Lens Model Approach for Understanding the Aesthetic Differences of Architects and Laypersons', *Environment and Behavior*, 32 (2), 163–187.

6 Joye, (2007).

7 Joye, Y. (2011), 'Review of the Presence and Use of Fractal Geometry in Architectural Design,' *Environment and Planning B: Planning and Design*, 38, 814–828.

8 Eglash, R., and Odumosu, T. B. (2005), 'Fractals, Complexity, and Connectivity in Africa', in Sick, G. (ed.), *What Mathematics from Africa?*, Monza, Italy: Polimetrica International Scientific Publisher.

9 Eglash, (2002).

10 Eglash, (2005), http://csdt.rpi.edu/african/African_Fractals/culture13.html

11 Geake, J. (1992), 'Fractal Computer Graphics as a Stimulus for the Enhancement Of Perceptual Sensitivity to the Natural Environment', *Australian Journal of Environmental Education*, 8, 1–16.

12 Salingaros, (2008).

13 Ostwald, M. J. (2001), '"Fractal Architecture": Late Twentieth-Century Connections Between Architecture and Fractal Geometry', *Nexus Network Journal, Architecture, and Mathematics*, 3, 73–84.

14 Tsunetsugu, Y., Miyazaki, Y. and Sato, H. (2007), 'Physiological Effects in Humans Induced by the Visual Stimulation of Room Interiors with Different Wood Quantities', *Journal of Wood Science*, 53 (1), 11–16.

15 Salingaros, (2008).

16 Crompton, (2002).

17 Crompton, A. (2002), 'Fractals and Picturesque Composition,' *Environment and Planning B: Planning and Design*, 29, 451–459.

18 Eglash, R. (2002). *African Fractals: Modern Computing and Indigenous Design*, New Brunswick, NJ: Rutgers University Press, 26.

19 Interestingly, Eglash notes that native peoples of North America and the South Pacific traditionally favoured Euclidian shapes like squares and circles in vernacular design – this is not a simple dichotomy of Euclidian western design versus fractal design in non-western cultures. But, as Crompton and others make clear, we find varying expressions of fractal patterns across the traditional buildings of various cultures, which we see less of as they become removed from vernacular traditions.

20 Alexander, C. (1980), *The Timeless Way of Building*, New York: Oxford University Press, 55.

21 Please note that Alexander uses a slightly different scale of analogy.

22 Alexander, C., Ishikawa, S., Silverstein, M., Jacobson, M., Fiksdahl-King, I., and Angel, Shlomo (1977), *A Pattern Language*, New York: Oxford University Press, 340.

23 Alexander, (1979).

24 Strickland, C. (2001), *The Annotated Arch*, Kansas City: Andrews McMeel Publishing, 126.

25 Strickland, (2001).

26 Mumford, L. (11 October 1947), 'The Skyline: Status Quo', *New Yorker*, 104–110.

27 Weingarten, D. (2004), *Bay Area Style: Houses of the San Francisco Bay Region*, New York: Rizzoli.

28 Mumford, (1947), 110.

29   Gregoire, Menie. (1971), 'The Child in the High Rise', *Ekistics*, May 1971, 331–33.

30   Alexander, (1980), 231.

31   Alexander at al., (1977), 881.

32   Alexander at al., (1977).

33   Alexander at al., (1977), dust jacket.

34   Paper Tiger TV (2013), *Rerouting the Motor City: Notes on a City in Transformation*, http://papertiger.org/?s=rerooting+the+motor+city

35   Forbes.com (26 October 2013) 'A Declining Population in a Widespread City in Photos: 10 Things to Know About Detroit', http://www.forbes.com/pictures/emeh45jimm/a-declining-population-in-a-widespread-city-13/#46ba34721daa

36   Herzog, T. R., and Shier, R. L. (2000), 'Complexity, Age, and Building Preference', *Environment and Behavior*, 32 (4), 557–575; Frewald, D. B. (1989).

37   Joye, (2007), 319.

38   Anderson, C. M., and Mandell, A. J. (1996), 'Fractal Time and the Foundations of Consciousness: Vertical Convergence of 1/f Phenomena from Ion Channels to Behavioral States', in MacCormac E., and Stamenov, M. I. (eds.), *Fractals of Brain, Fractals of Mind*, 75–128, Amsterdam, the Netherlands: John Benjamins.

39   Salingaros, (2008), 62–63.

40   Seresinhe, C. I., Preis, T., and Moat, H. S. (2015), 'Quantifying the Impact of Scenic Environments on Health', *Scientific Reports*, 5, 16899.

41   Eakin, E. (12 July 2003), 'Architecture's Irascible Reformer', *The New York Times*, http://www.nytimes.com/2003/07/12/books/architecture-s-irascible-reformer.html

42   Cunningham, W., and Mehaffy, M. W. (2013), 'Wiki as Pattern Language', unpublished article, http://www.hillside.net/plop/2013/papers/Group6/plop13_preprint_51.pdf

Chapter 7

1   GreenBiz editors (3 August 2004), 'Builders Break Ground on "World's Most Environmentally Responsible High-Rise Office Building"', GreenBiz.com, https://www.greenbiz.com/news/2004/08/03/builders-break-ground-worlds-most-environmentally-responsible-high-rise-office-build

2   Roudman, S. (28 July 2013), 'Bank of America's Toxic Tower: New York's Greenest Skyscraper is Actually Its Biggest Energy Hog', *New Republic*, https://newrepublic.com/article/113942/bank-america-tower-and-leed-ratings-racket

3   Roudman, (2013).

4   Druckman, A., and Jackson, T. (2009), 'The Bare Necessities: How Much Household Carbon Do We Really Need?', RESOLVE Working Paper 05–09, University of Surrey.

5   Institute of Hazard, Risk, and Resilience (2011), 'Climate Change Mitigation Begins With Every Household', IHRR blog, http://ihrrblog.org/2011/08/19/climate-change-mitigation-begins-with-every-household

6   Harris, S. (2016), *Fit-Out Environmental Good Practice On-Site Guide*, London: CIRIA (Construction Industry Research and Information Association).

7   LEED was launched by the non-profit US Green Building Council in 1998, while the UK-based BREEAM was created through a government initiative that has now been privatised.

8   Harvard Health Letter, (2012).

9   Altomonte, S., and Schiavon, S. (2013), 'Occupant Satisfaction in LEED and Non-LEED Certified Buildings', *Building and Environment*, 68 (2013), 66–76; Birt, B., and Newsham G. R. (2009), 'Post-Occupancy Evaluation of Energy and Indoor Environment Quality in Green Buildings: A Review', *Third International Conference on Smart and Sustainable Built Environments*, 2009, 1–7.

10 Alexander, B. K., Coambs, R. B., Hadaway, P. F. (1978), 'The Effect of Housing and Gender on Morphine Self-Administration in Rats', *Psychopharmacology*, 58 (2), 175–9.

11 Kennedy, R. F. (18 March, 1968), remarks at University of Kansas, https://www.jfklibrary.org/Research/Research-Aids/Ready-Reference/RFK-Speeches/Remarks-of-Robert-F-Kennedy-at-the-University-of-Kansas-March-18-1968.aspx

12 Brandmeir, K., Grimm, M., Heise, M., and Holzhausen, A. (2016), *Allianz Global Wealth Report 2016*, Munich: Allianz.

13 Behavioural Insights Team (5 December 2012), 'Measuring National Well-being', http://www.behaviouralinsights.co.uk/uncategorized/measuring-national-wellbeing

14 Office for National Statistics (2013), 'Personal Wellbeing in the UK, 2012/13', London: ONS.

15 Brandmeir, K., Grimm, M., Heise, M., and Holzhausen, A. (2015), *Allianz Global Wealth Report 2015*, 11, Munich: Allianz. https://www.allianz.com/v_1444215837000/media/economic_research/publications/specials/en/AGWR2015_ENG.pdf

16 Wilkinson, R., and Pickett, K. (2012), *The Spirit Level: Why Greater Equality Makes Societies Stronger*, London: Allen Lane.

17 World Commission on Environment and Development (1987), *Our Common Future*, Oxford: Oxford University Press.

Notes

18   Rybczynski, W. (1996), *City Life*, New York: Touchstone.

19   Harvey, D. (2008), 'The Right to the City', *New Left Review*, 53 (Sept–Oct), 23.

20   Budds, Diana (7 August 2016), 'How Urban Design Perpetuates Racial Inequality and What We Can Do About It', Slicker City, Co.Design, http://www.fastcodesign.com/3061873/slicker-city/how-urban-design-perpetuates-racial-inequality-and-what-we-can-do-about-it

21   Flint, A. (2009). *Wrestling with Moses: How Jane Jacobs Took on New York's Master Builder and Transformed the American City*. York: Random House.

22   Rybcynski, (1996).

23   Rothstein, Richard (2017), *The Color of Law: The Forgotten History of How Our Government Segregated America*, xi, New York: Liveright.

24   Katznelson, Ira (2006), *When Affirmative Action Was White: an Untold History of Racial Inequality in Twentieth-Century America*, New York: W. W. Norton.

25   Lewis, M. (December 2016), 'How Two Trailblazing Psychologists Turned Decision Science Upside Down', *Vanity Fair/HIVE*, http://www.vanityfair.com/news/2016/11/decision-science-daniel-kahneman-amos-tversky

26   Kahneman, D. (2011), *Thinking Fast and Slow*, citing Bruno Frey 269, New York: Farrar, Straus, & Giroux.

27   Example adapted from Kahneman (2011).

28   Lakoff, G. (2004), *Don't Think of an Elephant!: Know Your Values and Frame the Debate*, White River Junction, Vermont: Chelsea Green Publishing.

29   Murtagh, N., Nati, M., Headley, W. R., Gatersleben, B., Gluhak, A., Ali Imran, M., and Uzzell, D. (2013), 'Individual Energy Use and Feedback in an Office Setting: A Field Trial', *Energy Policy*, 62, 717–728.

30   Lewis, (2016).

31   Kahneman, (2011), 270.

32   Fritsche, I., Cohrs, J. C., Kessler, T., and Bauer, J. (2012), 'Global Warming is Breeding Social Conflict: The Subtle Impact of Climate Change Threat on Authoritarian Tendencies', *Journal of Environmental Psychology*, 32 (2012), 1–10.

33   Jugert, P., Greenaway, K.H., Barth, M., Buchner, R., Eisentraut, S., and Fritsche, I. (2016), 'Collective Efficacy Increases Pro-Environmental Intentions Through Increasing Self-Efficacy', *Journal of Environmental Psychology*, 48, 12–23.

34   Okasha, Samir (21 July 2017), 'Biological Altruism', *The Stanford Encyclopedia of Philosophy*, Zalta, Edward N. (ed.), https://plato.stanford.edu/archives/fall2013/entries/altruism-biological

35 Sampson, R. J., Radenbush, S. W., and Earls, F. (1997). 'Neighborhoods and Violent Crime: A Multilevel Study of Collective Efficacy', *Science*, 277(5328), 918–924.

36 Jugert et al., (2016).

37 Goldstein, N. J., Cialdini, R. B., and Griskevicius, V. (2008), 'A Room with a Viewpoint: Using Social Norms to Motivate Environmental Conservation in Hotels', *Journal of Consumer Research*, 35.

38 Mckenzie-Mohr, Doug (2000), 'Promoting Sustainable Behavior: An Introduction to Community-Based Social Marketing', *Journal of Social Issues*, 56 (3), 543–554.

39 Further resources are available at http://www.toolsofchange.com/en/tools-of-change

40 Harvey, (2008).

41 Compton, T. (2010), *Common Cause: The Case for Working with our Cultural Values*, Woking: World Wildlife Fund.

42 Paragon Ltd (2015), 'Are Hybrid Cars Becoming the New Status Symbol?', retrieved 20 January 2017 (link no longer working), http://hybrid.co.uk/hybrid-status-symbol.php

43 Ryan, R. M., and Deci, E. L. (2000), 'Intrinsic and Extrinsic Motivations: Classic Definitions and New Directions', *Contemporary Educational Psychology*, 25, 54–67.

44 Kasser, T., and Ryan, R. M. (1996), 'Further Examining the American Dream: Differential Correlates of Intrinsic and Extrinsic Goals', *Personality and Social Psychology Bulletin*, 22 (3), 280–284.

45 Deci, E. L. (1971), 'Effects of Externally Mediated Rewards on Intrinsic Motivation', *Journal of Personality and Social Psychology*, 18(1), 105–115, doi:10.1037/h0030644

46 Schwartz, S. H. (1996), 'Value Priorities and Behavior: Applying a Theory of Integrated Value', in Erlbaum, L. (ed.), *The Psychology of Values*, the Ontario Symposium, 8, http://www.palermo.edu/cienciassociales/publicaciones/pdf/Psico2/2Psico%2007.pdf

47 Brown, K. W., and Kasser, T. (2005), 'Is Psychological and Ecological Wellbeing Compatible? The Role of Values, Mindfulness, and Lifestyle', *Social Indicators Research*, 74, 349–368.

48 Zhang, W. J., Piff, P. K., Yer, R., Koleva, S., and Keltner, D. (2014), 'An Occasion for Unselfing: Beautiful Nature Leads to Pro-sociality', *Journal of Environmental Psychology*, 37 (2014), 61–72.

49 Crutch, S. J., and Warrington, E. K. (2003), 'The Selective Impairment of Fruit and Vegetable Knowledge: A Multiple Processing Channels Account of Fine-Grain Category Specificity', *Cognitive Neuropsychology*, 20, 355–372.

50 Joye, (2007).

Chapter 8

1 Haynes, G. (2008), *American Megafaunal Extinctions at the End of the Pleistocene*, Dordrecht, Netherlands: Springer Science and Business Media.

2 Personal communication, Tim Ahrensbach.

3 Shapiro, L. (2004), *Something from the Oven: Reinventing Dinner in 1950s' America*, New York: Viking.

4 White, M. P., and Dolan, P. (2009), 'Accounting for the Richness of Daily Activities', *Psychological Science*, 20, 1000–1008.

5 Lawrence, D. H., and Festinger, L. (1962), '*Deterrents and Reinforcement: the Psychology of Insufficient Reward*, Stanford, CA: Stanford University Press

6 Winston, A. (13 January 2016), 'Architects "are never taught the right thing," says 2016 Pritzker laureate Alejandro Aravena', *Dezeen*, https://www.dezeen. com/2016/01/13/alejandro-aravena-interview-pritzker-prize-laureate-2016-social-incremental-housing-chilean-architect/

7 The *Telegraph*, (15 August 2003), 'Cedric Price', http://www.telegraph.co.uk/news/obituaries/1438827/Cedric-Price.html

8 ArchDaily.com (31 December 2008), 'Quinta Monroy/ ELEMENTAL', http://www.archdaily.com/10775/quinta-monroy-elemental

9 Winston, (2016).

10 Winston, (2016).

11 Plans are available at http://www.elementalchile.cl/en/projects/abc-of-incremental-housing with the important caveat that these specifications may need to be modified for local context of climate and materials, and economic, political, and social landscapes.

12 Batty, M. (2008), 'Generating Cities from the Bottom-Up: Using Complexity Theory for Effective Design', *Cluster*, 9 (2008), 150.

13 Rybcinzski, W. (1996), *City Life*, New York: Scribner.

14 UN Department of Economic and Social Affairs. (2015), *World Urbanization Prospects, 2014 Revision*, New York: United Nations.

15 Lots can also be combined to form larger buildings and minimum height standards can be mandated if desirable.

16 Magdaleno, J. (8 February 2016), 'Build Your Own *Baugruppe* – Home for the Rest of Us', Impact Design Hub, https://impactdesignhub.org/2016/02/08/build-your-own-baugruppe-a-home-for-the-rest-of-us; Ben, (26 March 2013), House Planning Help, 'How Does Self-Build in the UK Compare to Germany?' http://www.houseplanninghelp.com/hph019-how-does-self-build-in-the-uk-compare-to-germany-with-mark-brinkley-author-of-the-housebuilders-bible

17 Cambell, K., and Cowan, R. (2016), *The Radical Incrementalist: How to Build Urban Society in 12 Lessons*, London: Movement Publishing.

18 Caldieron, J. M. (2013), 'From A Skyscraper to a Slumscraper: Residential Satisfaction In "Torre de David" Caracas, Venezuela', *The Macrothemes Review*, 2 (5), 138–152.

19 Risen, J. (18 September 1985), 'Poletown Becomes Just a Memory: GM Plant Opens, Replacing Old Detroit Neighborhood', *Los Angeles Times*, http://articles.latimes.com/1985-09-18/business/fi-6228_1_gm-plant

20 Paper Tiger TV, 2013.

21 'City of Bristol College Student Creates Artwork Celebrating Bristol Black Icons' (16 January 2015), *Bristol Post*.

Index

Note: page numbers in **bold** refer to illustrations.

Index

Index

Index

Index